The Soviet Union and the United States

A New Look at the Cold War

TWAYNE'S INTERNATIONAL HISTORY SERIES

Akira Iriye, editor
University of Chicago

The Soviet Union and the United States

A New Look at the Cold War

Linda R. Killen
Radford University

TWAYNE PUBLISHERS • BOSTON
A DIVISION OF G. K. HALL & CO.

Copyright 1989 by Linda R. Killen.
All rights reserved.
Published by Twayne Publishers
A division of G. K. Hall & Co.
70 Lincoln Street, Boston, Massachusetts 02111

Twayne's International History Series no. 3

Designed by Barbara Anderson.
Book production by Janet Zietowski.
Copyediting supervised by Barbara Sutton.

Printed on permanent/durable acid-free paper
and bound in the United States of America.

First Printing 1988

Library of Congress Cataloging in Publication Data

Killen, Linda, 1945–
    The Soviet Union and the United States : a new look at the Cold War / Linda R. Killen.
    p.   cm. — (Twayne's international history series ; no. 3)
    Bibliography: p.
    Includes index.
    ISBN 0–8057–7913–2 (alk. paper). ISBN 0–8057–9203–1 (pbk. : alk. paper)
    1. United States—Foreign relations—Soviet Union. 2. Soviet Union—Foreign relations—
United States. 3. United States—Foreign relations—1945–   I. Title.   II. Series.
E183.8.S65K55 1988
327.73047—dc19   88–16535
                                                                   CIP

CONTENTS

LIST OF ILLUSTRATIONS

FOREWORD

Twayne's International History Series was developed to provide reliable and readable accounts of post–World War II international affairs. Today, nearly fifty years after the end of the war, it is time to undertake a critical assessment of world affairs in the second half of the twentieth century: What have been the major themes and trends in international relations since 1945? How have they evolved and changed over time? What have been the connections between international and domestic affairs? How have states and peoples defined and pursued their objectives and what have these pursuits contributed to the world at large? How have the conceptions of warfare and visions of peace changed in the last fifty years?

Each of these questions must be raised to understand the contemporary world. That understanding must be both international—with an awareness of the linkages among different parts of the world—and historical—with a keen sense of what the immediate past has brought to human civilization. It is to be hoped that the volumes in this series will help the reader to explore important events and decisions since 1945 and to develop a global awareness and a historical sensitivity with which to confront today's problems.

The first volumes in the series deal with the United States' relations with other countries, groups of countries, or regions. The focus on the United States is justified in part because of the nation's predominant position in postwar international relations and also because far more extensive documentation is available on American foreign affairs than is the case with other countries. But the series is addressed not just to readers interested in international relations. Students of American history and of other countries' histories will find here useful and fresh insights into postwar domestic developments. Now, more than ever before, it is imperative that we understand the complex ties between national and international history.

This volume offers a fresh perspective on United States relations with the Soviet Union since the war. Most accounts of the bilateral relationship put it in the overarching framework of the cold war. But Linda Killen, a diplomatic historian who specializes in American relations with Eastern European countries, reminds us that the cold war has been just one of many themes of the postwar world. American–Soviet tensions and accommodations must be seen against the background of other developments in various parts of the globe. She thus represents unique, often controversial points of view about the ways in which American–Soviet relations are played out in Asia, Africa, the Middle East, and Latin America as well as in Europe. The book challenges the reader to retain a historical and global perspective as we ponder the meaning of the "cold peace" that has lasted for more than forty years.

INTRODUCTION

Like all great powers, the United States and the Soviet Union have grown fat, with noticeable tendencies to overhang their respective borders. The ideological baggage they carry has added to their girth, prompting both nations to take up more than their fair share of territory, resources, and media coverage. As a consequence, any study of Soviet–American relations defies the nice, neat confines one could draw for, say, Dutch–Mexican relations. How the two superpowers see each other, react to each other, and compete with each other directly affects some five billion people (the current world population). When one adds governments, interest groups, and the passage of time, the permutations on a variable analysis of the ins and outs of Soviet–American relations are literally endless. My approach in this survey is therefore unique, but also, far from definitive.

This book projects no single, overarching theme. I am championing no major revision of Soviet–American historiography. I am, however, trying to add an element of the unexpected, to challenge the ordinary, to shift the reader's mental axis. If this approach sparks discussion, encourages readers to transcend their ethnocentricities, or adds new dimensions to "the same old stuff," it has served its purpose.

Many Americans would probably choose post–World War II Soviet–American relations as that area of international affairs about which they are most knowledgeable. It makes writing this volume for the Twayne International History Series easier on one level, but it makes it more difficult in other ways: easier because the reader may be at least passingly familiar with many of the events, personalities, and policies; more difficult because that same familiarity makes it harder to rethink existing assumptions and presuppositions.

For over forty years now, Soviet–American relations have been among the most important influences on contemporary history; some would argue that they have been the single most important influence. For a while in the 1970s it looked like the cold war mentality had run its course, that the wheel of history had turned, and that other issues would supplant Soviet–American conflicts as the determining factors. But in recent years, cold war animosity has been revived, suggesting that hatchets have not yet been buried and that history is not yet done with this chapter. It was therefore no simple task to prepare a reasonably concise survey that does justice to the subject and that, in addition, asks readers to question their own ethnocentric subjectivity.

One of those ethnocentricities, reflective of American provinciality, is a tendency, even in the 1980s, to equate communism and even socialism definitely with things un-American and probably with the Soviet Union. Russia may have "been" communism (at least in practice and in power) as of 1941. It definitely does not have a corner on the market today. Yet, in large part because of this blanket association between things communist— or leftist or socialist—and things Russian, the American view of the countries' relations expands to a worldview: if leftists gain power in country Y, the Kremlin is either behind, or will benefit from, their actions. America's policy toward Y often becomes an extension of its policy toward the Soviet Union, which for forty years has been aimed at containing the Soviet Union and any spread of its influence. Soviet–American relations cannot, therefore, be as neatly bilateral as could be, for example, a recounting of Norwegian–American relations. Truth be told, Americans see US–Soviet overtones in their relations with even this inoffensive ally.

This book's approach to Soviet–American relations makes it clear that there are no *right* answers. An even remotely complete understanding of the impact these two nations have had on each other and on the world can be reached only by recognizing the existence and the legitimacy of other points of view. This need to see, acknowledge, and consider other perspectives is particularly true for citizens of these two nations that have historically been guilty of extreme insularity of vision.

One sees this almost every day in university classrooms. Several years ago my university brought the film *Apocalypse Now* to campus and about five hundred students went to see it. In one memorable scene, Robert Duvall's helicopter gunboats, with loudspeakers blaring Wagner, strafe a village in order to clear the way for the crews to go surfing. This particular audience cheered the gunboats and booed the villagers. Probably some very complex, as well as some not so complex, emotions were operating on that audience, but a blindered, uncritical, callous inhumanity was also at work. This incident prompted me to look much more closely at how Americans, and I as an

American, see the world and ourselves. It also piqued my interest in how others see us.

Another much more Russian—related but much less personally traumatic eye-opener occurred when the syllabi for survey courses on czarist Russia and US history arrived at the year 1861 simultaneously. Students in the Russian class had found serfdom barbaric but "not surprising" in a Russian context. Those in the US survey accepted slavery as a familiar but lamentable chapter in America's past. Both classes found it unsettling that an autocratic czar freed the serfs with, figuratively, a stroke of the pen, while the democratic United States had to fight the most devastating war in its history, against itself, to free the slaves.

One last anecdote. Students in a course on twentieth-century American diplomacy were asked to forecast the future. Would and should the United States remain the dominant world power? Approximately thirty percent saw no reason for American preeminence ever to wane. History, they seemed to be saying, was for other countries. The United States operated on history but was itself not limited by historical constraints. Major events might come and go in history, but the United States functioned in a kind of time-motion vacuum. Suggested means for guaranteeing American preeminence ranged from "nuking" the Russians to engaging in long-term, well-thought-out, conscious alteration of behavior in order for the United States better to deal with changing world problems. A few students suggested that democracy puts constraints on long-term, well-thought-out approaches to anything. Most of the class assumed, realistically, that no country would resign superpower status voluntarily. They also assumed, perhaps less realistically, that whatever happened was within America's power to determine, and that the Soviet Union was the biggest, baddest, and only real threat to our way of life. One person suggested that the United States should retire as a leader in power politics because it has much more to offer as an economic, technological, and social model. She did not find many supporters.

My students are normal, everyday people like the millions in colleges and universities throughout the world. They are different only insofar as they are American and, as such, reflect America's special rather provincial brand of ethnocentricity. Diplomatic literature refers to this as American universalism, a foreign policy that presupposes that America's values, goals, and interests are also everyone else's. American universalists find it hard to believe that "the American solution" is not necessarily the ideal solution.

Having recognized all these things about my own country, what could I as a teacher do to turn it around, to get beyond America's view of the world and of its place in that world? For a while I tried to teach the Russian point of view, but I soon discovered that subjectivity and provinciality are just as endemic to the Soviet Union's population, albeit for different reasons. Thus, to see both sides is to limit oneself to the American and Russian definitions of issues, problems, and realities, to assume that there are only *two* sides, and to accept the idea of bipolarity.

But what about everyone else? Most of the rest of the world is equally but differently ethnocentric. To be ethnocentric is to recognize and applaud your membership in a particular community of people. Most of the rest of the world cannot afford to be as provincial about its ethnocentricities as can the United States and the Soviet Union. Peoples of other countries must deal with problems—some of which are created by their relationship to the superpowers but many of which are the results of totally extraneous concerns. Much of the rest of the world has to live some kind of life *in spite of* the superpowers.

I am more than happy being an American and I would always opt to live in the United States; most Russians feel the same way about Russia. I also state categorically that life in the United States is preferable to life in the USSR. But then I am a white, middle-class, relatively affluent, employed, homeowning, healthy American. I do not know how I would feel if I were brown, poor, unemployed, homeless, and ill. I do know that, asked to choose whether they want their lives "messed around with" by Americans or Russians, developing nations see little difference between the two and prefer neither. Life as an American is different from life under America's tutelage. That is what we, as Americans, have trouble understanding.

It is not impossible that some historian writing centuries, or even only decades, from now could reasonably decide that either or both the United States and the Soviet Union had, by the 1980s, come to exist in fantasy worlds of their own making and had continued to compete for prizes that were no longer relevant. Would it not be embarrassing to discover that myopia had prevented the two most powerful post–World War II nations, obsessed by their own rivalries, from noticing that their military power and their rivalries had become irrelevant, that the rest of the world had stopped caring who won which particular round, and that they were shadow boxing imaginary villains in an empty arena? Americans and Russians may not like to see how others see them; that dislike does not make those other perspectives go away.

This book merges thematic and traditional chronological approaches. Most chapters concentrate on a specific theme and are internally chronological. Chapter 1 focuses on diplomatic recognition, an issue between Russia and the United States that prevailed in the years between the wars. Themes are often overlapping, however, and the chronology of one chapter may overlap with that of others. The 1956 Suez crisis, for example, appears in chapter 4's discussion of nationalism and nonalignment and in chapter 7's coverage of the Middle East in Soviet–American relations. In addition to having a chapter to itself, the arms race is an issue throughout the postwar years.

Most chapters have been assembled so as to make a slow but steady progression from early to most recent events. Chapter 3 concentrates on the early cold war (1945–50), chapter 4 on the 1950s, chapter 8 on the 1970s and 1980s, and so on. Alien but no less real perspectives on Soviet–American relations are introduced in chapter 2, which views World War II through Russian eyes, and chapters 4 and 7, which hint at how Yugoslavs and Arabs have looked at aspects of Soviet–American relations particularly relevant to them. Bilateral treaties, summit meetings, wars, trade relations—the stuff of political history—appear throughout, but with less emphasis on the players, episodes, and dates with which headlines are filled, and more on the political beliefs that have inspired the alignments, interventions, and other critical actions of the two governments. "Headline History," the first section of chapter 8, has been designed as a kind of "reconstruct it yourself" experiment. Using the headlines as points of reference, readers can research and reconstruct a fuller picture of events for themselves. Anyone looking for references to a particular person, event, or idea will find the glossary, chronology, and index helpful. The bibliographic essay suggests additional sources for a more in-depth study of particular issues or time periods.

I would like to thank Frank Ninkovich for introducing me to the Twayne Diplomatic History series and Akira Iriye for making an offer I could not refuse. A five-month Fulbright research grant to study in Belgrade, Yugoslavia, done in the midst of preparing this manuscript, reaffirmed my conviction that other people see things differently and provided several ideas that I have incorporated; thus my thanks to that program. My sister, Sandra Killen, and my colleague, Kenneth P. Werrell, both read parts of the manuscript and made valued suggestions. Ilia Jefferson prepared the maps. I owe particular debts of gratitude to my 1987 History 305 students at Radford University, to Mrs. Frederick H. Bunting, to Akira Iriye for editorial guidance, and to Meghan Wander for guiding me through the minefields. For better or for worse, however, I am solely responsible for this book's content.

Linda R. Killen

Radford University, April 1988

Starving in the Midst of Plenty.

Talburt, New York *World-Telegram*, 1933.

chapter 1

THE UNITED STATES, THE SOVIET UNION, AND DIPLOMATIC RECOGNITION

Prior to the Bolshevik Revolution in 1917, Russo–American relations had for some one hundred years been restrained but cordial. Traveling in the United States in the 1830s, Alexis de Tocqueville predicted rivalry between the two nations based on trade and territorial expansion, not ideology. After the United States purchased Alaska from an overextended Russia in 1867, however, it was not uncommon for years to go by with few if any significant contacts between the two countries. World War I and the Bolshevik Revolution sparked a much greater American interest in things Russian, but even then the official policy and interwar patterns of diplomacy kept the nations at a restrained, if this time hostile, distance. After World War II the Frenchman's prediction did come true, but it did so at least in part for reasons he would never have imagined.

Soviet–American relations after 1945 developed along lines mostly drawn during and after the war, but in an atmosphere of suspicion and ideological antagonism that most definitely predated the war. In a diplomatic context (Americans having never been particularly enamored of Marxism or communism) the antagonism manifested itself as early as the Bolshevik Revolution and was expressed in the US government's sixteen-year refusal to grant diplomatic recognition to the revolution.

Under normal circumstances, the granting of diplomatic recognition is a routine rather than a privilege. Few expectations arise as a consequence thereof. To withhold recognition implies a hostile relationship with minimal contact between the peoples, economies, and governments involved. Somewhat perversely, since recognition does not connote any expectation of national or governmental camaraderie, normalization of relations after an extended period of nonrecognition is often read as heralding major and positive changes. In other words, recognition coming *after* a period of nonrecognition has a different meaning than does that granted without such a period.

The United States withheld recognition from the Soviet Union for sixteen years. Between 1917 and 1933 no official relations existed between the governments: no treaties, no ambassadors, no invitations to inaugurations or May Day parades. During this time, however, relations between the countries were very different from more recent patterns of nonrecognition diplomacy. In the 1920s, nonrecognition of the Soviet Union was much less total; for example, it did not prevent Americans from trading with or traveling to Russia. These years are interesting in that light alone. They are also important as a preamble for understanding later relations between the postwar superpowers.

Diplomatic recognition is, by definition, something that must be given, not taken. However much the Soviet Union did or did not want recognition from the United States, the factors that determined whether or not it was granted were American policies and American perspectives. Thus the history of interwar Soviet–American relations is as much a history of American perceptions as it is of historical realities.

Diplomatic recognition acknowledges governmental or national legitimacy.[1] It opens the way to the exchange of diplomatic representatives, to trade negotiations, to treaty agreements, and to the granting of legal standing. National recognition acknowledges an entity as having a specific territory and population held together by a governmental structure free from external control. Many countries failed to recognize the new Russian government in 1917, but that does not mean they declared Russia a nonnation.

Governments, as opposed to nations, are recognized according to somewhat more complex guidelines. The standard practice has been to recognize any government that can demonstrate authority over its citizens. In such cases, the act of extending recognition loses any positive or negative connotation and assumes a neutral value, an acceptance, as it were, of what is. A more subjective criterion allows governments to judge each other on their willingness or ability to comply with existing international responsibilities and in a manner acceptable to international law. Here, political and ideological preferences help determine recognition policies. Theoretically, withholding recognition may or may not affect personal, economic, or other relationships between two countries. Each government can determine its own policies, although accepted parameters and consequences are written into international law.

Nonrecognition is relatively uncommon. It may be temporary after decolonization and the break-up of empires, while war normally leads to breaks in diplomatic relations that can be of fairly short or very long duration. Today Arab states commonly refuse to recognize Israel, arguing that a state of war has existed between them since 1947 even though no major hostilities have occurred since 1973.

As a policy that remains in effect over long periods of time, nonrecognition has negative connotations. To warrant nonrecognition, a government or nation must presumably have done something especially obnoxious or have failed to satisfy rudimentary definitions of independence. Transkei (a perceivedly artificial creation of South Africa) and Manchukao (a perceivedly artificial creation of Japan) were both denied recognition by most nations of the world as having failed to satisfy basic definitions of independence. The more recent case of the Palestine Liberation Organization (PLO) makes it clear that international agreement on definitions of nations and independence is not automatic; that is, the organization is recognized by some nations but not by others.

Because of the PLO's association with terrorism, the issue of its recognition also touches on the area of "special obnoxiousness." American nonrecognition of Cuba and black Africa's nonrecognition of the Republic of South Africa are examples of special obnoxiousness, or failure to behave in accordance with certain definitions of international law and morality.

During its own revolution, the United States set precedents in forcing European governments to formulate policies for recognition of both new states and new governments. Should the break-away colonies, preaching political dogmas radically different from most European governments of the time and setting dangerous examples for the European populus, be recognized and welcomed to the consort of power? Autocratic France, England's arch-enemy and consequently America's revolutionary ally, quickly granted de facto recognition. The equally autocratic czarist Russia withheld recognition for many years but then developed a friendly, if infrequent, relationship with the new democracy.

Recognition of new nations is one thing; recognition of revolutionary governmental changes inside an existing nation is another. Alexander Hamilton (who feared and disliked the French Revolution) believed that recognition was between governments. Thomas Jefferson (who sympathized with the goals if not the methods of the French Revolution) argued that it was between nations as well as governments, and that America's commitments to France were unaffected by the revolution. Woodrow Wilson's twentieth-century approach incorporated bits and pieces from both of these views plus precedents from the American Civil War. By insisting that new governments should take office only through constitutional means, Wilson gave himself the right to decide whether a foreign government was or was not legitimate. He sometimes had the United States assume the role of guardian in protecting the rights and interests of nations and peoples when he deemed their governments to be illegal. He followed American Civil War precedent in refusing to recognize the independence of separatist regions, in Russia for example, until or unless that independence had been acknowledged by the government from which the new nation was breaking away.

Wilson's use of these subjective criteria for recognition meant that Soviet–American relations got off to a bad start. Wilson believed that Russia was democratic at heart and that the March 1917 revolution, which overthrew the czar and promised to keep Russia in on the allies' side in World War I, represented a popular desire for democracy and what he called "progressive liberalism." Together with the European allies, the United States granted instant recognition (and war loans) to the self-proclaimed Provisional Government. The Bolshevik Revolution nine months later pulled Russia out of the war just as the United States was gearing up its own military involvement. Because of its timing, rhetoric, and actions, this second Russian revolution was greeted in much the same way that medieval Europe welcomed new outbreaks of the Black Death. Nobody extended recognition.

Americans resented Russia's separate peace with Germany, and Wilson resented Lenin's challenge to his own bid for moral leadership of a new world order. Officially, the United States declared the situation in Russia unstable and followed a wait-and-see approach that designated the defunct Provisional Government as Russia's legitimate governmental authority. Privately, Wilson and many other Americans saw the Bolshevik Revolution as a betrayal not just of the first, democratic, revolution, but also of the Russian people, of the allied war effort, and of what they saw as a universalistic world tilt toward Wilsonian progressivism. Rather than try to win the revolutionaries over with praise, loans, or even bribes, the United States backed away in horror.

Most European governments took an even more instant, more emotional dislike to the revolutionaries. Where the United States steadfastly refused to recognize separatist groups that periodically declared their independence within the old czarist borders, European governments were much more ready to extend such recognition since to do so was an indirect attack on bolshevism. Finding themselves without any friends, the Bolsheviks followed their own ideological blueprint, safe from outside contacts that might have moderated, contaminated, or corrupted the principles of the revolution.

Outbreak of civil war in Russia by mid-1918 led to military intervention. France, England, and Japan were the major players in this ill-fated adventure, with the United States a reluctant partner. National memories being what they are, the United States has tended to see its stay in Russia as minor, nonaggressive, and forgettable. The fact remains that America stationed about 12,000 troops in Russia for almost two years, and the Russians remember.

For their part, the Bolsheviks loudly proclaimed themselves the vanguard of a world revolution that would crumble the existing capitalist social and economic order. They played their own games with the concept of recognition. For example, they issued diplomatic initiatives by radio to peoples or workers rather than to governments. They ignored their predecessor governments' treaty agreements, denied responsibility for those governments' debts, and exposed the allies' secret treaties to public ridicule and disillusion. For a short while they even questioned the very legitimacy of nations, not to mention governments.

One might argue that the war had molded these initial responses and might theorize that peace would bring reassessments. Actually, at least between 1917 and 1919, the Bolsheviks had had doubts about their own ability to survive as a government and had not expected many governments to grant them full de jure recognition. By 1920, however, the war was over, Bolshevik authority extended across much of the nation, and the revolution's leaders had, at least rhetorically, agreed to play the diplomatic game by more traditional rules. With world revolution not immediately foreseeable, they put priority on safeguarding and expanding the revolution inside Russia. To do this, Lenin and his followers needed peaceful international relations, and they indicated a willingness to negotiate in traditional ways.

Recognition still was not immediately forthcoming. Ironically, there were more cracks in the European anti-Bolshevik stance than in the originally much less emotional and hostile American position. In fact, America's wartime wait-and-see policy solidified into formal denial of Bolshevik legitimacy. The Russians thought nonrecognition was premised on the assumption that if America and the other major powers withheld recognition the revolution would collapse. By this interpretation, nonrecognition represented active willingness to interfere in Russia's internal affairs. To attempt to destroy is to try to interfere, even if the interference is more of omission than of commission.

The United States was at the same time accusing the Bolshevik regime of interfering in other countries' affairs by fomenting revolution through propaganda. The revolutionaries' insistent distinction between government activities and party activities was, under the circumstances, as unconvincing as the American argument that leaving Russia completely alone to work out its own salvation—that is, quarantining it—was not a form of interference.

The American justification of nonrecognition was expressed most forcibly by Secretary of State Bainbridge Colby in 1920. The US government believed that the Russian people wanted a "stable government based on popular sovereignty." But those people were "helpless in the grip of a non-representative government, whose only sanction is brutal force" and "savage oppression," and whose policies reflected "the negation of every principle of honor and good faith . . . underlying the whole structure of international law." Colby declared that the revolutionaries had taken themselves beyond the diplomatic pale: "In the view of this Government, there cannot be any common ground upon which it can stand with a Power whose conceptions of international relations are so entirely alien to its own, so utterly repugnant to its moral sense."[2] The Wilson administration had responded to the radical Russian revolution with a radical recognition policy. The Bolshevik regime would not be granted recognition because it did not represent the popular will, had come to power by violence, was a promoter of world revolution, did not keep its promises or accept its responsibilities, and—an epithet with very broad interpretive possibilities—was morally repugnant. Harsh economic measures implemented during the Russian civil war (known as war communism) confirmed many Americans' beliefs that Marxist-Leninism was economically as well as morally destructive. The Bolsheviks' failure to accept responsibility for the Provisional Government's debts provided supporting evidence of deep-rooted international illegitimacy.

This, however, was the moralistic and therefore irrational Wilsonian criterion of recognition. In 1921 Wilson left office. The Bolsheviks, using Marxist theory to predict American behavior, thought that a more business-oriented leadership would respond rationally to profit-making opportunities. They expected the incoming Republican administration to extend recognition as an entrée to the economic concessions Lenin's government offered in a double-edged effort to attract foreign investment and to set off rivalries among capitalists.

While President Harding did in fact toy with the idea, Secretary of State Charles Evan Hughes was adamantly opposed. Hughes's position flew in the face of a Marxist reading of capitalism, but made sense as an emotional response to a perceived threat to the American way of (economic, political, and religious) life. Republican nonrecognition was somewhat less moralistic than Wilson's, stressing sanctity of contract, but it also emphasized Bolshevik tyranny and propaganda. In spite of periodic efforts toward recognition by some congressmen, businessmen, and internationalists, the twelve years of Republican rule saw no break with their Democratic predecessor's policy. While Herbert Hoover's Secretary of State, Henry Stimson, believed recognition of the Soviet Union could help keep an expansionistic Japan in check, Hoover himself had no intention of abandoning Wilson's policy toward their common ideological nemesis.

Like many Americans during the 1920s, Hoover continued to see the revolutionary government as Wilson and Colby had seen it: as a betrayer of the true Russian revolution; an unconstitutional tyranny; a foe of democracy, free enterprise, and rugged individualism; and an atheistic oppressor of individual freedoms. Russia served as a worst-case scenario to reaffirm arguments that the United States should hold at arm's length an Old World Europe that had spawned such an abomination.

For their part, the Bolshevik revolutionaries made clear their vision of the ultimate overthrow of capitalism, to be achieved when the working, producing people could free themselves from exploitation and oppression. Until that time, capitalist greed should itself be exploited to protect the revolution, to encourage socialist movements elsewhere, and to feed international capitalism's own ultimately self-destructive cannibalism. Formal recognition by individual capitalist governments was, of course, desirable because it would facilitate access to Western technology and finances, thus furthering socialism's goals. Access to America's awe-inspiring material, technological, and financial resources could be especially advantageous. But there were limits on how far the Soviets would compromise in order to obtain such benefits, particularly if half-measures were available without any compromise.

During the 1920s the Soviet Union concentrated on economic recovery from the devastation of world and civil wars. It preached and practiced a kind of international coexistence that would advance its recovery and encourage its survival in a hostile world. Concurrently, the United States enjoyed its own economic explosion and steered clear of balance-of-power political diplomacy.

With hindsight it is understandable that, given the world of the 1920s, both the American and the Russian governments could afford to talk *at* rather than *to* each other. Such was not the case in 1920s Soviet relations with Europe. The major European nations soon suspended their ideological antipathy toward bolshevism in the interests of other priorities.

This is not to say that Europe embraced the revolution. Germany and the Soviet Union found themselves paired as the two outcasts of postwar Europe. When it signed the 1922 Treaty of Rapallo, establishing economic and military ties with the Soviet Union, Weimar Germany became the first major European nation formally to recognize the revolution. Commercial motivation and fear of ties between Russia and Germany encouraged other European nations to recognize the revolution as well. In 1921 and again in 1923 the Soviet Union was invited to participate in European conferences. Great Britain opened diplomatic relations with the Soviet Union in 1924, although its economic parlays with the Bolsheviks implied at least de facto recognition as early as 1921. While Soviet–German friendship cooled noticeably after an aborted communist uprising in Germany in 1923, the mutual renunciation of war claims written into the Rapallo Treaty established a precedent that other recognizers would follow and that eliminated a major source of anti-Bolshevik sentiment. The Bolshevik government made no firm commitments to honor the war debts of earlier governments or compensate for foreign property confiscated during the war or by the revolution, but it did promise to halt the propaganda activities of its official foreign representatives.

Remembering postwar revolutionary efforts in their own region and still smarting from the memories of, or entangled in loyalties to, czarist Russia, much of Eastern Europe continued officially to denounce the Soviet Union. Yugoslavia, for example, as a parliamentary monarchy with no sympathy for communist ideology, and as sanctuary to thousands of anticommunist Russian emigrés, not only failed to recognize the new government but also outlawed its own rather sizeable Communist party. In this instance, normal diplomatic relations would not be established until just prior to the unwilling entry of both countries into World War II.

The Soviet Union was much less concerned about Eastern than about Western Europe. Recognition by the major powers would increase Russian prestige, open important economic contacts with the wealthier and more technologically advanced West, and provide the Communists with leverage with which, ideally, to turn the capitalist nations against themselves in their competition for Russian concessions. The Soviet propensity to advocate simultaneous economic coexistence and revolutionary agitation backfired in 1927 when the British accused Soviet diplomats of conspiring to subvert the British government and broke off relations for several years.

In general, even those European governments that extended recognition continued to hold Soviet Russia at arm's length and, ironically, trailed the United States in penetrating the communist economy. But the immediate postwar pattern of nonrecognition had been broken, and the United States stood alone among the major powers as formal censurer of the now ten-year-old regime.

The censurer by no means abstained from economic contamination, however. Whatever one might say about the logic of governmental nonrecognition as practiced by the United States in the 1920s, it allowed that country to have its cake and eat it too. During what may be the only instance of this variety of nonrecognition, the US government held fast to its castigation of the Soviet Union but left the American public and business community free to fraternize with the "enemy."

As a consequence, the sixteen years of nonrecognition were definitely not comparable to, for example, America's post-1949 ostracism of the People's Republic of China. Other than offering no support facilities, the US government made little effort to prevent private American individuals, organizations, or businesses from traveling to, cooperating with, working in, or doing business with the Soviet Union. In fact, during the famine years of 1921 and 1922, even the government, in the form of the American Relief Administration, dealt with what it considered to be an alien and repugnant government to facilitate the delivery of millions of dollars worth of famine relief to Russia.

This limited nonrecognition allowed Americans relatively free access to a Russia that was actively encouraging foreign contacts. Many of the major American newspapers and periodicals had permanent staff reporting from the Soviet Union, and American trade journals regularly commented on communism's successes and failures. Prominent American business leaders sought to negotiate concessions with the Soviet government, apparently undissuaded by its reputation for confiscation and debt repudiation. Henry Ford, an early critic of communism, agreed to design, staff, and provide complete operating specifications for a huge vehicle-construction project. Although he ultimately lost half a million dollars in the undertaking, he had no regrets, and for many years communist Russia moved almost exclusively in capitalist Ford vehicles.

Moral repugnance also did not stop Averell Harriman from negotiating for exclusive rights to exploit the huge and very important manganese deposits in Soviet Georgia, nor did it stop Socony-Vacuum Oil from buying large quantities of Soviet petroleum. These Americans and others worked closely with Amtorg (an American corporation that acted as Soviet agent in promoting bilateral trade arrangements) and the American–Russian Chamber of Commerce to develop, by the late 1920s, an economic connection that made the United States second only to Germany in the number of Soviet concessions it held and gave it one-third of all Russia's foreign trade. Over 1,000 American engineers worked in the Soviet Union, and American investment capital, machinery, and technology played major roles in Russia's march toward industrialization and collectivization. Americans also proved willing purchasers of Russian art. The dollar proceeds of such sales eased a foreign currency shortage that was caused in part by the US government's ban on the purchase of Soviet gold.

Officially, during the 1920s, little happened to change Bainbridge Colby's indictment. The Bolsheviks presumably were still as morally repugnant in 1930 as they had been in 1920. They had still come to power by violence, and Americans found it unbelievable that they might be representative of the popular will. Many Americans, such as influential labor leader Samuel Gompers, continued unabatedly to despise and fear all things Soviet. Secretary of State Frank Kellogg saw Soviet-inspired revolutionaries as responsible for 1920s unrest in Central America. Church leaders deplored communism's militant atheism, and other Americans had never forgiven its betrayal of the allied cause during the war.

On the other hand, clearly the Russians had changed. The harsh and destructive measures of war communism, which Americans had cited as proof both of communism's economic failure and its incompatibility with capitalism, gave way to the New Economic Program (NEP), which many of those same Americans now saw as evidence that communism would mellow into liberal capitalism. Just before the Great Depression, NEP in its turn gave way to the concept of centralized Five-Year Plans, which offered a potentially lifesaving alternative to a world drowning from too much capitalistic freedom. Ideologically, the Bolshevik party, speaking through the Communist International, was still preaching world revolution, but acceptance of the viability of socialism in one country (i.e., Russia) made the need for world revolution less urgent. Officially, the Soviet government presented itself as a champion of nonaggression and peaceful coexistence.

Formal American nonrecognition did not have a devastating impact on the Soviet Union and did not stop the revolution. Some Americans even argued that the policy was more harmful to their country than to Russia since the absence of official representation made it difficult to protect American interests, trade, and citizens. In addition, the United States government had no official sources of information about, or contact with, a country of potentially large influence in the world. There were still clear disadvantages for the Soviets, however. Nonrecognition did discourage some American businesses. Those that extended credit to the Soviets charged high rates and thus made trade more costly to the Russians. The American ban on Russian gold imports also made it that much harder for the Soviets to pay for American goods. For these and other reasons, the Soviet Union did want recognition.

The onset of world depression soured unofficial relations between the countries. Americans resented Soviet quips that the capitalist unemployed could find work in Russia. The United States accused the Soviet Union of dumping grain on the world market at below cost prices, thus further depressing American farm conditions. It refused to admit wood products allegedly made by "slave," or gulag, labor. Russia retaliated by dramatically cutting its purchases in response to what it saw as American discrimination against its goods. American business witnessed a fourteenfold decrease in its exports to Russia between 1931 and 1933. The US government's Reconstruction Finance Corporation tried to improve the situation (in spite of official nonrecognition) by establishing a $4 million credit for Russia to purchase American cotton, but by the end of the Hoover administration economic relations between the two countries were definitely cool.

All this time the United States government continued to recognize as the only legitimate spokesman for the Russian government, Sergei Ughet, who stayed on in charge at the Russian embassy in Washington after the Provisional Government's Ambassador Bakhmetev left in 1922 to teach at Columbia University. Therefore, it had no formal channels of communication through which to regain or protect its Russian market.

By the early 1930s more was at stake than just markets. The depression and the rise of German fascism led to a dramatic reorientation of Soviet–European relations. The depression and the rise of Japanese militarism had much the same impact on Soviet–American relations, especially after Franklin D. Roosevelt's election made realignment of Soviet–American relations politically and ideologically possible.

The Soviet Union was forced to put immediate national security considerations above the inevitable but endlessly postponable victory of communism over capitalism predicted by Marxist-Leninism. Militarism and fascism propelled the Soviets into seeking active collaboration (not just coexistence) with those capitalist governments themselves threatened by aggression. Concurrently, but ever so slowly, the United States realized that it might no longer be able to continue on its own while nonchalantly letting the rest of the world go by. Establishing normal relations was now much more important to both countries than it had been in the 1920s. Unfortunately, both sides came to expect more from recognition than seems in retrospect ever to have been reasonably possible. Failure to agree on mutually acceptable methods and goals led back to suspicions and animosities.

Roosevelt wanted to catch the imagination of the depression-fixated American public and convince it that dramatic changes were possible. Recognition of the Soviet Union after so many years of antipathy offered just such an opportunity. For most Americans in 1933, inertia may have played as much of a role in justifying continued nonrecognition as did anything the Soviets had or had not done. Nothing short of a new Russian revolution could win the support of those who continued to see the Bolsheviks as Antichrists, but such irreconcilables were few in number. Once an executive policy change broke the ice, Roosevelt's advisers foresaw few significant political liabilities domestically. Skeptical church leaders were assured that freedom of religion would be one of the prerequisites to recognition.

Some of the old problems still had to be addressed. The war debts remained unpaid and the Third International, spearheaded by the Soviet Communist party and providing direction to the American Communist party, still encouraged the overthrow of capitalism even as Soviet officials noted that communism and capitalism had proved they could coexist and argued for active collaboration. These were not insurmountable problems, however, if both sides were sincere in wanting to improve relations.

Sound reasons supported a shift in policy. Recognition would imply a positive, adaptive redirection of American foreign policy, eliminate an increasingly anomalous diplomatic embarrassment, improve trade relations, and possibly help to clip Japan's expansionist wings. Internationalists saw the chance to cooperate for world peace. Pragmatists applauded the practicality of opening communications in a time of rapidly increasing world complexity. Cynics noted that if nonrecognition was a result of nonpayment of debts, the United States should by now have broken relations with most of Europe after the almost total default of war debt payments by 1932.

In the climate of 1933 it was indeed hard to justify continued nonrecognition. The United States government had been able to ignore Russia with virtual impunity and avoid diplomatic entanglements in the 1920s. It could no longer do so without risk. Little chance of changing Russia's politics existed even if the United States was willing to continue the risk. Once other major powers had opened relations, unilateral nonrecognition could exert little influence on communist behavior. In fact, many Americans now argued that the United States could do more through recognition than through nonrecognition. Conversely, after sixteen years of propaganda efforts, the communists had had little success in fomenting revolution in the United States and could not realistically be seen as a domestic threat. In any case, recognition would probably give the government more control over radical activities at home rather than less.

It bears repeating that the Soviet Union could not itself determine American policy. It did, however, have its own priorities and its own prerequisites should recognition become a possibility. By the 1930s Stalin's control was complete and would become all the more so through a series of purges. The Soviet Union no longer lived in fear of imminent annihilation by a united capitalist onslaught. It could, in fact, congratulate itself on accurately predicting that greed would create rivalries among capitalists racing to exploit the communist market. Stalin's emphasis on socialism in one country, the relative lack of 1920s war fears, and over a decade of capitalist-communist cohabitation had made the Soviet Union a tolerated, if not actively courted, government. The country had made remarkable strides toward a mature economy, and it had done so without American recognition.

Now two traditional foes threatened Russia. Stalin's peace campaign gained momentum as he and his advisers tried to use nonaggression agreements as active, collective weapons against German and Japanese expansionism. In 1933 Stalin's most immediate concern was Japan, whose activities edged closer and closer to both the Soviet Union proper and Soviet interests in China. Japan might be unrestrainable without a cooperative Soviet–American effort, and Stalin had good reason to think the United States was concerned. As the other major Pacific power, America was equally leery of Japan's intentions, and while it was isolationist toward Europe, it was active in Pacific affairs. The Japanese problem was so prominent in 1933 that Soviet policymakers assumed it to be the primary impetus behind America's increasingly positive attitude toward recognition. Recognition, they hoped, would be followed by collaboration.

The Soviets wanted recognition for other reasons as well. Reversal of such a long-held American policy would represent a major diplomatic success in and of itself. It would also presumably improve access to American finances, especially important now that military preparedness was so vital. Depression to the contrary notwithstanding, the United States was still where the money and the technology were.[3]

Consequently, the Soviet Union responded favorably to unofficial feelers in 1933. Stalin sent to Washington Maxim Litvinov, a top Soviet diplomat with the prestige of high office, if not necessarily high party standing. During preliminary talks with representatives of the State Department, Litvinov presented a formidable front, but he was more flexible in his direct talks with Roosevelt. He may have been mirroring the attitude confronting him across the negotiation table. The State Department was not convinced that the United States had much to gain from recognition and was afraid normalization might come at America's expense. It tried to ensure that outstanding issues be resolved in detail before anything was signed. Roosevelt, more optimistic and less steeped in diplomatic formality and the Wilson–Hoover heritage, quickly reached agreement on issues over which earlier State Department talks with the Russians had produced impasses.

The Soviets readily agreed to guarantee freedom of religion for Americans in Russia. (A part of the American public would be dismayed when recognition did not bring guaranteed freedom of religion for Russians.) Relying on State Department groundwork, Roosevelt negotiated a promise from the Soviets to stop sponsoring, in America, political activities of a potentially subversive nature. Agreement was also reached on the protection of American nationals in Russia and on combating economic espionage.

But the Soviets staunchly refused to accept liability for that part of the Provisional Government's debts that had been expended fighting the Bolshevik Revolution. In fact, they presented their own bill of particulars demanding compensation for America's interventionist activities. They did accept responsibility, in principle, for other parts of the Provisional Government's indebtedness to the United States. Where the State Department had wanted detailed and prior agreement on specific amounts and methods of repayment, Roosevelt and Litvinov settled for a general statement setting upper and lower dollar limits, with details to be worked out in the future.

On 17 November 1933 sixteen years of this strange mixture of government nonrecognition and private-sector contact ended. Both countries expected significant benefits to accrue from the new relationship. Some analysts even thought that recognition could lead to a diplomatic partnership. Thus hopes were high for a brave new beginning in Soviet–American relations.

Much of the rest of the world welcomed the recognition, but from some very different perspectives. Whereas England and France both hoped it would mark increased American involvement in world affairs, Italy took it to mean that a more flexible United States would now accept changes in the status quo; that is, would acquiesce in Italy's expansionist plans. Almost everyone, including the Japanese, saw recognition as having implications for the Far East, in spite of there being no such reference in the Roosevelt–Litvinov agreements. In fact Japan responded as though Soviet–American cooperation had already been achieved. It backed away from activities along the Soviet border even though the US government repeatedly denied any anti-Japanese component to its new relationship with the Soviet Union.

Almost before the ink was dry on the agreements trouble developed. A roller coaster of diplomatic highs and lows quickly undercut the initial optimism. Negotiations on debt settlement fell apart when the United States refused to link American loans to Russian repayment and the Soviets refused to consider any other solution. The resulting charges and countercharges produced renewed ill will and suspicion that could not be offset by the signing of limited trade agreements. When the first Communist International meeting in years was held in 1935 and members of the American Communist party were prominently in evidence, many Americans questioned the sincerity of Soviet antipropaganda pledges.

Two years after recognition neither country had much to show for its efforts. For the Americans, there were no sizable gains in trade, and observers witnessed an increase, rather than decrease, in communist activism and Soviet oppression. The nay sayers could say, "I told you so," and disillusion dampened the enthusiasm and optimism of even the most ardent of recognition supporters, such as Roosevelt's (and America's) first ambassador to the Soviet Union, William Bullitt.

The Russians saw renewed US anti-Soviet rhetoric as an ominous failure to distinguish friend from foe. They had expected financial support and active cooperation in their peace campaigns. They had come away from the Roosevelt–Litvinov negotiations thinking it was understood that they would fund their war debts by paying a high interest rate on loans from America. The loans did not materialize, and neither, as a consequence, did the repayments. When the Soviets realized that the United States was unwilling to go beyond words and moral suasion in its role as peacemaker in Asia, they saw no security benefits to be gained by keeping America happy. As international tensions grew, Stalin increasingly relied on a united front tactic, which asked Socialist and Communist parties worldwide to support the Soviet peace campaign, and saw a positive Soviet–American working relationship less likely. He also sought defensive alliances with other governments. At home, Stalin embarked on massive purges, the reports of which rekindled American horror and further reduced the possibilities of cooperation.

In the five years after recognition, Soviet–American relations deteriorated relative to their prerecognition status. They suffered a major setback when Russia signed a nonaggression pact with Germany in 1939, fought a war with Finland, and annexed the Baltic nations and parts of Poland. The United States interpreted these actions as reaffirmations of Soviet perfidy. American ship-building firms were pressured into either cancelling their contracts with the Soviet navy or engaging in extreme delay tactics. By 1940, and in spite of Ambassador Joseph Davies's pleas for understanding, American relations with the Soviet Union had dropped to a low point, comparable to that of 1917.

Recognition had brought neither cooperation nor profit, but nowhere does it say that recognition *should* bring one or the other. Even William Bullitt, one-time Soviet supporter turned active Soviet critic and victim of the high expectation–disillusionment syndrome, understood that. He had left Russia in 1936 dismayed by what he witnessed and convinced that the two countries were incompatible. But he left still convinced

> that the value of recognition lay finally not in trade or in converting Russia in some marvelous burst of enlightenment but in simply being there: being in a position to exert subtle pressures on the government, giving visible examples of patience and determination, and most important of all being able to judge what really happened in the political and social sphere of Russian development and operations. These were as ample reasons for diplomatic relations as any that existed.[4]

Bullitt, as a now confirmed anticommunist supporting recognition of obnoxious regimes, was in a decided minority. His perspective would seem even less popular in the years after World War II when the United States' policy of nonrecognition was given a new gloss.

Once America's experiment in nonrecognition as an indictment of the Soviet Union's ideological obnoxiousness ended, it stayed ended in spite of post–World War II cold war tensions. But other, comparable ideological repugnances arose to which the United States responded with a revamped policy of nonrecognition. The policy involved much more sweeping ostracism than had nonrecognition of Russia. Beyond the absence of official contacts, American citizens, companies, organizations, and financial institutions were sometimes ordered not to trade with, travel to, or communicate with a nonrecognized government or its nationals.

For a long time, the People's Republic of China seemed just as happy to avoid recognition by, and thus contaminating contact with, the American "imperialists," just as America was happy to pretend China did not exist. Other targets of American nonrecognition might well have wished that the United States would revive its interwar approach to governments in official disrepute, however. If the current Vietnamese government, for example, had its choice, it would want full, normal relations. Assuming that, for whatever idiosyncratic American reasons, recognition is unlikely in the near future, it would settle for nonrecognition as practiced in the 1920s toward Russia, that is, a policy that would allow both parties at least the advantages of unofficial contact.

Recognition of formerly unrecognized governments, such as the People's Republic of China, has come, as with the 1933 recognition of the Soviet Union, not through any definitive change on the part of the unrecognized governments but, apparently, through very gradual awareness that nonrecognition was doing more harm than good. One consequence of nonrecognition has been that, by the time it decides to extend formal acknowledgment, the United States may have lost any chance to influence the recipient government's development. The Soviet Union and the People's Republic of China, for example, both found they could survive without American recognition and consequently, were unwilling to make many concessions just to obtain it.

The story of interwar Soviet–American relations offers at least one lesson as applicable now as it was then. While recognition under normal conditions is usually quite neutral in tone and rarely portends great expectations in future governmental camaraderie, recognition after years of nonrecognition often breeds false expectations. When reality fails to meet these expectations, frustration can make normalization all the more difficult. Disillusion was part and parcel of the consequences of extended nonrecognition. While earlier normalization of relations may not have changed history significantly, it might easily have improved the atmosphere, given both countries a better chance to learn and understand each other's foibles, and generally made that history more tolerant and much less traumatic.

NOTES

1. A full discussion of diplomatic recognition can be found in Gerhard von Glahn, *Law Among Nations: An Introduction to Public International Law,* 4th ed. (New York: Macmillan, 1981).

2. American note on the Polish situation, 10 August 1920, Box 3A. Bainbridge Colby papers, Library of Congress.

3. Some perspective on the way Russia viewed America in the 1920s and 1930s can be found in Hans Rogger, "America in the Russian Mind—Or Russian Discoveries of America," *Pacific Historical Review* 47:1(1978):27–51; and Nikolai V. Sivachev and Nikolai Yakovlev, *Russia and the United States: U.S.–Soviet Relations from the Soviet Point of View* (Chicago: University of Chicago Press, 1979).

4. For details of the failure of recognition to satisfy expectations see: Edward Bennett, *Franklin D. Roosevelt and the Search for Security: American–Soviet Relations, 1933–1939* (Wilmington, Del.: Scholarly Resources, 1985). For the quotation from Bullitt see: Edward M. Bennett, *Recognition of Russia: An American Foreign Policy Dilemma* (Waltham, Mass.: Blaisdell, 1970), 216.

The Big Three—Churchill, Roosevelt, and Stalin—at Yalta, 1945.
Courtesy of the Franklin D. Roosevelt Library.

American and Russian soldiers embracing at the Elbe, 1945.
National Archives.

chapter 2

THE GREAT PATRIOTIC WAR

For some twenty years after V-J Day (victory in Japan), World War II dominated American thinking about open, all-out military war. Since the mid-1960s the war has been overshadowed as memory and history by more recent events. Americans are not a very historically minded people to begin with; for most of them under age fifty, that war is as current and as relevant to their thinking as the War of 1812. Such is not the case for many Europeans. It is definitely not the case for Russians. In Russia, keeping the memory of World War II alive is a component to being patriotic. To understand the war's role in setting the stage for postwar Soviet–American relations, we must therefore try to see the war as Russians saw it. Not surprisingly, the Russians view the war very differently from how Americans remember it or learn about it in textbooks. Neither country has a monopoly on the truth of the matter. Both have hinged national policy and have molded public opinion on their own ethnocentric memories.

The orthodox, if simplified, American reading of the war projects an initially somewhat reluctant fight against Nazi Germany and Imperial Japan in which the United States played the role of primary victor. Hitler gobbled up as much of Europe as he could, with visions of extending the Aryan rule into Asia and Africa. An expansionist Japan was strangling China and imposing its "sphere of coprosperity" throughout Southeast Asia. The United States entered the conflict in Europe two years after it had begun and did so indirectly. After the Japanese attacked Pearl Harbor and Congress retaliated with a declaration of war, Japan's European ally, Germany, declared war on the United States. American texts divide the struggle into its European and Asian theaters, announce that American policymakers had decided to put first priority on defeating Germany, and then spend most of the ensuing chronology discussing the slow, tortuous naval battles in the Pacific. American texts tend to gloss over 1942 and 1943 in Europe and build instead toward the climactic invasion of Normandy in June 1944; thereafter, British and American troops sweep across Europe, and Germany surrenders in May 1945. Focus then shifts back to the Pacific, where the unexpected success of the atomic bomb brings about Japan's surrender in August 1945.

Russian texts take a somewhat different approach. To begin with, the war is not called World War II. It is referred to as the Great Patriotic War, and it is embedded in every Soviet citizen's historical consciousness. Russians learn that, with four years of sacrifice and courage, the Soviet Union put an end to the single most dangerous threat the world had witnessed to that date. Victory was achieved by the combined and coordinated efforts of the Communist party, the Red Army, the Russian people and institutions, and outstanding leadership and initiative. Russians are understandably proud of having defeated the Nazis. They see it as their victory, overlapping in time what the West calls World War II but really comparable with respect only to the enemy. If Germany was a rogue lion locked in combat with Russia, the wounded bear, then, from a Russian perspective, the role of the Western allies through mid-1944 could best be compared to a buzzing mosquito trying to distract the lion. By 1944–45 the allies' role had grown perhaps to that of a hawk, whose attacks injured the lion but were still secondary to the main struggle.

Like most Americans, most of today's Soviet citizens are too young to remember the war personally. They are not too young to know that twenty million Russians died rendering a service to the homeland and to the world. Nor are they too young or too ahistoric to wonder why much of the world is reluctant to acknowledge, much less applaud, Russia's role in the war. To give just one example of how alive and relevant World War II still is in the Russian mind, it is not unusual for couples to be married at one of the many war memorials. They pledge their fidelity to each other and, in memory of those who died during the war, to their nation.

This virtual obsession with World War II is not unique to Russia. The middle-aged Yugoslav is much the same, although in his case the war seems somehow to have centered on his country. The point here is not that people have accurate or inaccurate images of the war; rather, it is that we need to keep in mind that people and nations can have different interpretations of approximately the same sets of facts.

The Soviet Union spent most of the 1930s warning the world against fascism and militarism. Unfortunately, many in the West believed that communism was a greater threat than were Hitler, his thugs, and their fascist ideas of state supremacy. Others were reluctant to believe that these things were actually happening, or chose to read Russia's warnings as mere words disguising equally nefarious communist intentions. France, Czechoslovakia, and Poland all were hesitant to conclude binding defense treaties with the Soviet Union because neither of the last two countries was willing to allow Soviet troops to pass through its territories. Would Hitler have been eager, in 1938 and before he had experienced those early easy successes, to risk a joint Russo–French response to any aggressive move on his part? As it was, all of Europe found out what it was like to experience the presence of German troops.

In 1939 the United States was still pretending it had no vested interest in Europe's problems. Soviet–American relations were not particularly cordial. In fact, apparently more concerned about China and Japan than about Europe and Hitler, Roosevelt, Secretary of State Cordell Hull, and Secretary of War Henry Stimson spent much of their time trying to discourage Japan's expansion southward into China and Southeast Asia. If they had succeeded, Japan might well have opted to move north, against Russia. Since we would probably all be living in a very different, much less pleasant, world if Russia had been busy fighting Japan in the Pacific when Hitler invaded in 1941, this failure of American policy was probably a good thing.

When Hitler took Czechoslovakia and then eyed Poland, many in the West expected that he would move next against Russia. Some hoped the two "bogey men" of Europe would lock themselves into a duel to mutual death. Nothing could have made the Russophobes happier. England and France reaffirmed their promise to defend Poland, but many of their citizens and policymakers would happily have sacrificed Poland (as they had Czechoslovakia) on the altar of peace in their time and in the hope that Russia and Germany would destroy each other.

They misjudged the Soviet Union. In 1939, knowing that it was not militarily equal to the Third Reich's war machine, Russia refused to commit suicide. It signed the much-maligned neutrality agreement with Hitler. Neither country really expected Hitler to live up to the treaty's pledge of non-aggression, but the agreement did give the Soviet Union breathing space in which to make preparations. From a Russian vantage point, just as the harsh 1918 "peace" Treaty of Brest-Litovsk had been accepted so that the Bolshevik Revolution could survive and lead history's march toward a socialist world, so too this pact provided vital time in which to build defenses against fascism. At approximately the same time, but with much less international ballyhoo, Russia signed an armistice with Japan, thus allowing both countries to concentrate their attentions elsewhere with greatly reduced risk of having to fight on two fronts simultaneously.

The nonaggression treaty with Hitler was a public-relations nightmare then and later. Having refused to support Russia's anti-Nazi stands in the 1930s, and having ceded Austria and Czechoslovakia without a word, the Western powers now accused the Soviet Union of betraying civilization. Their after-the-fact reasoning assumed that if the pact had not been signed Hitler would have attacked Russia and not France. This would, of course, have been much better for France, but not for Russia.

In fact, Germany and the Soviet Union signed a number of agreements in 1939. One confirmed that the Baltic provinces belonged to the Soviet Union. None of the provinces had proved themselves economically viable in their twenty years as independent nations. They had broken off from Russia while civil war prevented the Soviet government from stopping them, and they remained independent during the interwar years only because the major powers deemed them to be so.

The treaties divided up Poland. Some may read this move as a callous Soviet land grab. Others see it as a miscalculation on Stalin's part since, by eliminating Poland as a buffer, it brought Germany right to Russia's door. In all probability, however, without such an agreement Hitler was prepared to take all of Poland himself. He would still have ended up at Russia's door, but the door would have been significantly nearer Russia's heartland. Once Hitler had put Poland in his sights, the question was not whether Russia and Germany, historically and ideologically hostile to each other, would end up at war, but rather where that war would begin. Stalin opted for it to begin in Poland, not Russia.

If the West gave Russia grief for having come to terms with Germany, it did not have much to gloat over itself. Germany's invasion of Poland in September 1939 did bring declarations of war from both Great Britain and France, thus beginning what is commonly referred to as World War II. But it was not much of a war. France was able to put up very little resistance and fell much more quickly than anyone had expected. England warded off a cross-channel invasion and then went on hold. The United States, pursuing domestic prosperity, finally readjusted its neutrality laws to allow arms sales to England; but while it castigated Russian behavior, it was itself unwilling actively to confront the Nazis. The first two years of World War II passed with little or no *war* and not much *world.*

Rather perversely, while Hitler kept building his strength, American attention focused on the Russo–Finnish war, during which the Finns benefited from the Anglo-Saxon mentality of cheering for the underdog and from sentimental attachments to the one nation that had repaid its infinitesimal World War I debts. Few Americans gave much heed to Finland's friendship toward fascist Germany or to Russia's strategic vulnerability had the Russo–Finnish border not been adjusted.

All of the early recriminations were at least temporarily muted when, in June 1941, Hitler did attack the Soviet Union. Thus began Russia's Great Patriotic War, and thus, in fact, began Russia's real world war: the war that tested the country's character, ideologies, courage, and commitment; that forced everyone to recognize just how serious a threat Hitler posed; that proved the 1917 Revolution and the resulting Soviet Union were not historical flukes but were, rather, beginnings; and that would shape the future of the world.

With the aid of hindsight one can argue that Hitler's invasion of Russia marked the beginning of the end of the war. Making the same mistake that others had made before him, Hitler tackled something that was just too big for him to handle and precipitated his own defeat. Also using hindsight one can argue that Hitler came extremely close to beating Russia. Had he done so, or had the Russians surrendered (not necessarily the same thing), the outcome would have been a very different story from everyone's perspective. In the context of Soviet–American relations, the relevant factor may be that Russia won and emerged a major force in world affairs. In the context of the war itself, the relevant factor was that Russia did not give up, and thus did not allow Germany the chance to use its energies elsewhere. At no point prior to 1944 at the earliest did the United States play as pivotal a role as did Russia. The Russians may have more reason than they know, therefore, to see their Great Patriotic War as the real war.

Few of these wartime and postwar ramifications were, of course, immediately apparent when Germany attacked Russia. The United States was not yet even a combatant, and in the early going the Third Reich seemed about to march all the way across the Soviet Union. Later in 1941 Japan and the United States declared war on each other and in so doing gave more geographic credibility to the world war rhetoric. When Hitler complied with the terms of the Axis alliance and declared war on the United States, America entered the Western Europe nonwar and spent two and a half years emulating Britain's cautious inactivity. By 1942 most of the world was committed to the war or had been engulfed by it. The real fighting was concentrated inside the Soviet Union, but because of the ethnocentricity and physical limitations of national news coverages, the American public read of American troops marching across Africa. They paid little attention to the concurrent and immeasurably more important battles for Moscow and Stalingrad, not to mention the siege of Leningrad.

Westerners have written that the June 1941 attack caught Russia by surprise. Most Russians disagree, arguing that it would be more accurate to say that the country was not yet fully prepared. No nation can spend all its resources planning for war; even a country as rich in natural resources and industrial bases and as remote from the battle as the United States took years to get up to real fighting strength. World War I and its civil war had lain waste to much of Russia's lands and industries. Recovery was a drawn-out process and, although Russia's growth under the NEP and Five-Year Plans was definitely impressive, the traumas of collectivization and later the massive purges of civilian and military leaders left the country psychologically and physically shaken. Consequently, Russia was not prepared to take on the

Third Reich in 1939; nor was it really ready in 1941. Both the navy and the air force were weak, in part because the US government did not allow American firms to undertake military contracts with the Soviet government. An old and proved Russian saying calls necessity the mother of the impossible, however.

When the Germans attacked, Russia made mistakes. It tried to do too much too soon (e.g., being unwilling to retreat in the face of overwhelming forces) and was particularly hampered by an insufficient air force. Russia suffered unimaginable deprivation and loss, and those who survived carried with them indelible memories of the horrors of war.

After Hitler invaded Russia, Great Britain and the United States quickly changed their tune, although Winston Churchill's often-quoted reference to having a good word to say for the devil if the devil were fighting Hitler makes it clear that this would be a cooperation of convenience, not of real cama-raderie. The United States shipped lend-lease supplies to Russia, and joint planning and coordination channels were established. Both the British and the Americans made these early overtures not at all sure that their efforts could do more than postpone the time when, after Russia's defeat, they would themselves once again be under German attack. Thus the two major Western allies underestimated the Soviet Union, and as a consequence they were reluctant to risk an early and logistically premature invasion of Europe just to relieve a Soviet army that might possibly have to surrender anyway. It was no surprise that the Russians did not appreciate that particular line of reasoning.

With quiet on their western front, Hitler's armies concentrated on Russia. At first the Soviet army had no choice but to retreat. Leningrad survived as an island of resistance in a sea of enemy troops. German troops ravaged the land and then made ready to march on Moscow. When Moscow held, the Germans tried to cut off its access to the Black and Caspian seas, and in September 1942 they attacked Stalingrad.

The Battle of Stalingrad, which lasted from September 1942 until the German surrender in early February 1943, marked the turning point in the war, and long before allied troops landed at Normandy. In fact, from one perspective, the allies waited until Russia had things well in hand before launching the D-Day invasion in 1944. The Russian counteroffensive began at Stalingrad with a fiery and bloody defense, with some German overex-tensions and miscalculations, and with a heroic Russian commitment of manpower and courage. Some might well say that the Germans lost their bid for world domination and the world was saved from fascism at Stalingrad. After that it was simply a matter of time and of graves as the Red Army slowly pushed the Third Reich back.

While the battle of Stalingrad was being waged, the wartime allies, En-gland, Russia, and the United States, did agree to fight the war against Hitler together, through to its conclusion. No one would sign a separate peace (as had been the case with Russia in World War I) and leave the others to face Hitler alone. While this agreement eased Western fears of a Russian separate peace, it did little at the time to ease Russia's need for relief against the German onslaught. The Soviet Union asked England and the United States to open a second front, attacking Germany in the west and forcing a division of the fascist forces. Roosevelt and General George Marshall agreed, but were then talked out of it by the British. Instead, a joint Anglo–American force attacked North Africa, where Rommel's troops were blocking the allies' supply routes to the Middle and Far East and trying to establish German access to the oil fields. The Western allies reasoned that they were not yet strong enough for a successful invasion of Europe, and that it was imperative to keep their own supply lines open and to cut those of Germany. Unfortunately, it was easy for Russians to interpret the North African campaign as proof that empire and economics took higher priority for the allies than did the continuing slaughter of Russia's people.

In 1943 Russia again asked for a second front, again received a positive answer, and again got nothing. The allies invaded Italy, insignificant from a Russian perspective but vitally important in maintaining control of the Mediterranean. During much of the war between one hundred fifty and two hundred German divisions crowded the Russian front; at no time between 1939 and 1945 were there ever more than fifty divisions on the western front and often as few as seventeen. By 1943 the Russians had good cause to feel that they were carrying more than their share of the war and that the allies, and especially Great Britain, were using the war for nationalistic and ideological purposes that were damaging to Soviet interests.

By 1944 the Red Army had retaken most of the motherland and stood ready to liberate Europe. The Soviet Union had suffered twenty million deaths, but it had routed and then demolished the finest fighting machine the world had ever known. Now the allies actually did open a second front with the Normandy invasion in June 1944. Generals Eisenhower and Patton and Field Marshal Montgomery marched across Western Europe. British and American air forces preceded this sweep with saturation bombing raids and accompanied it with massive air support that neutralized the Nazi air power. Russia had had the benefit of neither. Nevertheless, a last-ditch defense by Germany, the Battle of the Bulge, delayed the Western allies long enough to allow the Red Army to be the first troops into Germany and to have sole responsibility for the liberation of Eastern Europe.

World War II ended in Europe with the German surrender in May 1945. That victory cost the United States fewer than 200,000 lives and no physical damage inside its borders. America ended the war with the largest army ever put under arms (twelve million in 1945 to the Soviet Union's eleven million), the strongest economy ever witnessed, and a population about to become, as a direct result of the war, the most affluent in human history.

Still the Americans turned to the decimated and war-weary Russians for help. Convinced that a final assault on the Japanese home islands would cost them a million casualties, they pleaded with Stalin to declare war on Japan, and Stalin agreed. Obviously, he did not do so either for altruistic reasons or as a glutton for punishment. Although Japan and the Soviet Union had agreed to mutual nonaggression, Russia had long wished to reclaim lands taken in the Russo–Japanese war of 1905. In addition, Russia had a strong interest in the Far East, and with the Japanese in retreat, could not let the United States expand uncontested into the area. Stalin agreed, therefore, that the Red Army would deal with the Japanese forces on the mainland while the United States dealt with the home islands.

The Soviet Union declared war on Japan on 8 August 1945. This was exactly three months to the day after Germany's surrender in Europe and exactly as agreed seven months earlier at the February 1945 meeting of the Big Three (Stalin, Roosevelt, and Churchill) at Yalta. In less than a week the Japanese sued for peace, a full year ahead of American projections for an American solo effort. That, at least, is how Russian accounts tend to read.

American history downplays Russia's role in the Pacific and even manages to imply that its presence was undesirable. Since the United States had repeatedly asked for that presence, something must have happened to change the minds of American policymakers. That something was the atomic bomb, which plays very little role in Russia's interpretation of Japan's decision to surrender. Worried about Russia's military power in Europe, the United States had always wanted to keep the communist giant out of Asia and wished, ideally, to occupy a defeated Japan unilaterally. The atomic bomb helped turn wish into reality. It facilitated an American victory in Asia in which Russia had only a minor role, and allowed the United States to accept Japan's surrender and occupy that island nation with little or no participation by its allies. This obsession with control over the Pacific was not at the time so much a fear of communism (the real cold war had not begun in mid-1945) as it was a desire to do it the American way and do it without interference by *anybody*.

Throughout the war the United States and Great Britain coordinated their operations: the British assumed responsibility for most European activities and the United States took charge of the Pacific theater. After Stalingrad, the Western allies finally accepted the Soviet Union as a full partner. The Big Two became the Big Three as the top leaders held summit meetings at which they drew up guidelines for political, military, and economic coordination. From at least mid-1943 through V-E Day (victory in Europe), the personalities of these men dominated allied diplomacy and much of the national and international policy formulation, even though they met together as a threesome only twice, at Teheran in late 1943 and at Yalta in early 1945.

Roosevelt thought that ideological and national security differences could all be resolved through personal diplomacy. A man of great charm and persuasiveness, he was used to being able to "talk people around" to his view. Eager to avoid cracks in the allied front, he often assumed that everyone saw and interpreted agreements, joint communiques, and unspoken understandings exactly as he did. He frequently failed to pay close attention to detail, to his advisors, or to alternative interpretations.

Like many Americans, Roosevelt understood very little about actual social and economic conditions in the world. He believed that everyone would want to be as much like the United States as possible and felt, therefore, that the United States spearheaded a global commonality of interest. A self-proclaimed Wilsonian internationalist with a strong streak of pragmatism, Roosevelt rejected "spheres of influence" and eagerly championed universalist goals that were often either remarkably vague (e.g., freedom from hunger) or not even very universal within his own country (e.g., racial equality). Having learned the lesson of World War I's secret treaties and petty, nationalistic ambitions, he made very few advance commitments to the political and geographic makeup of the postwar world. This meant that, come the end of the war, Roosevelt had not thought through all the changes necessarily or potentially consequent to such a conflagration. Many would argue that he and American policymakers in general had not isolated American security interests, as opposed to the more nebulous Wilsonian universalist goals, in such a world.

Churchill was a masterful if conservative politician who championed the British Empire, feared both Russia and communism, and believed in the principles of backroom hard bargaining and power realities. He wanted first and foremost to preserve England's place as a world power and to protect not just the empire but also access routes. Since the British Empire was geographically dispersed, Churchill's actually rather specialized interests gave the impression of being global. A conservative in all the ways that matter diplomatically, he defended a codified status quo antebellum whenever possible, but was sometimes forced to accept temporary alterations. For example, he was a staunch supporter of Yugoslavia's monarchy until he became convinced that significantly stronger resistance to the Germans could be achieved by at least temporarily sacrificing nobility to the cause of victory. At that point, Britain shifted its support to Marshal Tito and the partisans. With victory in sight, England once again shifted to backing the monarchical claims in Yugoslavia and, more dangerously for the future, in Greece.

At Versailles in 1919 Churchill had wanted to move against the Bolshevik Revolution; in Moscow in 1944 Stalin and Churchill informally assigned influence percentages to each other in the immediate postwar administration of the various soon-to-be-liberated countries. In this percentage agreement, Churchill voluntarily acknowledged a preponderant role for his longtime villain, the Soviet Union, in much of Eastern Europe. The apparent inconsistencies were not really inconsistencies. In 1919 he had seen a chance to end communism before it had begun. In 1944 he grudgingly accepted Russia's inevitable postwar power and wanted to channel that power away from English interests. Thus he would concede parts of Eastern Europe in order to keep Russia out of the Middle East.

Stalin may have had less experience in the democratic art of public politicking than did Roosevelt or Churchill, but he surrendered no advantage to the others when it came to hard bargaining and face-to-face negotiations. Committed to protecting his own individual interests and the Soviet Union's political and security interests, he could be flexible on peripheral issues but held firm on questions vital to Russia's security. The Americans were especially eager to obtain agreement on a new version of the League of Nations. Stalin had little faith in such an organization and knew it would be controlled by the Western allies and their surrogates. Playing on the Americans' obsession with the United Nations Organization and their need for Russian help against Japan, Stalin hemmed and hawed. He gave in on several peripheral issues; for example, Nationalist China as a permanent member of the Security Council could only be explained as one of Roosevelt's misguided pipe dreams, but if that made Roosevelt happy, so be it. Similarly, Stalin accepted Great Britain's demand for equal voting rights for all Commonwealth members, a ploy that would assure Britain a large block of votes in the General Assembly. He could accept these inequities and political fantasies secure in the knowledge that the Soviet Union's own permanent membership on, and the veto power in, the Security Council would protect his country and the communist revolution from external reactionary interests. Stalin was equally determined to safeguard his country's interests in neighboring areas that historically had endangered Soviet security, to obtain financial and material resources with which to begin Russia's awesome rebuilding task, and to ensure a postwar Germany that could never again wreak devastation and tragedy.

Churchill and Stalin had the advantage over Roosevelt in that they both knew they were playing a diplomatic game at which they were masters. It is not always clear, on the other hand, whether either fully appreciated how badly America played the diplomatic game. Certainly neither foresaw how disruptive would be its later attempts to interpret literally statements that clearly had been designed for public consumption, and to interpret figuratively concrete statements that had been worded fluidly only to accommodate the naive sensibilities of British and American voters.

The Yalta agreements are a classic case in point. At Yalta, with Germany's defeat assured, the Big Three began real postwar planning. At the time, most of the terms were either secret or designed only as sops to various publics. The American furor later to play such a role in the cold war resulted from superimposing a postwar atmosphere onto a wartime setting. Everyone actually at Yalta thought they had worked out the best possible solutions to very complex issues.

The delegates spent much of their time discussing the future of Eastern

Europe in general and Poland in particular. They issued a Declaration on Liberated Europe, which promised self-determination in setting up new governments and made few other demands except that such governments should be friendly to the Soviet Union. All the delegates must surely have understood that the Soviet Union, victim of two invasions through Eastern Europe in less than twenty-five years and now one of the world's two strongest nations, could not and would not accept hostile neighbors. Many of these countries still had entrenched conservative, even fascist, political elites. Some of the governments in exile were openly hostile to the Soviet Union, did not want to legalize their indigenous Communist parties, and had no intentions of letting socialist or communist representatives take part in the postwar governments. A war was being fought to overcome such political oppression, and clearly the liberated nations would need to free their political structures as well. Churchill, in spite of his own political conservatism, recognized this reality in conceding primary Soviet influence in the area. Among the many causes of the cold war must be included later efforts by both the British and the Americans to minimize that Soviet influence. In these efforts, the United States evidenced disregard for the political conditions in those countries, for power realities, and for Eastern Europe's importance to the Soviet Union.

Germany's fate also rated much attention. While final arrangements were not made until the Potsdam summit in July 1945, at Yalta all agreed that Germany would temporarily be divided into occupation zones, with overall planning and development coordinated by a series of interallied committees. Stalin accepted the inclusion of France as a fourth occupational force only on condition that the territory assigned France be taken from the English and American sectors. A bureaucratic structure for postwar occupation of Germany provided few problems, but deciding the nature of that country and how much it should pay for its sins tore the wartime alliance apart.

The issue of reparations was inextricably tied to each participant's vision of Germany's future and to each participant's suffering at German hands. The United States, which had suffered no physical damage during the war, magnanimously "gave up" any claims to reparation payments and, remembering the reparation–war debt imbroglio of the two post–World War I decades, advocated that the other victors make minimal demands. Russia, which had suffered unimaginable material and personnel losses, could not, in good conscience to the demands of its people, agree. The Yalta participants finally arrived at a German reparation figure of $20 billion, of which the Soviet Union would get fifty percent. Given the extraordinarily heavy bombing to which American and British bombers subjected what would be the Soviet sector in Germany just before the war was over, the allies agreed at Potsdam that Russia should also receive ten percent of the industrial capacity, in plants and products, of the three other, less damaged sectors. When one realizes that the $11 billion in United States lend-lease shipments to the Soviet Union comprised only a small part of Russia's total military costs and did nothing to make up for its physical damages, it is clear that $10 billion would be more a symbol of Germany's crimes than an actual price tag on the damages done.

The agreements reached by the Big Three soon became the subjects of intense policy and academic debate. Much of the acrimony led directly back to charges that people were or were not living up to their Yalta promises. The Russians still see the agreements as evidence that acceptable and realistic relations between them and America could have been possible and were derailed only by Roosevelt's death and an abrupt change in American policy under Truman. American analysts are much less confident that even Roosevelt would have been able to keep the Russians in line or accept the Russian reading of what the Yalta agreements really amounted to.

No comparable problems plagued postwar relations in Asia. Not that there were no areas of potential disagreement; but America's position was strong enough, and may have been strong enough without the atomic bomb, that it was able simply to dictate a virtually free hand in the occupation and reconstruction of Japan. Many of the countries occupied by Japan during the war reverted, to the displeasure of their nationalist forces, to their prewar colonial status. That China would be reconstituted under the Nationalist government had long ago been agreed to by the Big Three, and the reopening of civil war in that country did not immediately impinge on Soviet–American relations. The division of Korea into a north occupied by the Red Army and a south occupied by the US Army would take several years to build to a center of cold war crisis.

When World War II ended the United States was still expanding, not yet having reached its full military and industrial capacities. For its part, the Soviet Union was exhausted. It had fought for over four years; it had shouldered most of the human cost of defeating Germany; it had lost immeasurable amounts of blood and resources, infrastructure and industry. Russia and the Russians needed desperately to have peace, to go home, and to begin the slow task of healing. In the four years during which the two countries had been allies against Germany, however, seeds of disagreement had been sown that would make peace difficult to achieve.

The Americans may not have called it the Great Patriotic War, but they definitely thought of "the Big One" as primarily their victory over two very different but equally horrific challenges to freedom. They were proud of their performance, saw the war as proof of what the United States could do when it put its mind to it, and expected a postwar world dedicated to the perpetual preservation of American-style freedom. In these perceptions they were ethnocentric and not a little naive, but they were not alone. To the Russians, their part in the war was an amazing display of stamina, patriotism, and sacrifice. They were proud of their performance, saw the war as proof of their nation's might, and expected a postwar world in which they could feel secure. In these perceptions Russia too was ethnocentric and naive.

Weapons testing: explosion of the atom bomb, Bikini, 1950.
UPI/Bettmann Newsphotos.

chapter 3

WAR OR PEACE?
THE COLD WAR RECONSIDERED

People in positions of power often seem instinctively to be suspicious or greedy, traits that frequently lead to belligerency. Although politicians and statesmen devote countless speeches to the virtues of peace, they (and their historians) seem so obsessed by war as to suggest that peace serves only to link the more compelling rites of militant passage. Histories often read like a conspiratorial, competitive game in which the rules are fluid and all that matters is winning or assessing blame. Wars honeycomb history. The artifacts of war are enshrined in museums. The artifacts of peace are another story; people find it difficult even to define them. It is no surprise that the twentieth century has distorted at least one part of its history and called it war when, in fact, it was peace.

The term *cold war*, used to describe those years after World War II during which unfriendly Soviet–American relations dominated world headlines, is a misnomer. The era witnessed tension, anger, suspicion, high rhetoric, and even some belligerency. To say that friction is war, however, is to say that history is war. History is full of tensions, suspicions, and bombast. Sometimes these lead to war but sometimes they do not. We cannot afford to confuse the two by calling forty odd years of peace a war. So far, the cold war has not been a real war, has definitely not been comparable to, for example, the Napoleonic wars or World War II. It has, however, been a very tenuous, very nerve-wracking, and very costly peace. Perhaps more accurately, the cold war should have been called a cease fire in the war that never was.

The so-called cold war began as a struggle over influence in Europe. For five hundred years Europe had been the driving force in Western, or modern, history. After 1945 it became the prize (or prizes) over which new driving forces haggled. Europe is a rather small land mass as continents go, further subdivided into even smaller nations most of which have spent much of their history fighting each other. Perhaps for that reason, the technological revolution began in Europe, as did the parallel move toward industrialization. In search of markets and raw materials, the more aggressive nations competed for territorial and commercial advantage. Sharp economic and class divisions characterized social structures. As domestic resources dwindled and economic stratification increased, interclass and internation conflict became common. Advances in technology made exploration, war, and exploitation easier.

The particularly destructive carnage of the Great War of 1914–1918 was followed only twenty years later by an even more widespread conflict that prompted the numbering of these wars. The consequences, if not the causes, of World War II led almost immediately to antagonistic relations between the United States and the Soviet Union, two territorially large nations that had been developing on the periphery of center-stage Europe. The three major prewar European powers, England, France, and Germany, all lost the war, although only Germany was placed under foreign occupation. Europe was left so weakened, and America and the Soviet Union left so strengthened (America absolutely and Russia militarily), that the world experienced a dramatic shift in its political equilibrium.

This shift must be seen as a kind of natural phenomenon, like the massive subterranean upheavals that created mountains or reshaped continents. While I would not argue that specific events in history qualify as truly inevitable, I would argue that change in one form or another is inevitable. More often than not, men have fought, literally and figuratively, against change. In spite of the rhetoric, the crises, and the hysteria, what the cold war witnessed was, rather amazingly, a peaceful accommodation to change.

Among other things, that change involved the shift away from Europe as center of the universe, constantly engaged in intra-European rivalries over extra-European territories, to the United States and the Soviet Union as two competing centers of world power engaged in rivalry for influence over first European and later more global stretches of territory. The change wrought dramatic and often terrible physical and psychological discomfort. That it occurred with so low a cost in actual human lives is remarkable; unfortunately, that fact is given relatively little good press. The more usual approach has been to recount all the disagreements between the new rivals and construct an illusion of war, complete with good guys and bad guys, that obscures the fact that there was no war. What I would like to stress is that all these things happened, but happened *without* igniting a third world war.

Russia and the United States were in uneasy tandem as covictors. Each was caught up in its own ethnocentricities, ideology, and concept of national security. After the war, with no common enemy to bind them together, these two formerly peripheral but now much more central powers gravitated away from their short-lived wartime unity into postwar rivalry. Economic and ideological antagonists long before World War II, their antipathies had been overshadowed by inter-European concerns. Reflecting the shift in world equilibrium, the old frictions, expressed in a variety of new ways, now assumed prominence. Since the realignment occurred simultaneously with the break-up of Europe's colonial empires, the weakened old and the developing new nations found themselves drawn reluctantly into the tug of war of a global bipolarity.

This competitive realignment is what is referred to as the cold war. The people affected saw it variously as preferable to or as a preamble to a third world war. Years before technology made it actually possible, many thought a final atomic war would destroy the world. Consequently, the cold war seemed both more and less dangerous than earlier hot wars. Many in the West assumed that, since it was called a war, there had to be a winner, an all-or-nothing resolution to a conflict that, if it did erupt into open hostilities, could annihilate life on the planet. Almost no one among the Western policy-making elite saw postwar developments as the rather natural, actually stabilizing aftershocks of a long-term equilibrium shift. In other words, they failed to read them as the beginning of a peace.

Incompatibility of plans for the occupied and liberated areas sparked some of the first frictions. Soon they moved from concerns about, for example, Poland per se toward a game in which winning Poland was a way to score points. Increasingly, both the new power centers evaluated nations and problems less in terms of their own intrinsic complexities, and more as pawns to be manipulated in the larger, but not necessarily more sophisticated, cold war strategy. Thus, for example, Americans viewed the Greek civil war as a global struggle pitting the United States against the spectre of Soviet expansion. The Soviet Union deposed a popular, stable, and economically efficient government in Czechoslovakia, at significant cost to its own most efficient road to recovery, simply to ensure uncontested authority and forestall the Americanization of Czechoslovakia. These are but two instances of cold war strategy that kept much of the rest of the world on tenterhooks for decades.

At least part of the reason for such behavior was ideological and thus more than a little irrational. Ideology provides very strong, often more robotic than reasonable motivations for actions and policies. It also offers an easy way to avoid self-doubt. By the middle of the twentieth century, most of the policy elites of the world identified themselves either as capitalists or socialist/ communists. National economies (while often a mixture of all three) trumpeted their allegiances to one system only and frequently declared any other to be inefficient, unjust, or even immoral and dangerous. Capitalists are by definition not Marxists. They see no need to evolve beyond capitalism, and they are particularly fearful of a communist ideology that not only preaches the evils of private property and projects capitalism's demise but is willing to help that demise along. Communists assume that capitalism will not go down without a fight and will even take the offensive to halt evolution. All of this should perhaps be taken with a grain of salt, but with a grain that recognizes that, when World War II ended, many many people believed in such ideologies literally and explicitly.

The jumble of labels, beliefs, myths, and obsessions contained within just the communist–capitalist chapter of mankind's many ideologies is, to say the least, confusing. Soviet communism seems to believe that freedom in the future can best be achieved through collective controls, centralized planning, and virtual negation of individualism in the present. Marxist-Leninism teaches that humanity is inherently good, but assumes that most individuals are not trustworthy. American democracy assumes that people have equal political rights and can be trusted collectively to make good decisions. Capitalism assumes that men are inherently unequal and probably evil, but will individually make self-serving decisions that somehow, mysteriously, work for the collective good. The United States and the Soviet Union each believes that it is right and that its way is synonymous with virtue. Each sees the other as not only wrong but evil. They seem equally unaware that American democratic capitalism is unique to the United States and Soviet communism is unique to the Soviet Union. Neither has really accepted that other people are committed to multitudes of other, equally appealing, equally confusing ideologies. The two new powers carried their ethnocentric, ideological baggage with them into the cold war. They also carried their own histories.

Russia has a long history of autocracy, restrictiveness, and gross administrative inefficiency. Socially, economically, and philosophically backward compared to Europeans, and aggressively expansionistic compared to their weaker neighbors, nineteenth-century Russians lived in a constant struggle against famine, unemployment, and the tax collector. Although rich in natural resources, much of the land mass was and is climatically uninviting. Its very size has always made effective administration and integration difficult. During the 1914–1918 war a series of revolutions brought a radical change in political orientation. The new ideologically communist system was committed, at virtually any cost, to expanding and advancing Russia's industrial base. Czarist rule, elitistly and immediately supportive of the upper classes, gave way to Communist rule, broadly but futuristically supportive of the workers.

During the war Russia mobilized a huge land force. The existence of that army did not in any way, however, lessen the domestic devastation with which the country had to deal. Thus the war's end found Russia militarily strong but economically decimated. Another major war right on the heels of this one was unthinkable. On the other hand, to compromise national security, having fought so long to regain it, was unimaginable. What the Soviet Union needed was peace, and to achieve it in what it saw as an ideologically hostile world, Russia needed power and security.

The Soviet army provided strategically well-located, conventional military power. The parallel pulls of peace and pride seemingly allowed Russia to ignore, or at least not be intimidated by, America's atomic monopoly. Economic power was going to be very hard to achieve, and demanded continued sacrifices of the citizenry. Awed by the task of reconstruction, Russia sought help wherever and however it could without threatening its security.

Russia's second prerequisite to peace, security, demanded psychological as well as physical well-being. The country's ability to achieve secure borders, friendly neighbors, and a guarantee that Germany could never threaten it again was dependent in large part on a coordinated policy, favorable to these goals, among the victor nations. One of the paradoxes, therefore, was that Russia could not feel secure (as opposed actually to being secure) until or unless the other victors felt secure with Russia.

A sense of national inferiority had dogged czarist Russia. Communist Russia had suffered early ideological isolation and ostracism by much of the world. By 1945 the ugly duckling may not have turned into a beautiful swan, but it had definitely grown into a very big duck. Russia wanted international recognition of its power, status, and legitimacy from a world that was not particularly eager to comply.

Convinced on the one hand that Soviet communism was destined to bring justice and collective, social order to the world, the Soviet Union had actively proselytized its beliefs. On the other hand, it was equally convinced that other nations, with very different ideas of an order that elevated political and individual rights above social and economic equality, and with the superficial glitter of capitalist wealth, were conspiring to humiliate, corrupt, or actually destroy a communist world order. In response, Russia defended itself through self-imposed isolation from external ideological and material contamination. It is difficult to know whether at any given moment Russia's actions were offensive or defensive, and whether it thought it was trying to spread its own power and its own beliefs, or to prevent its own destruction.

The other major power at the end of the war had much less historical reason to question its status in the world. Separated by ocean and environment from its mother countries, the United States had been the first colony to break away from European rule and rules. Extraordinarily rich in resources and unencumbered by the drag of tradition, America adapted the industrial revolution to its own needs. The majority white population came to expect guaranteed individual freedoms, private property rights, and a government that left it alone as much as possible. With no entrenched elites and no tax burden to drain personal wealth, the United States preached equality of opportunity (as opposed to equality in fact) and accepted economic stratification in the midst of what may be this planet's most bountiful environment.

The Americans fought small wars with their neighbors and one major civil war among themselves, but as of 1945 it had been one hundred and thirty years since they had suffered the humiliation and insecurity of serious enemy invasion. Possessing only a small territorial empire, increasingly they dominated the world economy, and they prided themselves on avoiding constricting international political commitments. Its brief participation in the 1914–1918 war actually strengthened America economically, as did its more considerable involvement in World War II.

America exited that war physically unscathed, economically unrivaled, master of the world's largest combined land, sea, and air forces, and in sole possession of the latest advance in destructive technology. Unlike the Soviet Union, the United States already had power, prestige, and prosperity. Nevertheless, the country felt insecure. The devastating depression of the 1930s was a real and living memory, brought on, many believed, by European mismanagement. The same was true, although to a lesser extent, with respect to the post–World War I recession, also linked in many American minds to European fiscal irresponsibility. Prosperity was not something Americans could take for granted, and much to their chagrin, threats to prosperity seemed linked, unfortunately and perhaps uncontrollably, to the vagaries of ideologically unstable European economies.

Physically and politically, most Americans wanted to put the war behind them and retreat into their ocean-buttressed cocoon. Having, they thought, again rescued Europe from Europe's own follies, they now hoped to leave it a better place—but definitely to leave it. Certain contractual obligations had been accepted, such as the temporary joint occupation of Germany, but ideally, postwar issues could be settled quickly, easily, and without benefit of large troop contingents. Demobilization was a high priority.

On the other hand, ideologically, many of those same Americans thought the rest of the world wanted to enjoy the same advantages and espouse the same values as they did. History and the nation's immaturity had conspired to prevent that in the past, but the allies' overwhelming victory against fascism and America's postwar military and economic power opened new doors. Americans had little sense of the magnitude of their own power, of the quirks of their own ideologies, or of the practical limits of either power or ideology. They simply assumed that any right-thinking nation would want to emulate them and could do so if it tried. Any significant deviation was deemed a betrayal not just of their country but of mankind in general. Americans had always thought like that; the postwar world provided an opportunity for them to do something about those beliefs.

Economically, Americans worried about a postwar depression. Many recognized a link that tied their nation's economic health to European prosperity specifically and access to the entire world generally. Anything that threatened to obstruct that prosperity and access was a danger that could translate into lost jobs and decreased sales. Capitalists believed that communism anywhere would impede economic prosperity everywhere. Thus most Americans viewed Russia, and especially a powerful Russia, as a threat that had to be met in a global context. Given the devastating impact of the war on the military and economic strength of other major capitalist nations, the United States found itself, almost by default, forced to assume the leadership role in meeting this challenge. It became ideologically impossible to retreat across the ocean, and this led to a dramatic turn-around in the character of America's international relations.

In such a context, an image of impending belligerency can easily be created. Thus one might say that in 1945 the world found itself vulnerable to the power of two very different nations. Their governments and people shared few views; they both had the potential to direct future events; and the clash of their different perspectives almost led to the outbreak of hostilities. Other words can suggest another reading. We could just as legitimately describe the world in 1945 as witnessing a realignment. Europe was replaced as the central focus by two new centers that were as alike in many ways as they were different. Under their leadership, the world would embark on a new and uncertain future, but one that maintained a precarious hold on peace.

Soviet–American relations, never cordial at the best of times, began to deteriorate even before World War II ended. Agreements reached at Yalta and Potsdam came unstuck when the participants discovered they had different ideas about the meaning of those agreements. The facade of allied unity was just that, a false front.

Major differences surfaced first in Eastern Europe. Both the United States and the Soviet Union had done some planning for postwar Germany but had no detailed contingency plans for liberated Eastern Europe. Russia and Eastern Europe shared intimate historical ties, positive and negative. The vehemently anticommunist position taken by interwar governments had precluded much friendly recent contact. America, outside its pockets of immigrant connections, had few ties with the region and had during the interwar years specifically rejected any political involvement.

Stalin expected the postwar future of occupied and liberated regions to be determined by whichever victor had the preponderance of military power there. In 1944 Churchill and Stalin had, by informally partitioning Eastern Europe into spheres of influence in the so-called percentage agreements, acknowledged Soviet political predominance. When the area was liberated by the Soviet army, Russia's undeniable military preeminence was established as well.

Americans may have thought the Yalta Declaration on Liberated Europe cancelled any earlier agreements, which in any case they had never sanctioned. The declaration promised free and democratic political self-determination, but, American hopes to the contrary notwithstanding, the British, Russians, and even many of the liberated nations themselves probably never actually expected Western-style elections. Certainly, under the existing stressful conditions, they should not have wanted the political instability of revolving-door coalition governments.

Russia wanted friendly governments in Eastern Europe, as, of course, did the United States, but for less strategic reasons. It is not clear how or whether Stalin defined, even to himself, just what a "friendly government" entailed or what he was willing to do to get one. Most probably no government that carried an anticommunist (much less a fascist) stigma, or that was chronically unstable would be able to satisfy Russia's need for security. Whether the Red Army was there as an occupation force, as a liberating army, or as an army that had not yet been able to be transported home, it gave a decidedly military dimension to Russia's role in government making.

The United States saw no reason why Eastern Europe would want to adopt any policies other than democratic capitalism. Since the area was geographically and culturally unfamiliar, however, American observers, nurtured on an undifferentiating two-party political system, had trouble distinguishing among the many political colorations and understanding the intricacies of hold-over prewar and interregional relationships.

Between 1945 and 1948 Eastern Europe was drawn more or less tightly into the Soviet orbit. When election results failed to produce communist majorities, the communist members of coalition governments demanded and, with Soviet backing, were given key administrative posts. Soon the elites who had been in office before the war were pushed out even of figurehead offices. The anchor nations, Finland, Albania, and Yugoslavia, retained the greatest degree of independence. Strong indigenous communist regimes had come to power in Albania and Yugoslavia during the war, and these voluntarily pledged their loyalty to Russia as leader of the world socialist revolution. Finland agreed to support Soviet foreign policy internationally in return for control over its own domestic affairs. The other nations were pushed, pulled, or prodded into adopting communism as government policy and the Soviet Union as guarantor of that policy.

Russia saw this as necessary, natural, in line with the Stalin–Churchill percentage agreements, and, within its own ideological definitions, reflective of the will of the people. By the same logic, Russia did little to stop the Western powers from instituting governments friendly to them in Greece, Trieste, Italy, and Japan. The US government was either unable or unwilling to halt Eastern Europe's slide toward Russian domination. America's own lack of early interest in and understanding of the region, its initial postwar tendency toward noninvolvement, and the reality of a strong Soviet presence led to what one scholar called a "nonpolicy" toward Eastern Europe.[1] Nevertheless, many Americans saw developments in that area as violations of the

Yalta agreements, verification of Soviet perfidy and oppression, and proof that Russia was out to dominate the world. The resulting rhetoric would make a more lasting impression on America's memory of those years than would the actual sequence of events.

Poland was the emotional focal point of early cold war conflict in Eastern Europe. Russo–Polish relations had a long and suspicion-ridden history. Partitioned out of existence by a European coalition in the eighteenth century, Poland reemerged as part of the czarist Russian empire. It won its independence during the first world war but a portion was reannexed by Russia in 1939. The Polish interwar government denounced the Soviet Union, and much of Europe saw Poland as a buffer that protected the Continent from invasion by communism and communists. Germany had twice attacked Russia through Poland. World War II simply exacerbated what amounted to centuries of conflict. No quick, simple, and electoral solution was going to settle Russo–Polish relations, but the Western democracies had made sizable emotional and political investments in the cause of protecting Poland's independence.

France and England entered World War II to defend Poland's independence and, some said, to preserve Poland as a buffer against Russia. The outcome had done little to change such goals, although by 1945 men like Churchill must have recognized the inevitability of Soviet involvement in Polish affairs. Poland was of less diplomatic but more domestic significance for the United States. Elected officials could not ignore the large and vocal Polish-American communities that spoke out against communism and against Russia's takeover of Poland. Since those officials had little chance of actually altering events in Poland, they responded to their constituents with gratifying but impotent oratory. Generalizing from this, Americans took issue with Soviet actions and motives throughout Eastern Europe.

Actually, the Soviet Union did not exercise unilateral fiat in Poland. As had happened before, Poland was redrawn by agreement among external powers. To compensate for territories lost to Russia, the allies gave several hundred miles of Germany to Poland, thereby also reducing, territorially at least, fears of a revived Germany. This made Poland's internal readjustments that much more difficult, since it introduced a new population into the already complex political equation.

Staunchly anticommunist, but rife with in-fighting, the London-based wartime Polish government in exile had won support from the British, French, and later American governments, all of whom had pledged to return it to Poland. Germany's invasion of Russia in 1941 did little to change the Polish government's anti-Soviet feelings and, as the Germans retreated back across Poland in 1944, Russia supported the new procommunist Lublin government in situ. At Yalta, the Big Three agreed that the postwar government should be a coalition containing elements from both the London and the Lublin organizations, and the Poles had no choice but to comply. Under the circumstances, this was like telling oil and water that they must mix. By 1947, feeling that it had been more hindered than helped by Western anticommunist pressures, the remnant London group admitted the coalition's failure. Thereafter Poland was under Soviet tutelage.

The liberated nation had, from a Western perspective, become a captive nation. From a Russian point of view, Poland had joined international communism's struggle against reactionary capitalism. From a third perspective, the world's political plates had shifted, dividing Europe and ending its earlier preeminence. At the time, the effects of this shift on places like Poland were viewed by most Americans as tragic harbingers of an inevitable renewal of hostilities.

Americans found the loss of Eastern Europe in general and Poland in particular difficult to accept. They looked for a villain, and they found the Soviet Union. For their part, the Russians, trying to understand why they still felt insecure even after achieving territorial security, found the United States, with its atomic monopoly and its castigation of Soviet actions. At no time, however, did the US government indicate that it would fight for Poland, or even for all of Eastern Europe. The Soviet Union might force America to defend its vital interests, but the next war, if there was one, would not be over Eastern Europe.

Although it was also on the political fault line of the shift in world equilibrium, Germany presented the victors with a very different situation. No single occupation force dominated the entire country; the allies acknowledged that Germany's future was in their hands, not Germany's, and they all played an active role in making and administering policies affecting Germany.

Minus the territory given to Poland, Germany was partitioned into four occupation zones—American, British, French, and Russian—with the city of Berlin (inside the Soviet sector) itself divided into four similar zones. All these divisions were supposed to be temporary. The United States and Russia each saw the ensuing indefinite postponement of reunification not as a solution to Germany's historical role as a destabilizing agent but as verification of the other's nefarious intentions.

The German question assumed increasing importance when economists began calculating just how serious the war's devastation had been and how important Germany was to the European economy as a whole. One school wanted to destroy Germany's war-making potential and, in the process, distribute its resources (i.e., reparations) among its victims to aid in their rehabilitation. Another school looked at how slowly Western Europe was recovering and took a broader view, concentrating on generalized economic well-being, world peace, and the communist–capitalist rivalry. For these theorists, Europe's economies might well depend for their prosperity on the vitality of the German economy. A destitute Europe would be vulnerable to communist propaganda, which they believed finds poverty and despair much more fertile hosts than prosperity and contentedness. Even without succumbing to the ideological onslaught of communism, weak European nations would not be able to withstand a military assault—and the Red Army sat poised, within easy reach of Paris. A reunified, working, prosperous, de-Nazified Germany was, many thought, the lynchpin to containing communism.

On the other hand, France and the Soviet Union both still had nightmares of a revived and reunited Germany. Russia desperately wanted German resources, including manpower and the transfer of complete industrial plants, to help rebuild its own shattered economy and permanently weaken Germany's. Some Western planners, who hoped to use an operating German economy to prime their own economic recoveries, saw this as a cunning plan to weaken Europe, undermine capitalism, and spread communism. Russians interpreted resistance to their ideas as proof that the West was sorry a fascist Germany had not destroyed the communist revolution and was perfectly willing to let a reformed Germany try it again.

As victors bickered over amounts and kinds of reparations, the German economy stagnated and threatened to become a drain on the allies' already strained resources. Many believed that Hitler's rise had been the direct consequence of too punitive a peace after World War I, and these people were concerned that the Russians, obsessed as they were with fear of a revived and rearmed German monster, were repeating that earlier mistake. The United States, with a lower emotional and economic stake in Germany's future, was, in 1945, not of one mind. Several years of chronic interallied disagreement elapsed, during which time cold war suspicions intensified in Germany and elsewhere, before the United States came out firmly in support of a healthy and therefore strong German economy. Such a Germany, by buttressing a Europewide recovery, would not only hold the line against communism (physically and ideologically) but also provide markets for America's dramatically increased industrial capacity.

The clash of these ideas at interallied coordinating sessions led to words, warnings, and even war scares. Germany offered the nearest thing to open war between the United States and Russia, in a European context, that the cold war ever produced. In the end, East and West went their own ways in Germany, but they did so unwillingly and in spite of recurring crises and fears of open conflict. By 1948 all pretense of joint occupational administration had been abandoned everywhere except on paper.

Berlin fell victim to the anomaly of its own geographic location and to the growing cold war atmosphere. In 1948 Russia blockaded the city's western sectors in an unsuccessful attempt to forestall a political consolidation and economic revitalization plan about to be implemented in the western sectors of Germany. The Western allies responded with a year-long airlift. The Russians finally acknowledged the futility of their actions and reopened ground access routes. This first of many Berlin crises further fueled suspicion on both sides and turned West Berlin into a symbol of capitalist "freedom" held hostage by and fiercely fighting off communist "tyranny."

In 1949 even the facade of joint occupation ended when the western sectors instituted a trisector government and recognized the German Federal Republic. Russia responded by creating the German Democratic Republic in its sector. So the situation remained, with the two Germanies and the city of Berlin the leading edges of cold war emotion. Not until 1975 was the de facto division of Germany given de jure international recognition. In the intervening thirty years, German unification, as a hoped-for but unattained goal, remained an open wound potentially capable of reinfecting the European body politic and turning a cold war into a fever-pitch real war.

Germany offers the strongest European evidence for the legitimacy of cold war terminology. But the economies of East and West Germany today argue convincingly that from every point of view except gamesmanship and ideology, reunification was neither necessary nor particularly desirable.

One wonders in retrospect why the idea of German reunification remained so popular, even outside Germany, for so long. Reunification, of course, would have removed Berlin as a cold war tinderbox but, alternatively, would have rekindled fear of a resurgent Germany, which had already, in its first seventy years' existence, been a key figure in three major conflicts. The root causes of these conflicts were different from those of the cold war. Rather than concentrate on issues germane to East–West problems, however, the United States and Russia became sidetracked, even trapped, by German issues. They might better have served their respective interests by championing a permanent separation and by doing so immediately. For the world to risk a new war over the issue of reunifying the last war's "arch villain" seems, in hindsight, less than logical. In fact, rather than try to ease the pressure by holding the juxtaposed plates apart, both the United States and Russia reveled in pushing them together. In the process, of course, raw nerves were repeatedly exposed to irritation.

Between 1945 and 1950 a whole range of issues, in addition to Eastern Europe and Germany, fed the belief that America was fighting a new kind of war, a cold war. Many Americans were slow to accept a new international role for their country. They had optimistically expected postwar allied cooperation and the new United Nations to assure a safe, free world. They also recognized that the power of the atomic bomb offered the greatest hope for, and threat to, peace. Therefore, the Soviet Union's refusal to cooperate in making atomic research an international effort through the United Nations under the Baruch Plan was decidedly disquieting.

So too was Russia's behavior in Iran. In 1946 the Red Army's refusal to evacuate Iran's northern provinces and Russia's active encouragement of militant separatist groups sparked an international mini-crisis. The Soviets finally retreated across the border, and with their departure Iran was able to pacify the renegade movements and maintain its sovereignty. Russia's actions, however, occurring as they did even before it was clear how the wind was blowing in Eastern Europe and Germany, suggested an ominous Soviet adventurism.

Americans soon thought they saw a similar behavior pattern in Greece and Turkey. One could say that in Eastern Europe Stalin did no more and no less than the 1944 percentage agreement with Churchill had given him the right to do. According to that agreement, Russia was to stay clear of Greece (he and Churchill had agreed that England had a ninety percent to Russia's ten percent interest in Greece). Turkey, as a neutral during most of the war, had not been mentioned at the Moscow meeting. By 1947 Great Britain and the United States thought Russia was threatening both of these nations. Their case for Turkey was in hindsight stronger than that for Greece, but Greece received most of the attention.

Massing troops on its Turkish border, the Soviet Union pressured its weaker neighbor to grant it rights of passage and defense along the Bosporus. The Turks had no desire to do so but needed help from the Western allies to buttress their refusal. In Greece, a revolutionary Communist party fought against centrist and rightist factions in a bloody and destabilizing civil war. The Western allies believed (erroneously as it turns out) Russia to be behind the revolutionaries. For this and other reasons England had provided financial, material, and personnel support to the recognized rightist government. When in 1947 the British could no longer financially afford to continue this assistance, the United States reassessed its traditional policy of noninvolvement. President Truman convinced a conservative Congress that not only did America have a moral obligation to defend free peoples against aggression, but the security of the Western world was simply an extension of America's security. This Truman Doctrine is one of the best-known examples of cold war rhetoric. The president told his audience:

At the present moment in world history nearly every nation must choose between alternative ways of life. The choice is too often not a free one.

One way of life is based upon the will of the majority, and is distinguished by free institutions, representative government, free elections, guarantees of individual liberty, freedom of speech and religion, and freedom from political oppression.

The second way of life is based upon the will of a minority forcibly imposed upon the majority. It relies upon terror and oppression, a controlled press and radio, fixed elections, and the suppression of personal freedoms.

I believe that it must be the policy of the United States to support free peoples who are resisting attempted subjugation by armed minorities or by outside pressures.

I believe that we must assist free people to work out their own destinies in their own ways.

I believe that our help should be primarily through economic and financial aid which is essential to economic stability and orderly political processes.

The world is not static, and the *status quo* is not sacred. But we cannot allow changes in the *status quo* in violation of the Charter of the United Nations by such methods as coercion, or by such subterfuges as political infiltration. In helping free and independent nations to maintain their freedom, the United States will be giving effect to the principles of the Charter of the United Nations.[2]

An initial appropriation of $400 million and open American support enabled Turkey to resist the Soviet pressure, the Greeks to defeat the leftists, and the United States to guard its self-defined national security interests.

The Soviet response to this Truman Doctrine and, more specifically, to events in Greece and Turkey offers a sample of Russian rhetoric. An editorial in *Izvestia* gave the same situation referenced by Truman a totally different interpretation:

> The US government has no intention of acting in the Greek question as one might have expected a member of UNO [United Nations], concerned about the fate of another member, to act. . . . Truman did not even consider it necessary to wait for the findings of the Security Council Commission specially sent to Greece to investigate the situation on the spot.
>
> Truman, indeed, failed to reckon either with the international organization or with the sovereignty of Greece. What will be left of Greek sovereignty when the "American military and civilian personnel" gets to work in Greece by means of the 250 million dollars brought into that country? The sovereignty and independence of Greece will be the first victims of such singular "defense." . . .
>
> We are now witnessing a fresh intrusion of the USA into the affairs of other states. American claims to leadership in international affairs grow parallel with the growing appetite of the American quarters concerned. But the American leaders, in the new historical circumstances, fail to reckon with the fact that the old methods of the colonizers and die-hard politicians have outlived their time and are doomed to failure.[3]

Quite clearly, Russia and the United States were not seeing eye to eye.

American aid to Greece and Turkey was soon followed by plans for a massive economic recovery program for Europe. Originally introduced to the world in a brief address by Secretary of State George C. Marshall, the Marshall Plan (also called the European Recovery Program) was elaborated on in a May 1947 speech by the eloquent Assistant Secretary, Dean Acheson, who would later become secretary of state:

> These measures of relief and reconstruction have been only in part suggested by humanitarianism. Your Congress has authorized and your Government is carrying out a policy of relief and reconstruction today chiefly as a matter

of national self-interest. For it is generally agreed that until the various countries of the world get on their feet and become self-supporting there can be no political or economic stability in the world and no lasting peace or prosperity for any of us. Without outside aid, the process of recovery in many countries would take so long as to give rise to hopelessness and despair. In these conditions freedom and democracy and the independence of nations could not long survive, for hopeless and hungry people often resort of desperate measures. The war will not be over until the people of the world can again feed and clothe themselves and face the future with some degree of confidence.[4]

Ambassador Andrei Vyshinsky delivered an official Soviet reply in the UN General Assembly in September 1947:

> It is becoming more and more evident to everyone that the implementation of the Marshall Plan will mean placing European countries under the economic and political control of the United States and direct interference by the latter in the internal affairs of those countries.
> Moreover, this Plan is an attempt to split Europe into two camps and, with the help of the United Kingdom and France, to complete the formation of a bloc of several European countries hostile to the interests of the democratic countries of Eastern Europe and most particularly to the interests of the Soviet Union.[5]

Much to America's relief, the Soviet Union refused to participate in the plan; nor would it allow its Eastern European dependents to do so.

The Marshall Plan provided some $17 billion in credits and grants to participating European nations. A blueprint for recovery was worked out by the Europeans, with American advice; the United States provided funding, materials, and technical assistance. This largest, coordinated mutual aid program ever undertaken proved a remarkable success. Even though most of the funds went to military defense, by 1952 Western European economies were on the mend.

The West spent huge sums on defense because the Red Army continued to hover over Eastern Europe and because, in 1949, Russia shocked the world by detonating its own atomic bomb, years ahead of Western projections. As of that year Russia had atomic weapons, control of Eastern Europe, and control of North Korea. Already shaken by these advances, Americans were horrified to learn of the 1949 communist victory in China's long-fought civil war.

In spite of what nay sayers would later argue, the United States did not "lose" China. The Nationalists lost the civil war, aided by their own corruption, by conditions indigenous to China, and by the perseverance of the Chinese Communist party. Nevertheless, it seemed, almost overnight, that the world balance of forces had shifted (which in fact is exactly what had happened), and that the United States could do nothing to alter the situation. This sense of impotence was, of course, very traumatic for a nation that just four years earlier had had good reason to feel virtually omnipotent.

The creation of the North Atlantic Treaty Organization (NATO) was both a consequence of and a cure for this perceived power imbalance. A beginning had already been made on a coordinated anticommunist European defense, but progress had been slow and hampered by the question of Germany's role in such a system. The 1949 NATO alliance, to which the United States was a signatory, pledged America's atomic might as a shield against communist aggression. This first peacetime defensive alliance in American history illustrated America's decision to play an active and central role in world affairs. (For more detailed discussion of arms and defense agreements see chapter 6.)

An imaginative observer could reasonably have predicted World War II, its outcome, and a Soviet–American rivalry (after all, de Tocqueville had done so in the 1830s). It would have taken a very fertile imagination to have foreseen the extent to which postwar America globalized the definition of its national security interests and demonstrated a willingness actively to pursue those interests. With the exception of the brief Wilson era, the US government until 1945 prided itself on avoiding European political affairs. The change was as surprising to many Americans as it was to most of the world.

Part of the cold war tension emanated from the US government's new and uncharacteristic willingness to involve itself—physically, if necessary—in the internal affairs of nations far removed from the western hemisphere. Additional sources of tension can be traced to the difficulties other nations had in learning to recognize and adapt to America's changed persona. The transformation was not total. The United States did not intervene everywhere, and other governments found it unsettling that they could never predict how it would respond to any given situation. The United States did little to stop what it saw as the imposition of a communist government on Czechoslovakia, even though it had already agreed to immerse itself in the task of preserving a conservative regime in Greece during a clearly civil war. Having pulled most of its troops out of Europe, the acknowledged center of its postwar foreign concerns, the United States then accepted a full-scale commitment of military forces to Korea within weeks of having declared that country outside its sphere of interest. It advocated capitalistic free enterprise and then underwrote with billions of dollars a planned, collective recovery program for Europe. It overturned a centuries-old tradition of avoiding military and political commitments to Europe by joining NATO.

The United States itself had difficulty in adjusting to this new role. Limited by the constraints of frequent elections, budget debates, skepticism about foreign affairs, and their own lack of information, American policymakers, much less the general public, could not possibly assimilate the information that a sophisticated global role required. Their response was to oversimplify, to define each new issue (if and as it caught their attention) as a crisis, and to see in that crisis the superhuman, not to say inhuman, hand of an evil, paranoid, perhaps even insane Soviet dictator wreaking havoc on the world. For an American public uncomfortable with an ambivalent world of gray ambiguities and unfamiliar with many of the issues involved, the resulting images of belligerency were traumatic but easier to understand than would be the complexity and convolution of actuality.

The same simplification soon infected official policy. A 1947 policy paper by George Kennan spelled out a sophisticated, complex, and nonbelligerent long-term approach to the Soviet Union. Kennan described an unquestionably expansionist Soviet government that on the one hand sought to exploit any capitalist weaknesses to spread its ideology and power, and on the other justified its own economic and political repression as necessary to protect the revolution against its ubiquitous capitalist enemies. Recent history gave credence to this image of a Russian homeland surrounded by physical, military foes as well as ideological rivals and made it easier for the totalitarian communist government to legitimize its repressive policies domestically even as it pursued expansion internationally. Thus, Kennan argued, it was essential that the West contain Soviet expansion, but it was equally essential that such containment not be aggressively militaristic. Projecting a bipolar struggle that would last decades, Kennan hoped containment, which he saw primarily in economic terms, would prevent the spread of communism outside its current borders while at the same time undercutting the Russian people's fear of capitalism's physical threat to them. Over time (and again, Kennan was thinking in terms of decades, not months or even years), the Russian people would grow increasingly restless under communism's oppressive rule, and the government, unable to maintain its paranoic charade, would be forced to liberalize or face revolt. According to this view, peace would be a much better weapon against Soviet communism than would war. Much to his dismay, Kennan's containment theory was soon distorted into a much more simplistic, more immediate policy of confronting and, it was hoped, repulsing, by whatever means, military as well as economic attempts in any part of the world by the Soviet Union to expand its control or influence. This blanket acceptance of a global responsibility to contain Russia was a major departure from American tradition. It also undercut the perhaps too subtle idea of a firm but nonthreatening peace as the way to force positive change in Russia.

The postwar Soviet Union did not experience so drastic a behavioral and psychological change as did the United States, even though Russia also found itself more involved internationally and also assumed that an adversarial, bipolar relationship existed. The country had a tradition of acting on its national security and ideological responsibilities. It had, however, defined its national self-interests rather more narrowly, and continued to do so after the war. It bears repeating that most of the territorial early cold war crises occurred either very close to the Soviet Union or in lands actually contiguous

to it. Russian policymakers also tended to read into events the more imper-
sonal historical forces of capitalism and communism, and that perspective
meant that contretemps were less likely to be viewed as crises.

Defining the cold war years not as a series of crises but as a continuing
play of historical forces, the Soviets spent 1945–49 in an anxious cohabitation
with the West. Initially, and on a physical level, a rearmed Germany worried
them more than did America. Russian Communists saw capitalism struggling
to save itself, but they believed the balance was shifting in socialism's favor.
Russia had a responsibility to help usher in the socialist future. The increased
number of socialist/communist governments conveniently reaffirmed the
inevitability of history while providing greater immediate security for the
Soviet Union.

In its new role, the United States made little distinction between its
ideological and its national security interests, but gave both global dimensions, and was willing periodically to pursue both with active worldwide
involvement. This was America's radical change, and it emerged as such in
oratory.

Much of the strongest cold war rhetoric was not readily available for study
until many years after it was delivered. American policy planning papers—
in-house studies, recommendations, analyses, and plans—suggest strongly
that policy elites used their own words on themselves to induce a kind of
uncritical self-hypnosis.

In 1947 the US government created the National Security Council (NSC),
intended to coordinate interests, ideas, and intelligence from all relevant
branches of government. This agency wrote analyses of the world situation
that were pivotal in formulating policy and that, classified as top secret, were
kept from the public. The council's document 7 dated 30 March 1948 summarized the government's view of America's position vis-à-vis the Soviet
Union and communism:

> . . . 2. The ultimate objective of Soviet-directed world communism is the
> domination of the world. To this end, Soviet-directed world communism
> employs against its victims in opportunistic coordination the complementary
> instruments of Soviet aggressive pressure from without and militant revo-
> lutionary subversion from within. Both instruments are supported by the
> formidable material power of the USSR and their use is facilitated by the
> chaotic aftermath of the war. . . .
> 5. In addition, Soviet-directed world communism has faced the non-
> Soviet world with something new in history. This is the worldwide Fifth
> Column directed at frustrating foreign policy, dividing and confusing the
> people of a country, planting the seeds of disruption in time of war, and
> subverting the freedom of democratic states. Under a multitude of disguises,
> it is capable of fomenting disorders, including armed conflicts, within its
> victim's territory without involving the direct responsibility of any com-
> munist state. The democracies have been deterred in effectively meeting

this threat, in part because communism has been allowed to operate as a legitimate political activity under the protection of civil liberties.[6]

There followed a series of recommended policies for the government to implement, including domestic suppression of "the Communist menace in the United States." Official and still secret US policy remained virtually unchanged for years thereafter.

Although screened from the rhetoric of NSC documents by their classification as secret, the public did hear and read things specifically targeted at them. There are litmus tests to detect rhetoric. Did the speaker use unnecessarily value-laden words and expressions? For example, is the enemy described as "infiltrating" an organization rather than "entering" or "joining"? Another test is the use (the greater the usage the heavier the rhetoric) of catch words and phrases such as *democracy, capitalism, communism, imperialism,* and *exploitation.* The Chinese talked of America as imperialist; Americans used "international communist conspiracy" almost religiously; the Russians had an affinity for "capitalist exploitation."

As a rhetorician, Secretary of State John Foster Dulles was anything but subtle. In 1954, when the cold war had moved out of Europe to encompass most of the world, the US government supported the military overthrow of an agrarian reformist government in Guatemala. Talking to an American public that knew little or nothing about Guatemala, Dulles explained events in words designed to win public support of the new government and of American policy:

> For several years international communism has been probing here and there for nesting places in the Americas. It finally chose Guatemala as a spot which it could turn into an official base from which to breed subversion which would extend to other American Republics.
>
> This intrusion of Soviet despotism was, of course, a direct challenge to our Monroe Doctrine, the first and most fundamental of our foreign policies. . . .
>
> Communist agitators devoted themselves to infiltrating the public and private organizations of Guatemala. They sent recruits to Russia and other Communist countries for revolutionary training and indoctrination in such institutions as the Lenin School at Moscow. Operating in the guise of "reformers" they organized the workers and peasants under Communist leadership. Having gained control of what they call "mass organizations," they moved on to take over the official press and radio. . . .
>
> The judiciary made one valiant attempt to protect its integrity and independence. But the Communists, using their control of the legislative body, caused the Supreme Court to be dissolved when it refused to give approval to a Communist-contrived law. Arbenz, who until this week was President of Guatemala, was openly manipulated by the leaders of communism.
>
> Guatemala is a small country. But its power, standing alone, is not a

measure of the threat. The master plan of international communism is to gain a solid political base in this hemisphere, a base that can be used to extend Communist penetration to the other peoples of the other American Governments. It was not the power of the Arbenz government that concerned us but the power behind it.[7]

No one who reads that speech analytically can see it as an objective discussion of events.

There was a great deal of that kind of talk during the cold war. Russia did not explain that it could never feel secure until it controlled Poland. Instead it talked of liberating Poland from imperialist oppression. The United States did not say it had decided to play a much larger role in world affairs in order to spread its influence and protect its beliefs. Instead it talked about protecting universal values. In both cases the statements were self-deluding, automatically antagonistic, and needlessly exaggerated. Many on each side even came to believe their own words, but words are not wars.

Such comments from the two sides led directly to the mislabeling of the early postwar years as a cold war. Those years might just as accurately have been described as a cold peace, or even just as peace. After years of being told they faced imminent outbreak of war, Americans, Russians, and Europeans all came to believe it, even in spite of much evidence to the contrary.

Within ten years of World War II's termination, Western Europe, Eastern Europe, Russia, and Japan had recovered economically, and they and the United States were prospering as never before. During the so-called cold war major advances were made internationally in technology, health care, food production, energy consumption, and most other areas generally used to measure progress. Changes of this nature are a function of peace, not war. Individual nations continued to kill, imprison, and oppress people, but most often this was internal, not international, behavior. Domestic tyranny is not war, it is simply domestic tyranny. The Greek civil war was a civil war, not an armed Soviet–American confrontation. Even the Korean War, which began in 1950, was a decidedly limited and, some might actually say, civil war. The Pakistanis and Indians slaughtered each other and the world stayed at peace. What distinguishes peace from war in a nuclear era is the absence of world war and planetary annihilation.

The peace was, in fact, to mankind's credit. By the early 1950s both the United States and the Soviet Union had nuclear weaponry that neither side used. Stalin harangued at capitalist imperialism, and Truman raged against communist imperialism. Invective flew fast and furious, but both sides realized that, more than anything else, this new and terrible means of destruction had to be used as a guarantor of peace. While it is a fact that the so-called cold war was not a war, it is also a fact that very few people in power recognized it as peace. Yet, in spite of their comments and flag waving, the antagonists managed not to follow their own ideological fantasies to destruction. It is even possible that the late 1980s and the 1990s will witness, in the Gorbachev reforms, a partial validation of Kennan's hope that peace would bring positive changes to the Soviet Union.

NOTES

1. See Geir Lundestad, *The American Non-policy Towards Eastern Europe, 1943–1947: Universalism in an Area Not of Essential Interest to the United States* (New York: Humanities Press, 1975).

2. Cited in Thomas G. Paterson, ed., *Major Problems in American Foreign Policy: Documents and Essays*, vol. II, *Since 1914*, 2nd ed. (Lexington, Mass.: Heath, 1984), 309.

3. *Izvestia*, 13 March 1947, cited in Alvin Z. Rubinstein, ed., *The Foreign Policy of the Soviet Union*, 2nd ed. (New York: Random House, 1966), 230–31.

4. State Department *Bulletin*, vol. XVI, 18 May 1947, 991–94.

5. UN General Assembly, *Official Records*, plenary meetings, verbatim record, 18 September 1947, 88.

6. Cited in Thomas H. Etzold and John Lewis Gaddis, eds., *Containment: Documents on American Policy and Strategy, 1945–1968* (New York: Columbia University Press, 1969), 164–68.

7. Cited in Walter LaFeber, ed., *America in the Cold War: Twenty Years of Revolution and Response, 1947–1967* (New York: Wiley, 1969), 118–21.

Leaders of the Nonaligned Movement—Nasser, Nehru, and Tito—in Yugoslavia, 1956. *Wide World Photos.*

chapter 4

THE YUGOSLAV HERESY

Yugoslavs would disagree with the image of global bipolarization as described in chapter 3. The Socialist Federal Republic of Yugoslavia in 1948 broke with the Soviet Union and became the first "communist" state not subject to Soviet dictate. A multicommunist party federation, Yugoslavia rules itself through principles of worker self-management, nationality autonomy, and international nonalignment. At various times damned as an ideological heretic by both the United States and the Soviet Union, Yugoslavia sees itself as proof of the fallacy of bipolarity.

While Americans have disagreed over which pole, Russia or the United States, was primarily responsible for the cold war, most accepted the conceptual structure of bipolarity. Much of the rest of the world, together with Yugoslavia, did not. We must keep that in mind, and following Soviet–American relations in the 1950s with a focus on how those years looked through Yugoslav eyes is one way to do so.

Yugoslavia's history during the 1940s and 1950s is as much a chapter in Soviet–American relations as it is its own story. Within the larger world context, Russian and American policies toward Yugoslavia reflect some lessons learned and some not learned by these rival powers. Yugoslavia broke the Soviet Union's monopoly on socialist exclusivity. It did so unwillingly, trying desperately to preserve an idealized image of the Soviet Union that Russia was itself destroying. Nevertheless, as of 1948 there was no more reason to identify communism with the Soviet Union alone than there was to identify capitalism exclusively with the United States.

The Yugoslavs did not start out as enemies of bipolarity. Led by Joseph Broz Tito, in the middle of World War II they rebelled against their monarchist past and joined the socialist workers movement. They revered the Soviet Union as the center of the communist revolution and Stalin as that revolution's guardian. In the rather naive and idealistic afterglow of a hard-fought victory, Yugoslav Communists expected to continue the struggle, arm in arm with Russia, against remnants of their own nation's past and against what they saw as the collective colossus of Western capitalism. Their stereotyped image of the United States as the personification of evil capitalism was as strong at that time as was their idealization of the Soviet Union as the guardian of socialism.

Caught up in fast-moving postwar developments, the United States did little to dissuade Yugoslavs of this image. Giving little weight to the economic, ethnic, and national issues involved, US policymakers insisted that the port of Trieste remain under Italian control. Italy had been a recent member of the Fascist alliance, whereas Yugoslavia's status as an ally had been more than paid for in blood. The Istrian peninsula had a clear Slavic majority, and before the war, Italy had used Trieste to exploit Yugoslavia economically. Yet here were American troops prepared to fight for Italy's claims to a city of no American interest and of vital importance to Yugoslavia. Somehow the United States had decided that a decades-old struggle between these two Adriatic rivals was a newly born, Moscow-inspired plot to spread communism. Coming on top of the openly ideological clash, this and similar incidents produced mutual suspicion, not to say hostility, between Tito's Yugoslavia and the United States.

Although Yugoslav Communists took pride in their status as the second nation to bring about a successful, indigenous communist revolution, they still looked to the Soviet Union for leadership. Tito supported Russia and the socialist revolution at the United Nations; his government signed trade agreements and began joint economic undertakings with its socialist neighbors and with the Soviet Union; it encouraged other socialists struggling against their own reactionary past. In fact, Yugoslavia provided most of the assistance to Greek leftists for which the United States blamed Russia.

Yugoslavia's commitment to socialism never wavered. What did waver were its early, idealized images of Stalin and the Soviet Union. Yugoslavs discovered that the Soviet Union, in addition to championing its own definition of socialism, was championing the Soviet Union. It had no intention of sharing leadership or power; nor was it willing to learn from fellow socialists. Stalin feared Yugoslavia's strong sense of self. He saw it as a direct threat to his own personal and to Russia's national supremacy among socialist nations. He balked at a planned confederation of Bulgaria, Yugoslavia, and perhaps Albania because, instead of socialist solidarity, he saw in such plans a challenge to Soviet preeminence. Ultimately, Stalin masterminded Yugoslavia's expulsion from the Cominform (the postwar successor to the Communist International and firmly under Soviet control) when Yugoslavia proved unwilling to eviscerate itself at the altar, not of communism or socialism, but of immutably Stalinist Russia.

Stalin accused Yugoslavia of counterrevolutionary nationalism. A Yugoslav would respond that, at the time, it had been a nationalism of self-awareness forced upon it by the Cominform's behavior. If Yugoslavia was ever guilty as charged, that guilt followed, rather than preceded, the accusation. What Yugoslavs began to learn in 1948 was that, while the end goals of international socialism remain the same for all believers, the path to that future must be flexible enough to accommodate human, historical, economic, and even geographic differences. The Yugoslavs' heresy was the impudence of thinking they understood their country better than did the Russians—or Americans or Greeks. Like Russia, the United States would have trouble differentiating between nationalism of the Yugoslav type and "the enemy."

Stalin's betrayal of international socialism came as a shattering blow to stalwart Yugoslav Communists who had seen in him the embodiment of all their ideals. Equally traumatic was the quick realization that Stalin might well try not only to expel but also to obliterate them for their so-called affronteries. Yugoslavia prepared to defend itself against Russian chauvinism even as it refused to betray its commitment to socialism.

Both Yugoslavia and the Cominform initially tried to downplay the controversy. With Yugoslavia's very survival as an independent nation at risk, its leaders still wanted to prevent capitalism from profiting from division inside the socialist community. For a long time the West failed to see the intrasocialist rupture for what it was. The British, for example, hypothesized that reports of a Yugoslav–Cominform split were ploys to mislead the West, that the break was a charade, and that communist Yugoslavia had always been and was still a Soviet puppet.

Only when troops from Cominform member neighbors were reported massing on the Yugoslav border did some in the West take a closer look at the crack in socialist solidarity. If the split were real, this could be a great propaganda victory, which was exactly what Yugoslav Communists did not want. The Soviet Union had created a socialist dilemma, but in so doing, Russia brought the West face to face with a dilemma of its own. Would capitalism benefit more by doing nothing to avert an attack on Yugoslavia (thus "proving" the West's perception of communism's perfidy but allowing Russia to tighten and spread its control) or by supporting one communist nation against others (thus perhaps driving a wedge into socialist unity)? The West, now firmly under American control, opted for the latter course. It began quietly to offer Yugoslavia military and later economic assistance. Tito accepted, but only on the condition that there be no conditions. He made no promises to change his ways.

The US State Department wanted to keep as low a profile as possible in its Yugoslav assistance program. For one thing, many Americans, including a large portion of the population of Yugoslav origin, could not understand why they should help a communist nation, and one that had a negative public relations image among Americans at that. For another thing, if America was too belligerent in its actions, Russia could use this to justify its own repressive behavior in the name of defending socialism against a capitalist attack. The position America took and how it took it could also affect internal Yugoslav politics. Many Yugoslavs inside and out of the country disapproved of the communist government and had hopes of counterrevolution. American support *to* Tito suggested support *of* Tito and would undoubtedly defuse or at least delay any such plans. Although in a more perfect world the United States had no desire to see Yugoslavia remain communist, it knew that the anti-Tito elements were far from united, with little chance of installing a stable pro-West government. Thus the State Department found its Yugoslav policy more than a little tricky. It decided, after much discussion, that a stable anti-Soviet government, even if communist, was preferable to either an external Soviet takeover (and events in Czechoslovakia in 1948 suggested that was a real possibility) or to an unstable, however anticommunist and anti-Soviet counterrevolution, which in all probability could not hold the country together and would therefore be a target for some new, pro-Soviet regime or renewed chaos in the Balkans.

At least in part as a consequence of America's decision to help Tito, Yugoslavia survives to this day as an alternative route to socialism. In the intervening forty years it has experimented with a range of political and economic policies. The West, which acted in its own best interests, has no claims on Yugoslavia and neither does the East. Both blocs owe it unacknowledged debts. The 1948 split unmasked Russian chauvinism that matched capitalist chauvinism in its threat to international peace and in its insensitivity to national idiosyncracies. After Stalin died, Russia did begin trying to rectify the damage, but it found it difficult to change old patterns. The Soviet Union has crushed, often with brutal force, most other Eastern European attempts to pursue independent paths to socialism. Until 1953 it defined Titoism as heresy toward Marxist-Leninism. After 1953 Russia eased its rhetoric and became a little more tolerant of socialist experimentation, particularly in developing nations.

In 1948 neither East nor West recognized the historic implications of the Yugoslav–Soviet split. Both continued to talk of a sharply divided world in which rival ideologies went hand in hand with the power struggles of two contending national identities. When the renegade Yugoslavs failed to reject communism along with their forced rejection of the Soviet Union, the United States could still not divorce itself from the idea that all communism was Russian. It continued to see Yugoslavia as a very suspicious anomaly within

Russian communism, not as a communist development different and divorced from Russia.

The Yugoslav case was the only time during the late 1940s and the 1950s that the United States supported a socialist/communist experiment. Even Titoism was almost more than Americans could handle. Funding for the Yugoslav assistance program was an annual struggle, with an ideologically hostile but realistic State Department having to steer support for the heretic through the rocky shoals of an irrationally, emotionally, anticommunist Congress. Much more commonly, the United States government offered support to rightist, definitely less than democratic regimes in order to avoid even the possibility of leftist governments. Certainly it did so in Greece.

Yugoslavs would argue that, by failing to encourage non-Soviet paths to socialism, the United States sometimes pushed new or weak nations that were trying to avoid capitalist exploitation into seeking Soviet assistance. Americans argued that they were struggling to contain Soviet expansion.

BIPOLARITY

The American and Soviet responses to Yugoslavia highlight their shared proclivity toward seeing the world in hostile, mutually exclusive, black-and-white terms. Both nations saw the Yugoslav heresy as an exception that somehow proved, rather than disproved, the rule, but much of the world saw it differently. Much of the rest of the world wished it could be like Yugoslavia, aligned with neither East nor West.

Bipolarity is a Marxist concept—the struggle between capitalism and communism—that, ironically, Americans embraced even more wholeheartedly than did Marxists. The America of the 1950s perceived the world as divided into two blocs. Depending on one's outlook, each bloc hoped or plotted to destroy, contain, or overcome the other. The lesser members in each group followed a prime mover whose role was seen as dictatorial, exploitive, and oppressive in reference to "them," and as benevolent, beneficial and democratic in reference to "us." This meant that the United States often tried to fit new or emerging nations into a two-sided context that had little relevance to those nations' problems and policies. Cold warriors on both sides were so wrapped up in their own perspectives that they lost sight of other social, economic, ideological, and political dimensions.

For those who espoused this image, the world lost all of its colorfully rich and very human complexities. For them, history played on a much sharper, but more simplistic, and more regimented screen. The rival ideological frameworks were drawn so tightly that variables that defied inclusion were necessarily ignored, while others, which really did not belong, were manipulated into line forcibly.

Such a picture of international structure did not accurately reflect the issues about which much of the world was most concerned. Neither communism nor capitalism has much to do with why Arabs fought Jews or why Vietnamese fought the French. Neither explains why Hitler set out to destroy the gypsies.

Bipolarity never existed as an indivisible economic dichotomy and was expounded in an excess of ideological zeal, or in pursuit of power and national self-interest, rather than as a description of fact. Even in the late 1940s and 1950s, when the rhetoric peaked, "we" were not homogeneous and neither were "they." Labels broke down. The "free" capitalist West (a term, of course, that should be taken no more literally than "communist East") included, for example, an increasingly socialist England as well as many very poor, very backward economies administered by very undemocratic regimes. The communist world ranged from the technological and industrial sophistication of Czechoslovakia to the wastes of Mongolia and wilds of Albania. In Europe, nations such as Switzerland, Yugoslavia, Sweden, and Finland remained outside the dichotomous structures and demonstrated the viability of mixed political and economic systems. As part of colonial empires or otherwise dominated by economic or military "big brothers," much of Africa, Asia, and Latin America was overlooked or ignored in bipolar thinking. To discount those people just because they did not fit into the current structure was to prove that structure invalid.

The West had particular trouble with the impetus and legitimacy Yugoslavia gave to two major postwar phenomena: nationalism and nonalignment. A strong sense of the first may have been a prerequisite to having the fortitude, in the world of the 1950s, to pursue the second. Both played havoc with hegemonic constructs based on bipolarity, and both affected Soviet–American relations and relations between each of those powers and other nations.

Nationalism creates in peoples a powerful desire to be their own masters, make their own decisions, be responsible for their own successes and failures. One of the strongest forces in the world, it was behind wars of independence and sparked the break-up of colonial imperialism. Nationalism and the nonaligned movement went hand in hand in that many nations wished to avoid the neodependency that often came with being absorbed into the East–West tug of war. Nationalism is not democracy, communism, or any other political ideology; nor is it capitalism, socialism, or any other economic ideology.

World War II, not the cold war, precipitated the end of colonialism. It was in the world of the cold war, however, that many nationalists fought their final battles; into the cold war that the new nations emerged; and with conditions brought about by the cold war that they had to cope. Reversing that image, the chief protagonists in the cold war had to learn to handle nationalism and its consequences. It was not surprising that newly independent nations, often still scarred by their experience under capitalist imperialism and often pragmatically attracted to socialism, looked to the Soviet Union or to the nonaligned movement for guidance. Both of these options made American policymakers uncomfortable.

KOREA

Although the first major military engagement of the cold war was not between Russia and the United States, it was a sharp illustration of how Soviet–American relations, and the cold war those relations engendered, distorted and sometimes even destroyed nationalism. Korea had been under Japanese domination for decades. After Japan's defeat, Korea was divided and occupied by Soviet and American forces. As with Germany, the assumption was that this status would be temporary. Also like the German case, each occupier proceeded to install a government of its own ideological bent, and each wanted to bring all of Korea into line with its particular camp. Both also repressed Korea-wide nationalist sentiment, which wished a plague on both their houses and wanted a united Korea run by and for Koreans. Nationalists probably represented majority Korean feeling, but they had no external big power backing. They wanted neither Soviet communism nor American capitalism per se. What they did want was the expulsion of foreign masters and ideologies. Unfortunately for the nationalists, the politicians who fell into ideological line behind their respective occupiers received ample material and moral support to overwhelm any political opposition, into which category nationalists in both north and south were placed.

When the Korean War began in 1950, the opposition nationalists were lost in the shuffle. The movement was caught and crushed under the weight and firepower of cold war ideology. While the question of who fired the first shot may still be at issue, in June the "Soviet" government of North Korea launched a massive attack against the "American" government of South Korea. At the time America had no significant number of its troops in South Korea; Soviet forces in the north were apparently caught unaware of, and played no significant role in, the attack.

Although just months previously Secretary of State Acheson had declared Korea outside America's sphere of national security interests, Truman responded to the invasion quickly and decisively. Under the command of General Douglas MacArthur, American (and later United Nations) troops were rushed in to reinforce the overpowered South Korean army.

The Soviet Union was at the time boycotting UN Security Council meetings (because of that body's refusal to accept the People's Republic of China as the rightful holder of China's seat) and could not veto international support for America's unilateral decision to contain by force the spread of "international communism." This Soviet boycott at so crucial a time strongly suggests that Moscow was as surprised by the North Korean action as was Washington. Had it known in advance, it could easily have blocked United Nations participation and left the United States to explain its unilateral and massive military involvement in what many saw as a Korean civil war. Although the Soviet army doubled in size during the war (to some six million men), it was never an active participant. Korea was not a Russian war.

When the United States moved the war north to the Chinese border, the People's Republic of China did intervene. Still recovering from the turmoil of its own civil war, China nevertheless felt compelled to protect its borders and to support fellow communists. The United States assumed international communist conspiracies were operative, but stopped short of making war on China proper. There was always the risk of touching off a world war if Russia, indirectly through both China and Korea, were pushed too hard.

A seesaw war resulted that lasted about a year. For two more years the fighting continued, although the battle lines stayed rather stable, very close to the original 38th parallel dividing line between north and south. An armistice was finally signed in 1953, spurred by military stalemate, the costs on both sides, Stalin's death, and a new American president's hint at the use of atomic weapons if agreement were not reached.

The United States assigned direct responsibility for the war to Moscow; saw it as a military move by the Soviets, using Korean surrogates, to expand their empire; and made Korea into a test of America's determination to contain communist aggression. Originally designed as an economic and political policy, containment had by now been redefined to include military force if necessary. Although most American policymakers assumed, correctly, that Russia would not enter the war, the possibility existed that it had even grander plans than the conquest of South Korea. The West hurriedly built up NATO forces in Europe, including the introduction of West German troops. Not wanting to extend the hostilities any further than necessary, however, the United States also moved to "leash" the Nationalist Chinese government on Taiwan, which had declared itself eager to enter the war and thus risk heightened mainland Chinese, and possibly even Russian, involvement.

Any chance of reaching a truly Korean solution disappeared. Korea became less a nation at war than an expendable pawn in the game of international power politics.

A new administration, with Eisenhower as president and John Foster Dulles as secretary of state, escalated the rhetoric of anticommunism, talked glibly of using nuclear weapons to contain the threat, and even suggested that Russian satellite states should be "liberated." There was now even less room in the American plan for undecided nations. Korea had raised the emotional stakes of the cold war and made those years much more difficult to perceive as the basically peaceful years they really were. Americans read Korea as communist militancy writ large. The war validated their darkest fears and made it doubly difficult for them to break out of a bipolar worldview. Korean nationalism was a casualty of that view.

INDOCHINA

Indochinese nationalism was also victimized by the cold war, but in a different way. Although used by the postwar rivals for cold war purposes,

Indochinese nationalists were able to gain the leverage of at least partial recognition as members in the governing elite. Indochina (today's Laos, Kampuchea/Cambodia, and Vietnam) has a long and proud history during much of which it struggled to preserve its independence from China's grasp. In the nineteenth century, when China itself was the target of European imperialism, Indochina fell to the French. In spite of France's ploy of technically incorporating its empire into France proper, in truth Indochina became French colonies. The Viet Minh, a popular front united by a desire for national independence, fought the French and then the Japanese. When World War II ended, the Viet Minh resumed the struggle against their reinstalled French rulers. The Vietnamese resistance leader, Ho Chi Minh, was committed both to Vietnam's independence and to communism. Ho was to Vietnam much what Tito was to Yugoslavia: a charismatic national leader. Like Tito, Ho had spent time in Russia; like Tito, he remained a person who knew his own mind.

The United States became involved in Indochina through France. After the war, it subsidized the French fight against the Viet Minh not because it opposed Vietnamese nationalism or even because it opposed Vietnamese communism. It needed French cooperation in its postwar anticommunist program for Europe, the continent deemed at that time most vital to American national security and most threatened by Russia. France in the late 1940s was wary of American plans for Germany and not one hundred percent certain it wished to follow America's lead. Financial support in Vietnam was the price France demanded for cooperation in Europe.

The Communist Chinese victory in 1949 and then the Korean War prompted a now much more insecure America to see communist victories everywhere and to take a closer, if not necessarily clearer, look at Indochina. The communist aspect of what it saw overshadowed the nationalist. No longer colonialists suppressing legitimate Vietnamese nationalist ambitions, the French were transformed in American eyes into crusaders fighting a Vietnamese outbreak of monolithic, Soviet-inspired, communist expansion.

The French did not win in Indochina. In 1954 an uneasy US government watched as an international conference decided the region's future. The resulting Geneva Accords eased France out, granted Laos and Cambodia independence, and led to a temporary division of Vietnam. Ho controlled the north while the stridently anticommunist Ngo Dinh Diem soon held sway in the south. The United States assumed responsibility for preserving a noncommunist South Vietnam as one more arena in its policy of containment. The nationalist aspect of Vietnamese politics became basically irrelevant in American eyes.

The Geneva agreements had drafted plans for a 1956 nationwide election to determine majority sentiment for leadership of a united Vietnam. Unable to differentiate between communism and Moscow, Americans labeled Ho a Soviet puppet and thought his very probable electoral victory would be a

Soviet victory. At the time, Russia was too absorbed in its own domestic post-Stalin reorganizations to devote much time or attention to Vietnam. As did China, the Soviet Union contributed economic assistance to the Ho government, which in its turn accepted aid and ideological affiliation even as it strove to preserve its political independence from either of the communist giants.

Having been forced to accept a divided Germany, and having failed to reunite North and South Korea, American policymakers saw division as preferable to unification under Ho in Vietnam. Diem, with the United States' approval, decided not to hold the promised elections. Much to Ho Chi Minh's distress, Russia accepted Vietnam's permanent division and even introduced a resolution in the United Nations that would have granted full recognition status to both the north and the south. Unable to vote their wishes, indigenous nationalist groups in the south began antigovernment guerilla actions and soon the second Indochinese war was under way. The United States had replaced France as the foreigner against whom Vietnamese nationalists fought.[1]

During the 1950s American efforts in Vietnam were largely political and economic. Significant military involvement did not begin until the 1960s. Certainly the Eisenhower administration never envisioned half a million American troops fighting in Vietnam. Nevertheless, in that decade South Vietnam became a key factor in America's increasingly global containment efforts. The Eisenhower administration made this clear when it applied the domino theory to the region and suggested ominously that the loss of South Vietnam could set off a chain reaction of other nations falling to the communists. This it was not about to let happen without a fight.

America's concern about Vietnam intensified when a three-sided civil war erupted in Laos in the late 1950s. After years of working against each other, in 1961 the United States (under the new Kennedy administration) and the Soviet Union agreed to accept a neutralist regime. That made for a balanced, or stalemated, outcome on paper but satisfied almost no one, including the Laotians, and the war soon resumed. Vietnam, as the largest and most developed part of Indochina, became increasingly important from a regional perspective.

There was by now no third side in Vietnam. Unlike Korea, where nationalist sentiment was caught between communism and capitalism, in Vietnam nationalism merged with an indigenous communism as it had in Yugoslavia. The United States saw communism and refused to lose any more ground to what it had decided was another case of international communist aggression. In the 1960s it became even more deeply embroiled in a war against Vietnamese nationalism that would last longer than any other military conflict in American history.

One must assume that that was not really what America wanted. We can hypothesize, in hindsight and using the Yugoslav lesson, that there was a logical alternative. Had the United States opted for an Asian version of

Yugoslavia, had it supported the holding of elections in 1956 and then dealt with the national government (of whatever ideological hue), the result most probably would have been an Asian version of Yugoslavia, complete with Vietnam's nationalistic perception of a need to defend itself against another communist nation, China.

The United States was looking at a different picture in the mid-1950s, however, and it saw Vietnam not as Vietnam, with unique, indigenous idiosyncracies, but as one of several disquietingly similar areas of communist aggression. Secretary of State Dulles had seen communism threatening Guatemala in 1954 and, with remarkably little difficulty, had achieved the elimination of that threat. Might not the same be done in Vietnam? That was the up side. On the down side, Dulles saw the formation of the Warsaw Pact in 1955, and in 1956 the world witnessed the Red Army's suppression of a revolt in Hungary. Soviet communism (and most Americans did not think there was really any other kind) posed a threat to the West that America could not afford to take lightly, and Ho was most definitely a Communist.

THE MIDDLE EAST

Secretary Dulles also thought he saw communism in the Middle East. In the 1950s, both the United States and Russia failed to grasp the irrelevance of their particular ideologies relative to the needs, interests, and cultures of that part of the world. Never as totally colonized as India or Indochina, most of the Middle East had in one way or another been under British or French influence most of the twentieth century. Europe had dabbled in Arab politics enough to instill bitter resentments.

During the late 1940s and early 1950s, the Middle East was too peripheral and too securely tied to the West to divert much attention from the European and Asian cold war theaters, but things began to change. As Arab nationalism matured both in individual countries and as a cross-cultural phenomenon, British and French ties in the region weakened while the importance of oil grew. The creation of Israel in 1948 began a long and protracted Arab–Israeli conflict. Although many career diplomats and, of course, the oil companies thought that America's vital interests were with the Arabs, Israel's staunch anticommunism, coupled with sentimental and religious attachments, led presidents and the public to see Israel as a natural ally and as, to use the popular term, a "bulwark against communism." Given Arab hatred of Israel, the Soviet Union saw a chance to court new allies. Neither rival realized just how unwilling both Arabs and Israelis were to be molded by cold war narrowmindedness. (For a more detailed discussion of the Middle East in Soviet–American relations see chapter 7.)

As the first of the region's truly nationalist postwar leaders, Gamal Abdul Nasser championed both Egyptian and Arab nationalism. He served as international spokesman for much of the oil-rich Middle East even though

Egypt itself has no significant oil reserves. Although it was the most developed country in the region, Egypt's efforts at modernization were hindered (as was true for many new and nonaligned nations) by an economic backwardness that was insurmountable without infusions of foreign capital and technology.

The Soviet Union was not Nasser's first choice as a source of developmental assistance. Like most Moslems, he was repelled by communist atheism and preferred dealing with the more advanced and much richer United States, even though America had close links to France and England (the old colonial foes) and to Israel (which Egypt saw as the most destabilizing force in the area). Nasser was at the same time determined not to be tied to the West. When he bought arms from Eastern Europe, the United States read his purchase as a tilt toward Russia. Secretary Dulles first tried to counter that tilt by offering to finance the massive Aswan Dam project intended to revolutionize Egyptian agriculture and provide much-needed hydroelectric power. Nasser accepted the American offer but refused to cut all ties with the Eastern bloc. Thereupon Dulles cancelled the agreement, expecting this to pressure Nasser into a change of policy.

Instead, in 1956, saying he would find domestic financing for the dam, Nasser nationalized the privately owned Suez Canal, Europe's gateway to oil, to its empires, and to the Far East. In quick retaliation, France and England, the major stockholders in the Canal Company, and Israel launched coordinated attacks against Egypt that ended only under the combined, if not cooperative, pressures of America and the Soviet Union. Although Egypt suffered a humiliating defeat and although the canal was blocked to traffic and produced no revenues for years thereafter, Nasser emerged as a hero of Arab nationalism in the face of Zionist and colonial aggression.

The Suez crisis was, at bottom, the result of forces that had little to do with the cold war; it sprang from nationalism, from the conflicting pulls of nations trying to free themselves of imperialism and others trying to preserve the vestiges of imperial power, from Arab–Israeli hostilities, and from perceived economic necessity. The crisis also suggested that American and Soviet interests were not always at variance. This preview of the 1970s detente saw both rivals working to restrain their allies, to limit the damage, and to contain not communism but chaos. The crisis was outside bipolar boundaries. It was therefore unacceptable to both sides, and both made that resoundingly clear.

Once the crisis eased, things got back to cold war normal. The Soviet Union offered to build Egypt's dam. When Nasser accepted, the United States tried to pressure him back into the fold by scaling down all contact with Egypt. The plan backfired. Nasser refused to knuckle under, and the Eastern bloc became his chief supplier of military arms and advisors as well as the source of technological assistance. Contrary to American interpretation, however, the relationship remained professional, not ideological. Holding Egypt away from commitments to either East or West, Nasser tried the risky game of playing the two sides against each other. For moral support he looked to the nonaligned movement, which had been formed for just such purposes.

None of this sat well with the United States. American policymakers were particularly sensitive to Russia's increased influence in the Middle East because of that region's all important oil reserves and the Arab–Israeli tensions. They also saw the Middle East, as they had seen Vietnam in 1954, within a global perspective that still had Europe as its pivot. The Middle East's oil was essential to European economies.

From an American point of view, the Suez crisis had another unfortunate consequence. It diverted attention from a concurrent crisis that could have given the West a huge propaganda victory had the Suez issue not created its own propaganda nightmare. The new Eisenhower administration had brought a change of position to American policy. Secretary of State Dulles told the world that containment was not enough, America would support the "liberation" of countries already under Soviet domination. This, combined with a thaw in Soviet policies after Stalin's death, awakened nationalist aspirations in Eastern Europe. Liberal elements demanded more autonomy and less compliance with Soviet dictates. They asked for too much too fast, however, and in 1956, at exactly the same time as the Suez crisis, Russian troops and tanks marched on Budapest forcibly to suppress Hungary's liberal experimentation. The West lambasted the Soviets and praised Hungary's freedom fighters and their gallant resistance against overwhelming odds. Although Dulles did nothing tangible to liberate Hungary, he could not have asked for better proof of communist tyranny.

In 1956 Eastern Europe came to understand that, rhetoric to the contrary, it could not look to the United States or to the West in general for help. America had decided to accept Soviet hegemony there much as Russia accepted American hegemony in Japan. The Hungary experience also made it clear that the Soviet contribution to world socialism was at best a mixed blessing. The invasion hurt Russia's international prestige much the same way as Suez hurt France and England's.

NONALIGNMENT

Both Suez and Hungary reaffirmed Nasser's and Tito's earlier decision to reject association with either bloc. That decision had already led to the creation of a nonaligned movement. Nasser, Tito, and India's Jawaharlal Nehru organized this association of nations, which offered members much moral and some material support. More and more nations were breaking away from colonial imperialism. Newly independent, many of them had no desire to be dictated to by the pulling and pushing, much less the attacks and counterattacks of a cold war. At the same time, given the economic and military pressures available to the two camps, opting out of their confrontation often demanded both sacrifice and courage, especially for nations with few financial resources, little industrial base, and many, many problems to tackle.

A 1955 meeting in Bandung, Indonesia, of twenty-nine nonaligned nations (many of which had been former colonies) produced a joint resolution applauding Russia's call for peaceful coexistence. Under different circumstances, such a position would hardly have raised eyebrows. Times were such, however, that the United States interpreted the resolution as indicating a preference for communist socialism over capitalist freedom. That thinking explained Secretary Dulles's generalized displeasure with the movement and its founders.

The nonaligned movement was designed as a kind of support group. It encouraged self-help and development molded to the perceived needs and potentials of each individual nation *as expressed by that nation.* American assistance programs (there simply was not much Soviet foreign aid), which in theory were usually more than welcome, did not always match the needs or wishes of the recipients and sometimes seemed to be trying to mold developing nations in America's image. In other cases, of course, the United States withheld assistance, which made support from the movement that much more desirable. In either case, nonaligned nations fought desperately to preserve their sense of self and to survive economically. To this day, the nonaligned movement, with a fluid membership that represents huge portions of the world's land mass, population, resources, and brainpower, provides depressurized alternatives to the high-intensity economic and political regimentation of bipolarity.

From the beginning, the movement faced impressive obstacles both internally and externally. It allowed anyone to join, and some members used the meetings to proselytize their own ideology. Rejection of bipolarity could not in and of itself guarantee agreement on other subjects. Interests and ideas clashed. Over time, as the posturing of both sides eased somewhat, the need for a structured organization of nonaligned nations seemed to be less important. Ironically, that may have been the movement's most important contribution: it forced the eastern and western blocs to question their opposite constructs and accept the legitimacy of nonalignment.

East–West tolerance of the nonaligned movement did not come easily and may still be more superficial than real. Initially, both cold war camps tended to label anyone who did not subscribe to their rules as ipso facto the enemy. The United States found it especially difficult to accept nonalignment from nations looking to its resources for developmental assistance. While it was more willing than was Russia to accept idiosyncratic behavior from the already aligned, firmly anticommunist nations (compare its response to Israel in 1956 with Russia's response to Hungary), it was much less tolerant of any sign of socialist ideology or economic experimentation (leftist leanings) among emerging and nonaligned nations.

The Soviet Union reacted more sympathetically toward nonalignment, partly for ideological and partly for financial reasons. Its increased international activism, and that of the United States, made clear its still significant economic limitations. It simply did not have as much to offer developing nations as did the United States. Stalin's death made a more flexible policy possible, but among ideological hard-liners that very flexibility also raised doubts about Russia's ability to retain leadership of the international socialist revolution. In particular, the People's Republic of China challenged Moscow for title to ideological purity. As an international power, Russia needed flexibility; as an ideological power, it found flexibility to be a double-edged sword.

By the late 1950s Russia had opted to downplay rigid dogmatism in its relations with non-Eastern European nations. Flexibility would help wean insecure new nations away from love-hate relations with former rulers. Aided by a more tolerant Soviet Union, these countries might cut their colonialist–capitalist economic umbilical cords. The Russians had begun to grasp the Yugoslav lesson, and although this understanding could not settle their differences with a dogmatic China, it did prompt them to re-establish ties with Yugoslavia.

Shortly after Stalin died the new Soviet leaders expressed a desire to heal the Soviet–Yugoslav division. Khrushchev visited Belgrade and agreed that there were, indeed, many roads of socialism. Relations improved, but the Soviet response to Hungary in 1956, and Yugoslavia's commitment to the nonaligned movement and to national independence, precluded any reversion to pre-1948 intimacy.[2]

The United States continued to have trouble rationalizing its support of Yugoslavia under these circumstances. The Eisenhower administration responded to the ups and downs of a post-Stalin Soviet–Yugoslav rapprochement with much less tolerance than the Truman administration had shown when Yugoslavia was an orphan communist regime under siege. The United States did continue, in fits and starts, to give economic and military aid, but the relationship was always a little shaky. By the 1960s Yugoslavia no longer needed direct economic assistance and did not have to suffer the vagaries of big power pique. Other countries could only hope that both the United States and the Soviet Union would understand that, while assistance was needed and welcomed, it did not come at the expense of national integrity.

CHINA

China's emergence as a self-proclaimed prophet of socialist revolution contributed both to the Soviet Union's increased tolerance of nonalignment and to the weakening of the movement. Like Yugoslavia, China brought about a revolution through its own energies. Unlike Yugoslavia, China had a messianic streak. Announcing that Russia had betrayed the cause and was trafficking with the devil, China declared itself to be the orthodox authority on revolutionary dogma and set out to convert others to its own, particularist, socialist ideology. In the 1960s it tried to do this through association with the nonaligned movement.

China may not have had a corner on revolutionary socialist dogma, but it had sound historical reasons for distrusting both the United States and the Soviet Union. Sino–American hostility was apparent even before the Korean War. The United States saw the Chinese Communist victory in a bipolar context, labeled Mao a Russian protégé, and assumed that China did as Russia dictated. When China entered the Korean War, the United States declared it ideologically anathema and diplomatically nonexistent. During the 1950s the United States continued to recognize the Nationalist government in Taiwan as the true voice of China, and the People's Republic continued to attack America as a paper tiger.

Sino–Soviet disagreements took a little longer to surface. Dubious of its potential for success and eager to maintain postwar allied harmony, Stalin had kept Mao's Communist party at arm's length during the protracted Chinese civil war. When the People's Republic emerged victorious, Russia was leery, as it had been with Yugoslavia, of indications that China would go its own way. By the mid 1950s the Chinese were, in fact, accusing the Soviet Union of ideological impurity. Among other things, they did not think Russia was taking a strong enough stand against capitalist imperialism and its chief proponent, the United States. They also harangued Russia for its overtures to Titoist heresy on the one hand and on the other announced their independence from Russia by joining the Yugoslav-sponsored nonaligned movement. China's membership in the movement did not reflect its acceptance of alternative paths as much as it reflected a rejection of Russia's path. While the formal Sino–Soviet split dates from the early 1960s, tensions had already become so strained that troop clashes along the two countries' very long shared border were common.

Thus, by the late 1950s China had become something of a thorn in Russia's side even while the United States still depicted it as being little more than a Soviet puppet regime. China's membership in the nonaligned movement doubly condemned that group's efforts in American eyes, while announcing to the Soviet Union that China rejected Russian guidance. Continuing friction between Yugoslavia and China surfaced in the movement, with China convinced that Yugoslav communism was a heresy rather than a true alternative route to communist socialism. With the Russians and the Americans now competing for influence in emerging nations not only against each other but also against the collective (if ideologically nonspecific) prestige of the nonaligned movement and China, the two-sided dogmatism of as little as five years previously was increasingly politically and diplomatically impossible. Yugoslavia played no small role in bringing some awareness of the fallacy of bipolarity to the world and to the concept's architects.

The world had never been bipolar, nor had it ever been exclusively concerned with cold war issues. In the 1950s it was divided into Eastern and Western blocs only in the eyes of the blocs themselves. Admittedly, the Eastern bloc had ruthlessly brought a rebellion in Hungary under control using tanks against sticks; and the Western bloc had overthrown a reform government in Guatemala and a nationalist government in Iran. All these shows of force gave the illusion of bipolarity maintained by force as well as by ideology.

Closer examination showed serious cracks even within the blocs. Albania's communist leader Hoxha operated a Stalinist regime long after the Soviet Union had de-Stalinized. Romania showed signs of siding with China, and China was calling Russia a capitalist stooge. So much for communist unity.

On the capitalist side, during the Suez crisis and again in the early 1960s, France asserted an independence in Western Europe that threatened to undermine Western solidarity. France's leader, General Charles de Gaulle, was a kind of Western Europe Tito: a thorn in the side of demands for unthinking conformity. Elsewhere in Europe, "creeping" socialism made inroads into the bastions of free but definitely unequal capitalist enterprise. Elsewhere in the world, decolonization ate away at imperial claims to loyalty. The "free world," as America loved to call its allies, relied more and more on the Central Intelligence Agency (CIA), military strong men, and reactionary regimes to keep populist unrest in check. More and more countries like Yugoslavia were able to exist free of ownership or control by East or West. Nations like Egypt and India mapped their own courses and managed to separate themselves from the either-or of Soviet–American bipolarity.

Marx, who knew little about the non-European world, developed a dichotomy between capitalism and socialism that one hundred years later was distorted into Soviet–American rivalry for hegemony. As early as 1948, however, the Yugoslav example raised questions about the dualism and suggested that alternatives to this irrationality did exist. The nonaligned movement's fundamental premise was that individual nations, struggling against particularist problems, can best reach their full and unfettered potentials by avoiding the cold war. Strongly nationalistic nations often found themselves unwillingly ensnared in the prevailing machinations, but some nonaligned nations benefited from Soviet–American rivalry. Belonging to neither bloc but courted by both, an independent, nonaligned Yugoslavia was able to examine and compare their respective offerings. Egypt and India felt America's wrath but were nevertheless recipients of both American and Russian economic assistance. A measure of success as an independent, nonaligned nation became the ability to take advantage of bipolar thinking without being dragged in to it. That was the Yugoslav heresy.

NOTES

1. For a study of the Soviet relations with Vietnam see Douglas Pike, *Vietnam and the Soviet Union: Anatomy of an Alliance* (Boulder, Colo.: Westview Press, 1987).

2. For more information on Yugoslavia and the nonaligned movement see Alvin Z. Rubinstein, *Yugoslavia and the Nonaligned World* (Princeton, N.J.: Princeton University Press, 1970).

Spirit of Camp David, 1959:
Eisenhower and Khrushchev.
UPI/Bettmann Newsphotos.

The Berlin Wall. *Roger Malloch, Magnum Photos.*

chapter 5

THE SECRET SIDE OF SOVIET–AMERICAN RELATIONS

Many Americans were troubled by nationalism, the nonaligned movement, and the Yugoslav heresy, and perceived these developments to indicate a dangerous world over which their country was losing its grip. The flip side of that assessment was, of course, that communism and the Soviet Union were on the rise, and that, unless something beyond traditional diplomacy was done and done soon, America's national security was in danger.

Before World War II, the US government had little call for master spies, much less for an entire agency devoted to intelligence gathering and covert operations. The war changed all that. At President Roosevelt's request, Colonel William Donovan organized the Office of Strategic Services (OSS), which quickly rivaled the State Department in its ability to gain access to information and policy-making, and which definitely surpassed the department in its ability to conduct undercover and behind-the-lines operations. The OSS closed its doors when the war ended, but the need for a permanent, centralized, and coordinated intelligence capability, in which networks of spooks and spies were but one facet, remained. The cold war turned covert activity into a major arm of the making and implementation of US foreign policy. The Truman administration also wanted an umbrella coordinating agency that would facilitate the government's much-expanded foreign operations. The National Security Act of 1947 addressed these needs by creating two new executive branch agencies. The National Security Council (NSC) would coordinate the containment of communism among all relevant US government offices and advise the president on national security issues. Assisting it in this effort, the CIA would provide data on which to base informed, rational, and relevant policy. It would also, when called upon, implement covert policies beyond the scope of traditional diplomacy. By law, the CIA was barred from operating inside the United States, as the Federal Bureau of Investigation (FBI) protected domestic national security interests. Other than this, the CIA had few legal limitations and was not particularly accountable to congressional oversight.

Over the years the NSC has evolved from an almost invisible coordinating mechanism into an autonomous policy formulator and implementer. Its exact function and how it shares policy and power with other branches of the government have varied from administration to administration. The CIA has, from its very beginning and with great consistency, been a major foreign policy player and thus a critical factor in Soviet–American relations.

In 1947 America's major foreign policy and national security concerns were Russia and communism. The CIA used a cloak-and-dagger approach to containing Russia, while the State Department pursued more traditional and formal diplomatic means. Career diplomats have definitely not always seen eye to eye with the often much more singleminded and more adventuresome undercover operatives. In some cases, the department has fought against CIA activities; more often, it has provided a front behind which the real action unfolded. By the 1950s analysts began to talk, with justification, about a front door (State Department) and back door (CIA) diplomatic duality in which the front door was not always told exactly what back door initiatives were.

Almost by definition, the CIA's unilateral anticommunist and national security nature meant that it mirrored the views of America's stridently anticommunist and staunchly nationalistic conservative wing. For many conservatives, communism may not be the first evil to confront mankind, but it has definitely been the most dangerous. As they see it, whether transmitted by force or by the more insidious corrosion of social and political values, communism destroys individual freedoms and human dignity while stripping its victims of political, economic, and religious rights. As such, it warrants taking strong, even harsh, preventive measures at home and abroad. At the very least, communism should be contained; ideally, it should be stamped out. The latter, of course, was exactly what the CIA had been born to do.

While the huge majority of Americans, conservative and liberal, shared a dislike of communism and suspicion of Russia, the conservatives distinguished themselves by the intensity of their feelings and by their nationalism. Unlike Wilsonian internationalists, for example, they openly set national security first, had little faith in collective security, and assumed America's interests could best be served by hard-nosed, energetic, unilateral action. They had little sympathy with any limits that misguided liberal do-gooders, allies pushing their own national self-interests, or even the constitutional niceties of separation of power power might try to impose on America's freedom of action. Diplomatic conservatives were cold warriors; they lived in constant fear that the United States was losing its rightful place as the world's preeminent military, economic, and ideological force. Many were willing to put at least part of the blame for cold war crises not just on the actions of foreigners operating abroad but also on those of disloyal Americans operating inside the United States. Time has not significantly altered this position: strong support for a superior military defense, distrust of any suggestion that relations between the United States and the Soviet Union might be mellowing, preference for unilateral action, and acute anxiety about domestic security.

Thus, by dint of either their personal ideology or their job descriptions, political conservatives and intelligence planners both focus on nationalistic, unilateral, foreign policy options; both usually see Russia and communism as the primary causes for concern. The impact of these two forces, working sometimes in tandem but more often independent of each other, has been felt both at home and abroad, and has done much to keep Soviet–American relations at a boil.

Before World War II men like Senators Robert Taft and Arthur Vandenburg had argued long and hard that Europe was no place for American troops and that Europe's problems were for its own nations to solve. They were not quick to be convinced that the United States had new global responsibilities. They were also convinced that communism was abhorrent. When the 1946 Iran crisis was followed by civil war in Greece, by the Soviet takeover of Eastern Europe, and by the problems with Russia in Germany, one-time isolationist conservatives decided that, in order to protect itself, America had to protect the world.

Although the Truman administration hoped the United Nations (collective security) could resolve some of the postwar problems, it balked at putting all of its eggs in one new and unproved basket. The NSC and the CIA (national security) enhanced America's ability to do it on its own if necessary. This pleased conservatives, who had almost no faith in organizations such as the United Nations and saw the carefully shrouded CIA as an alternative to such open, international policy.

Whatever its pros and cons, collective security could do little or nothing to eliminate weaknesses inside the United States and even inside its government. Neither, theoretically, could the CIA. Domestic security had to be handled internally. The discovery in 1946 that Canadian scientists had passed atomic research to the Russians awakened Americans to the reality and risks of disloyalty and espionage. Foreigners had easy access to the United States (unlike the restrictions imposed on outsiders entering Russia), and nothing guaranteed that there might not even be Americans sympathetic to or actually working for the Soviet Union. Some members of an anxious public complained that the administration was not hard enough on Russia, was soft in its dealings with communists, and was peppered with communist sympathizers who betrayed America's interests.

Partly to defuse security as a partisan issue and partly because it was a legitimate government concern, in 1947 Truman instituted a loyalty program to screen government employees and protect the nation against possible security breaches. Civil libertarians protested against the need for such police state scrutiny; conservatives feared the program did not go far enough. By 1948 the NSC recommended that the government "urgently develop and execute a firm and coordinated program (to include legislation if necessary) designed to suppress the communist menace in the United States," which policymakers feared included "disruptive and dangerous subversive activities."[1] The FBI ran extensive security checks on government employees, and the Justice Department began monitoring the activities of hundreds of organizations deemed suspect. For some, to be on the Attorney General's list was a badge of courage; for others, it was proof of disloyalty.

The fall of China was a major blow to America's psyche. If, as many believed, the United States had lost China, then someone must be responsible. Had people in the government wanted China to fall, been secretly in sympathy with the Communists, and done nothing to prevent this disaster? China experts in the State Department who had followed the course of that country's years of turmoil found that their analyses spelling out China's own failings as the cause of its fall to communism did not exonerate them personally from suspicion. Men like John Carter Vincent and John S. Service of the State Department were driven from government or refused new security clearances in the face of repeated, if unproved, accusations. These valuable information resources were victims of a growing national insecurity that would culminate in McCarthyism and leave scars to hamstring the flexibility of American foreign policy at least into the 1970s.

Formed by Americans for religious, economic, and ideological interests, a China lobby campaigned to prevent any rapprochement between the United States and the People's Republic. Hoping for the eventual return of the Nationalist government to the mainland, this amorphous, conservative organization successfully lobbied for active military and economic support of the Formosa government and against granting "Red China" the China seat on the UN Security Council. Having designated itself as guardian of traditional American values, and functioning as a kind of adjunct private arm of the FBI and CIA, the China lobby had a tremendous impact on America's China policy in the 1950s and 1960s. Yet most Americans have never heard of it. They have, however, heard of McCarthyism.

In 1938 Congress created the House Un-American Activities Committee (HUAC) with a mandate to investigate domestic organizations whose activities threatened American security. Revived after the war, HUAC concentrated on leftist organizations almost exclusively, and its members, including then-Representative Richard Nixon, conducted lengthy investigations most notably of labor organizations and the film industry. Individuals who could not convince the committee of their loyalty (and certainly anyone with proved communist connections) found themselves fired, blacklisted, or discredited in the public eye.

In 1950 Senator Joseph McCarthy undertook to, in his words, "ferret out" the hundreds of communist sympathizers he declared to be working inside the US government. Buttressed by one proved case of perjury (the State Department's Alger Hiss had lied during an earlier investigation about his prewar associations), the conviction of two Americans (the Rosenbergs) for selling nuclear weapons secrets to the Russians, and a public eager to find scapegoats for perceived foreign policy shortcomings, McCarthy embarked on a four-year crusade that knew few ethical bounds but found no communist agents. President Truman and former Secretary of State George Marshall were, according to McCarthy, manipulated directly from Moscow. Even President Eisenhower, although of McCarthy's own Republican party, was of doubtful loyalty since he refused to eradicate all those spies and agents from the government.

In 1954, as suddenly as it had begun, McCarthy's personal reign of abuse and harassment came to an end. The anticommunist witch hunt that bears his name remained a force, however, demanding conformity and unquestioning loyalty to hardline anticommunism long after his demise. By restricting foreign policy options, McCarthyism helped keep the cold war very close to the borderline of a hot war. Policymakers, fearing accusations of being soft on communism, supported the status quo, and the status quo had no room for rethinking either the NSC's analysis of Soviet intentions or America's containment policy.

These 1950s reflections of conservative America—HUAC, McCarthyism, the China lobby, and an ever-vigilant FBI under J. Edgar Hoover's overly firm control—played prominent roles not so much in formulating foreign policy as in determining public opinion and in stagnating policy by preventing it from evolving. Communism came to be thought of as a monolith; anyone who questioned the premises of the cold war or questioned America's relentless opposition to all forms of communism faced an immovable barrier of suspicion and fear. Since much the same atmosphere, in mirror image, characterized Soviet policy, the chances for a significant breakthrough toward bilateral coexistence, not to say cooperation, were minimal.

Premised on the evils of Soviet and communist expansionism, the CIA had trouble dealing with the concept of harmonious coexistence. Unlike HUAC and McCarthy, the CIA operated outside the United States in a world where suspicion and fear were supported by hard evidence. At one point in McCarthy's prime, he sent two assistants on a tour of Europe where they stripped US Information Service libraries and reading rooms of allegedly un-American holdings. (They were making the world a safer place by guarding it from Mark Twain; McCarthyites declared *The Adventures of Huckleberry Finn* un-American because it raised doubts about the justice of racial segregation, still legally sanctioned in the United States at that time.) On their fools' errand, these two men romped through many of the same cities where CIA operatives risked their lives in defense of national security.

The secret side of Soviet–American relations began before the CIA. During the war, various, often uncoordinated, civilian and military branches of the US government built networks of American and foreign national intelligence agents to monitor and, if necessary, manipulate events. Most of this happened in Europe. Anti-Soviet sentiment was strong enough, at least in some quarters, to sanction the use (and later protection) of such people as known Nazi war criminal Klaus Barbie to aid in uncovering communist cells and Soviet spies in liberated Western Europe.[2] Because some documentary records of these early cold war years are still classified, the whole picture of just whom the United States used and what those people did is not yet clear. Certainly some Americans went to extremes to establish a counterintelligence base. The Russians can use this behavior as "proof" that the United States never expected to deal fairly with them and as justification for their reaction in kind. On the other hand, the Russians had a long track record of their own use of sophisticated secret police and intelligence networks that operated at home and abroad with equal efficiency. Even if one eliminates the ideological side of Soviet–American rivalry, Russian espionage required some measure of counterintelligence.

Although the secret side of the cold war in Western Europe rarely affected the constitutional or political nature of governments, it did affect people, did guard or expose secrets, did increase knowledge about the other side, and did involve national and international security interests. Both the CIA and its Russian equivalent NKVD/KGB (plus, of course, other national intelligence networks) played a kind of game to see who could learn the most about the other, who could infiltrate the other's intelligence networks, and who could steal whose economic, military, or intelligence secrets. Counterintelligence efforts tried to stop the other side from doing its job.

This was the CIA's original raison d'être. The Soviet government has been so shrouded in secrecy that espionage and information analysis offer two of the few ways to learn the inner workings of its corridors of power. Convincing KGB agents to switch allegiance, finding "moles," and recruiting defectors who can then be debriefed may not be everyday occurrences, but these spy thriller images of intelligence work do happen and are taken seriously by all sides. Like all intelligence work at any time and under any circumstances, spying is a mixed bag ethically. According to Ross Thomas's cynical 1966 fictional description, cold war spies were "engaged in a business which follows no set rules or laws. It is a hard, filthy business that goes on in its peculiarly arcane fashion, fed by overweaning ambition, by greed, by intrigue, blundering often, and then blundering again to cover up the original mistake."[3] Most recently, Colonel Oliver North of the NSC gave much the same assessment, without the cynicism and with a firm conviction about its importance to national security, to the Iran-Contra arms-for-hostage activities with which he was associated in 1985 and 1986. According to North, lies and deceit are the name of the game.

During the height of the cold war, Europe was the prize over which the United States and Russia exchanged lies. Thus, in spite of the Continent's relatively stable politics and steadily improving economy, it was awash in spies, field agents, intrigues, drop points, and information exchanges. Berlin was the field center of both sides' operations. Periodic disclosures of highly placed Russian agents having access to Western intelligence sent recurrent shock waves through the public and rekindled the need to be that much more secretive, fearful, and aware of Soviet perfidy. Undoubtedly the same reactions periodically shook Moscow as well, but the Russian public was rarely apprised of its government's security failures.

Because both sides were fairly well matched and able to contain each other, their intelligence work in Europe was usually limited to information gathering and the periodic individual assassinations or defections. Covert operations in other parts of the world offered more freedom of movement and more dramatic results. Outside Europe, the CIA felt even less need to coordinate with its French and British counterparts, for example, and inexperienced governments in new or undeveloped countries were much easier targets for persuasion.

During most of the Eisenhower administration, the overt (State Department) and covert (CIA) arms of American foreign policy worked in close tandem. As Secretary of State and devout cold warrior, John Foster Dulles firmly believed that the United States had a responsibility to contain communism. Although Dulles was the architect of several regional collective security pacts, he was convinced that the United States could and should act unilaterally much of the time. He thought many of his own State Department career diplomats temperamentally incompatible with the policy needs of the day. Together with his brother Allen Dulles, Director of the CIA, however, John Foster devised alternative means of policy implementation. Under these men, covert diplomacy came into its own.

One of the Dulles brothers' first ventures involved the very volatile Middle East. When the Iranian nationalist leader Mosaddeg threatened to distance Iran and its oil resources from Western influence in 1953, the CIA, working with the young, pro-West and anti-Mosaddeg Shah, helped organize a change in governments and bring Iran back into line. The CIA provided the anti-Mosaddeg forces with guns, vehicles, and means of communication. It even paid for street demonstrations to project popular support for the coup. For twenty-five years thereafter the Shah, as a stalwart if demanding ally of the

West, maintained close ties with the CIA. He let the United States install monitoring devices along Iran's border with the Soviet Union and relied on the CIA for help in training his own secret service, SAVAK. Under the Shah, Iran became a member of the Baghdad Pact–cum–CENTO which, especially in the 1950s and working closely with the United States, created a collective security alliance against Russia that spread from Turkey to Pakistan.

The Dulles CIA expressed an active, if not always successful, interest in keeping the Middle East aligned with the West. Those in the know, American and Arab alike, learned that visiting CIA men more often voiced operative US policy than did ambassadors or the State Department's political officers. The agency found the hodgepodge of emotional, religious, nationalist, and personal forces in the region difficult to mold, however (see chapter 7). Much more politically sophisticated than many Americans (or Russians) gave them credit for being, Arabs had no qualms about slanting cold war politics to their own purposes. Although firsthand accounts of the CIA in the Middle East give the impression of a US government covertly trying to play god with Arab politics, a notable lack of success with countries such as Egypt and Syria suggests that here, at least, the god was not omniscient.

Closer to home the Dulleses achieved another Iran-like, cold war victory in Guatemala. When the Guatemalan government initiated socialist agrarian reforms that threatened large American landowning interests, Dulles saw Soviet aggression at work. Reflective of McCarthyistic thinking and of a rather simplistic, black-and-white view of the world, American Ambassador to Guatemala Peurifoy later used his famous duck analogy to explain why he, for one, was convinced the Arbenz government was communist: if something looks, walks, and quacks like a duck it makes sense to call it a duck until something better comes along. Although Arbenz was not a communist, the cold war atmosphere was such that not only did the United States label him as such, but it also took the next step and assumed him to be a Russian duck. The CIA outfitted a handpicked opposition force that overthrew Arbenz and installed a new government. (See chapter 3 for Dulles's speech explaining this action to the American public.) Private property rights were protected and Guatemala became a staunchly anticommunist, if definitely rightist and elitist, ally in Central America.

In Asia, the Eisenhower administration worried about Vietnam, Laos, and the domino theory. In 1958 and in the midst of a three-sided civil war, the CIA engineered the overthrow of Prince Souvana Phouma's neutralist Laotian government. John Foster Dulles was never comfortable with neutral or non-aligned policies. Anything short of complete commitment to the West represented at best a weak link in global containment and at worst a facade behind which the Soviet Union could insidiously expand its influence.

Dulles died in 1959, and the Democrats were in the White House in 1961. Much to the dismay of diplomatic conservatives, and in spite of his own activist campaign pledges, Kennedy accepted Laotian neutrality. Souvana

Phouma returned to office as part of an international agreement signed by Laos, Russia, and the United States. Then the CIA's self-fulfilling prophecy came true: Souvana Phouma proved unable to hold the country against Soviet-backed rebels on the one hand and CIA-supported rightists on the other. Officially, both the United States and the Soviet Union maintained overt support for the neutralist government; unofficially, Laos continued on as a surrogate battlefield where nationalistic and cold war emotions ran riot.

The CIA predictions of doom and gloom also proved out in Vietnam, where the agency served for many years as a chief source of American intelligence information, as well as policy implementor. In the mid-1950s, having assumed responsibility for protecting South Vietnam's independence, the United States sponsored the South East Asia Treaty Organization (SEATO) to defend member nations and South Vietnam (not a member) from communist aggression; however, SEATO could not do anything about internal South Vietnamese problems. Diem's government was corrupt, nepotistic, and insensitive to the needs of the people. The CIA issued pessimistic progress reports to both the Eisenhower and the Kennedy administrations, but neither was willing either to get out or to apply enough pressure to force so firm an anticommunist ally to change his ways. Finally, in 1963 even Diem's own generals recognized that he had alienated so much of the population as to be a boon to the Viet Cong insurgents. Although the United States played no active role in removing Diem, it did voice advance if covert support for the coup, hoping that a new government could conduct a stronger, more unified offensive against the rebels. By then the seeds of much deeper American involvement had been planted, and American policy in Vietnam went beyond CIA control.

In the late 1950s, during the calm before the storm, as it were, Vietnam experts burgeoned in both the CIA and State Department. Like the earlier China hands, these men were well aware of the Diem government's shortcomings. Given the China experience, they were also committed to preserving an anticommunist government. Unable as a matter of US national policy to accommodate a communist South Vietnam, they wrote objective analyses of current difficulties but based future policy on the assumption that somehow things could be made to work out. In hindsight, one can say this was ideologically motivated self-delusion.

In Africa, the covert side of American containment enjoyed more success. The 1950s and 1960s witnessed a rapid breakup of colonial Africa and the emergence of neophyte nations with little experience of self-government. The United States used overt (foreign aid) and covert (CIA) approaches to steady shaky governments and counterefforts by both the Soviets and the Chinese to gain influence and ideological converts. The dark continent was a hotbed of complex political intrigue, where skilled and callous intelligence operations often proved more effective than the maneuverability limitations of more traditional State Department diplomacy.

How the Belgium Congo, with its huge copper holdings but almost no experience in self-government, dealt with independence was of particular interest to a West with sensitive natural resource needs. In 1960, when a popular nationalist leader, Patrice Lumumba, evaded total alignment with that Western bloc, the CIA was told to eliminate the problem. It bungled several attempts to assassinate Lumumba, however, and had to be satisfied with news of his death at the hands of a rival Congolese leader who was able, soon thereafter, to establish a pro-West government. The new government put an end to any chance of a flirtation with leftist policies. The Congo (renamed Zaire), plagued by corruption and economic distress, has remained aligned with the West in spite of problems with rebel insurgents.

Much of the CIA activity mentioned so far was, of course, secret. Until documents were declassified or information was leaked, even the informed American public was unaware of the extent to which the CIA manipulated the internal affairs of foreign countries. One reason for secrecy was concern about how that public and a public-sensitive Congress would respond to using assassinations and blatant violations of national sovereignty as weapons of diplomacy. Many Americans were not convinced that desirable ends justified any means. For its part, the CIA (and the other US government intelligence agencies that emerged over time) assumed that security interests should override squeamish public and congressional sensibilities that the agency saw as naive. Covert operations fought fire with fire, or so they believed; one could not afford to turn the other cheek against communism, the KGB, or risks to America's national security.

In the late 1950s and early 1960s the United States experienced a series of shocks that, from a conservative perspective, seemed to threaten that security. All of these set the stage for one of the CIA's most publicized operations and most embarrassing failures: the 1961 Bay of Pigs invasion of Cuba.

At home, resistance to the civil rights movement prompted the movement's supporters to see America's self-proclaimed leadership of the free and equal world as a sham. The movement itself prompted other Americans to see communism invading their home shores and undermining tried and true traditional values. The fanatically right-wing John Birch Society linked communism and integration; the FBI looked at Martin Luther King and saw a potential revolutionist. For those who agreed with the John Birch Society and FBI Director Hoover, strides made by the civil rights movement went hand in hand with revolutionary events in Cuba to suggest communist inroads into the very heart of America.

Internationally, the tentative beginnings of a Soviet–American thaw, presaged by a 1955 Geneva summit and Premier Khrushchev's 1959 visit to the United States, began to freeze over again. In 1960, and during another summit, the Soviets shot down an American U-2 reconnaissance plane deep inside Russian territory. The United States had been using such overflights to monitor Soviet weapons deployment. The incident was more embarrassing than anything else, but it soured bilateral relations and seemed to put the United States on the wrong side of Russia's call for peaceful coexistence.

A new crisis in Berlin was also in the works. Throughout the 1950s, thousands of East Europeans escaped to the West through Berlin. Above and beyond the bad publicity consequent to such large numbers of people trying to leave socialist states, these refugees represented a major drain of skilled and professional manpower from the Eastern bloc. Tensions mounted to a point at which, in 1961, the communists felt compelled to build a physical, concrete and barbed-wire wall through the city. For an American public prepared to believe the worst of Russia and its East German satellite, communism was still a clear and present danger.

As if all that was not enough, the arms race had made tremendous and terrifying advances in the 1950s, Russia having launched Sputnik and inaugurated the era of the intercontinental ballistics missile in 1957. Senator John F. Kennedy, campaigning for the presidency in 1960, accused the Eisenhower administration of allowing a missile gap to develop, which, if it actually existed, would put the United States behind Russia defensively.

It was in this highly charged atmosphere that Americans learned of a revolution in Cuba and the victory of a scruffy but charismatic guerrilla fighter who loudly proclaimed the United States responsible for his island's atrocious economic and social inequities. Almost no one mourned the Batista regime, but thousands of Cubans fled the island and its new reformist government under Fidel Castro. Those who came to the United States told tales of terror and helped assure a decidedly, not to say fanatically, anti-Castro reaction in America. The United States had been Cuba's major export market, and the government tried to force Castro out by cutting off Cuban imports. With his economy in a shambles, Castro turned to the Soviet Union for help. The chance to have a foothold in the Western Hemisphere was an offer Russia could not refuse.

Relying heavily (too heavily, it turned out) on Cuban emigrée informants, the CIA decided that Castro did not have the support of most of the Cubans still in Cuba. Given a chance, the agency thought, many of these people could move to oust the regime and bring democratic capitalism to power. Anti-Castro refugees not only agreed but volunteered to train for a "liberating" invasion to be manned by Cubans backed by US material and air support. Plans that were drawn up in the last months of the Eisenhower presidency were presented, almost as a fait accompli, to the incoming Kennedy administration. Taking much of what he was told at face value, the new, action-oriented president nevertheless had qualms about so heavy an American interference in Cuba's internal affairs. He approved the invasion, but at reduced levels of US air support.

The 1961 Bay of Pigs invasion was a fiasco. No internal uprising to support the liberators materialized, and Castro brought a quick end to the matter. America's role in the operation was internationally embarrassing and made the CIA the brunt of innumerable jokes. It was an internal debacle for the CIA as well. Beyond the immediate demoralization of so publicized a failure (and this CIA operation could not be kept secret), the Bay of Pigs damaged the agency's credibility. Did it really know what was going on, or was it seeing only what it wanted to see? How intelligent was America's intelligence agency?

The invasion did nothing, of course, to improve Cuban–American relations and much to tighten Cuban–Soviet friendship. Eighteen months later, discovery that Russia was deploying medium-range missiles in Cuba and within easy striking range of the United States prompted a tense naval confrontation and the most traumatic instance of brinkmanship in Soviet–American relations: the Cuban Missile crisis broke (see chapter 6). After that, Soviet–American and Cuban–American relations were for a while so acrimonious that, when Kennedy was killed in late 1963, a horrified America found it logical to assume that the assassin had Cuban or Soviet connections. It also assumed that Cuban–American relations had become a kind of subset of Soviet–American relations. When Castro announced his determination to support and spread communist regimes throughout the hemisphere, the marriage of things Cuban with things Soviet was sealed.

Kennedy also moved away from the Eisenhower–Dulles defense strategy of all-or-nothing massive retaliation. He preferred flexible response and counterinsurgency, both of which would allow the United States to conduct a foreign policy of precision more suited to the 1960s. Laos was Laos, and it needed to be dealt with specifically as such, not as another indistinguishable repeat of Soviet–American clashes anywhere in the world. Definitely Laos was not as critical as Berlin and should not be allowed, in a misguided, brinkmanship display of power, to spark a world war. By their very nature, flexible response and counterinsurgency implied the need for greater knowledge at specific, detailed levels, about particular areas of concern. Fighting communism was not enough. One had to know the particular field of battle, the personalities involved, and the relevant indigenous details. The Kennedy team expected its intelligence agents to be knowledgeable, up-to-date specialists. Ideally, they should even speak the language. Kennedy often went outside the still-chagrined CIA to find such men. New ideas meant new implementers, and there began a proliferation of sub rosa offices, departments, and agencies all playing their part in America's covert diplomacy.

Covert, particularistic containment offered an attractive alternative to open, melodramatic confrontation. After the Cuban missile crisis, which was a classic example of brinkmanship, Kennedy and Khrushchev both tried to cool cold war tempers. The 1963 Test Ban Treaty and the installation of a hotline communication link between Washington and Moscow symbolized a new willingness to coexist, at least overtly, for fear that, if they did not, the two powers might take the entire world hurtling to disaster.

These lessons were most poignantly learned by the individuals involved at that time; they did not become part of either nation's consciousness. Kennedy's assassination brought a veteran cold warrior into office who would give the Republicans no cause to accuse him of being soft on communism. Ironically, Lyndon Johnson ran for president in 1964 against Barry Goldwater, who campaigned on just that issue. The Democrats were soft on defense, giving the Russians the edge, not taking a strong enough stand in foreign policy, or so Goldwater said. Although this conservative challenger lost his bid for the presidency, on a foreign policy level he and Johnson were not as far apart as the campaign declamations suggested.

In 1965 Johnson sent some 22,000 troops to the Dominican Republic. Publicly, he was protecting American lives and property; practically, he was making very sure that no leftist regime came to power in the western hemisphere during his presidency. One Cuba was more than enough, and American policymakers found the concept of a Yugoslav heresy in the New World unimaginable, not to mention unacceptable.

In Russia, Khrushchev's fall from grace in 1964, in large part because of his humiliation over the missile crisis, meant that for some years to come the Soviet Union would not be interested in making deals with America. In fact, it began a major military buildup and diplomatic push that brought new concerns to US foreign policymakers.

By the mid-1960s the United States was embroiled in Vietnam. With presidential attention focused on Southeast Asia, the rest of the world was left relatively free to run itself. Direct Soviet–American rivalry let off public steam through competitive space races and quadrennial Olympic games. The arms race (see chapter 6) continued unabated, but none of the new super-weapons were used in anger, and their destructive potential reached such proportions as to be mind numbing and thus, in a weird way, irrelevant. The East–West focus of the cold war bipolarity finally began to soften a little. Fictionalized accounts of cloak-and-dagger espionage no longer assumed that American agents always operated from noble motives, although their Soviet opposites remained incorrigibly bad or played a muted, off-stage role. In *The Cold War Swap*, published in 1966, Ross Thomas painted a damning fictional picture of the CIA and, by extension, of the US government as seen through foreign eyes:

> You Americans are still very insular people. You have your violence, to be sure, and your thieves, your criminals, even your traitors. You wander the world trying to be—how does the slang go?—the good guys and you are despised for your bungling, hated for your wealth, and ridiculed and mocked for your posturing. Your CIA would be a laughing stock, except that it controls enough funds to corrupt a government, finance a revolution, sub-

vert a political party. You are not a stupid or stubborn people, Herr McCorkle, but you are an ignorant people, a disinterested people.[4]

The real CIA may have substituted money for finesse, but it had a lot of money to do it. Still in pursuit of threats to a definition of America's national security interests written twenty years earlier, the CIA plodded on, finding monsters everywhere. Dismayed at Soviet and Chinese inroads in the developing nations, made while President Johnson concentrated on his plans for a Great Society and sank more money and manpower into Vietnam, the CIA kept on gathering information and running its own side-show operations.

Agency fears of a deteriorating international situation prompted its covert and clearly illegal targeting of the antiwar movement inside the United States for surveillance and infiltration. By the late 1960s Vietnam had divided the country. Some Americans visited North Vietnam as a gesture of peace and humanity, and opponents of the war criticized the military government in the south as not worth defending. To conservatives, the FBI, and CIA alike, this smacked of treason and raised the possibility of communist sympathizers gaining a powerful voice inside America. With antiwar protests, race riots, and student uprisings, revolutionary outcries rang down the length of Main Street, USA. Both the FBI (legally, if perhaps overzealously) and the CIA (illegally) investigated, infiltrated, and created files on thousands of organizations and individuals whom those agencies felt endangered American security. As in the early 1950s, some Americans were horrified; others thought the government was not doing enough to control the radicals.

Richard Nixon's election reassured the true blue silent majority that domestic law and order would be restored. The civil rights and protest movements did in fact soon seem to disappear. But those who had voted for Nixon in his 1950s role as a hard-liner were in for a surprise.

Nixon's appointment of Henry Kissinger as National Security Advisor elevated the NSC to a new and powerful position. No longer the passive coordinator of national security needs, the council became an active policy formulator. With Nixon as a silent partner, but ultimately the majority shareholder, Kissinger conducted selected foreign relations from the executive offices. He used the State Department and the CIA, but felt no compulsion to rely on or confide in either. The two key features of Nixon–Kissinger diplomacy were detente with the Russians and rapprochement with the Chinese. Anything but classic cold war goals, both dismayed conservative Americans and astonished liberals. The Nixon White House's obsession with secrecy in the pursuit of these and other goals dismayed liberals and amazed conservatives. Ironically, Kissinger's later move to the State Department gave him less flexibility of action and decreased his proclivity toward secrecy.

On one level, the easing of tensions with Russia and reopening of contacts with China (the latter achieved through Kissinger's masterful use of secret diplomacy) dramatically altered the course of Soviet–American relations.

On another level, things stayed remarkably the same. Communism was still the number one threat to American security, and containing the spread of Soviet influence was still the number one goal. Detente simply meant that the United States and Russia would calm their rhetoric, work together on issues of mutual concern (e.g., medical science), and try to prevent crises, whether between themselves or involving third parties.

Detente did not mean Nixon liked communism. Rather, he accepted both the Soviet Union and the People's Republic of China as near equals in order to play them off against each other. He hoped that, by creating a more stable superpower relationship, world peace and increased prosperity would decrease Soviet and Chinese influence among the poorer, weaker nations. Detente was a kind of public containment through kindness, and it put renewed emphasis on covert relations.

Theoretically, detente implied some degree of overt disengagement from antagonistic diplomacy. Disengagement fit in nicely with the American public's reaction to the last years of the Vietnam war. This so-called post-Vietnam syndrome witnessed an unwillingness to risk any foreign involvements that might escalate into another no-win situation. Congress even tried to assert its authority with passage of the 1972 War Powers Act, intended to decrease the chances of presidential wars (such as the invasion of Cambodia) and increase its own control over the commitment of American military forces abroad.

By the terms of its own charter, the CIA could not accede to the post-Vietnam syndrome, but had to be perpetually alert to any risk to American security. It found itself pursuing national interests in opposition to public opinion. It was not bound by the War Powers Act, however, since its operations rarely involved extensive, much less protracted, military engagements. Nor was it particularly limited by detente. After all, the purpose of detente was to contain through cooperation. Certainly this did not mean that the United States would stand idly by and watch new leftist regimes come to power.

All of this became particularly relevant when Chileans voted in a leftist government. The election of Salvador Allende, a moderate leftist who promised to reform the economy, sent chills through that country's upper classes and worried American investors much the way similar Guatemalan promises had worried them in 1954. Working through the Chilean military and American multinational corporations, in 1973 the Nixon–Kissinger team unseated Allende. His "suicide" in the course of the coup may have surprised, but probably did not dismay, CIA–NSC observers.

A vocal minority protest in the United States followed the Allende affair. Americans who cheered Henry Kissinger's secret trips to and opening of talks with mainland China could not understand how the two seemingly contradictory policies dovetailed. The Nixon administration, calculating the pros and cons of establishing normal relations with China, decided that its ability to play one major communist government off against another could weaken the overall threat of either to the free world. It also calculated, by the same logic, that a leftist Chile had no advantages and many disadvantages. It acted accordingly. Kissinger's ability to play this kind of game earned him his reputation as master of realpolitik. He also was adept at dovetailing overt and covert foreign policy, which often left his own State Department and CIA support staffs, not to mention the Russians, Chinese, and US allies, guessing as to his next move.

Kissinger was stymied in Angola, however. Upon gaining its independence from Portugal, that former poorly administered colony in southwest Africa was besieged by a civil war that pitted Soviet- and American-backed surrogates against each other while the superpowers themselves maintained detente cordiality. Angola's natural resources and geographic location made it a strategic as well as ideological prize. Castro provided manpower and Russia money to support a leftist faction. The United States and China each covertly supported rival anti-Soviet contenders, with South Africa piggy-backing on America's side. Thus racism and anticommunism were dumped into the muddy waters already disturbed by the post-Vietnam urge to disengage. Angola became a battle the American public would not wage aggressively, but one in which the CIA, by continuing covert support, linked America to the racist South Africans in the eyes of black Africans. Kissinger was never able to find a way out of that dilemma.

Congress balked at furnishing funds, much less troops. The Soviet-backed faction established the semblance of a government, although fighting continued. Ironically, Cuban troops diligently protected American-owned oil refinery installations from rebel saboteurs. Thus Cubans, acting for a leftist black African regime, guarded American property against forces armed with white African racist and American weapons.

Decolonization had led to the creation of a host of new nations in Africa, most of which by the 1970s were nonaligned or leaned actively toward the West, although Angola, Somalia, Ethiopia, and Mozambique all had leftist governments of one sort or another. In the view of an agency committed to containing the spread of communism, Russia was definitely gaining ground.

The Soviet Union might not have been so sure about that. It is very difficult to detail what role, if any, Soviet intelligence and covert operations—or for that matter Soviet diplomacy in general—played in establishing these leftist African governments. The KGB records on the early cold war years, much less current events, are not open to researchers. Few personal and unofficial accounts have appeared. Obviously, Russia's covert diplomats do not always get what they want. This was brought forcibly home to them in 1948, when their personnel and Yugoslavs acting on Russia's behalf were unable to bring the Yugoslav Communist party back into line. The Soviet Union provides covert support to some, if not most, leftist insurgent movements, but not all such movements want that help. Those that do may not live up to optimal Soviet expectations.

Mozambique's leftist government, for example, came to power immediately after independence and, in spite of chaotic internal problems, has assiduously avoided ties with the Soviet Union. Communist support in Angola was blatantly overt. The same can be said of American and South African support on the other side. The Soviet Union intervened in Somalia and the Sudan, but was soon evicted from both by the indigenous and still-leftist governments. Its involvement in Ethiopia was costly, not terribly gratifying, and also not very covert. Future historians will have to try to discover what role the KGB played in the actual military coup that overthrew Ethiopia's emperor Haile Selassie.

There is no reason to think that, within its own self-defined spheres of influence, the Soviet Union's covert policy was any less zealous than America's, always recognizing that it had fewer resources to devote to such efforts. There is also, as of yet, no way to document such successes and failures with anywhere near the reliability one can document American efforts. Russia may simply be better at keeping secrets than is the United States.

By the late 1970s America's foreign policy was feeling the consequences of an administration that tried to redefine the nation's role internationally. Shortly after assuming office, President Jimmy Carter rejected the thirty-year-old idea that containing communism was America's number one issue. Thus together with its emphasis on human rights and its support of nationalist sentiment, the Carter presidency downplayed covert diplomacy. Revelations about the Nixon administration's use of the CIA and various electronic surveillance tactics against Americans, inside the United States, brought the agency itself into disrepute. Its new director, Admiral Stansfield Turner, sent out a strong signal that covert diplomacy was on the wane and that intelligence activities would be increasingly limited to information gathering.

Carter's actions reflected a short-lived attitudinal change in the United States. They also reflected a more permanent change in the world. By the late 1970s there were very few new nations. The political instability of decolonization and nationalism was in large part over. Increasingly sophisticated governments and diplomats left less room for the kind of manipulations of which the CIA had been so fond.

The Carter administration witnessed, but did not preside over, the collapse of the Shah in Iran and of Somoza in Nicaragua. Both were rulers American conservatives had thought sound allies; both were ousted by internal revolutions, one fueled by religious fundamentalism, the other by leftist agrarian reform. Carter gave moral support to the black nationalists in Rhodesia/Zimbabwe and lashed out, rhetorically and economically, against rightist (as well as leftist) regimes with unacceptable human rights records. An administration that could aid socialist revolutionaries in Nicaragua and publicly castigate allies for using terror to quiet their opposition was not the kind of administration with which old-school CIA operatives could feel comfortable.

An anxious intelligence community and some very skeptical conservatives saw the United States voluntarily reducing its grip on international politics. As if that were not enough, in Russia old men became more set in their ways, and the hard-line anti-Westerners seemed to be on the ascendancy. Russia grew stronger and stronger. Nixon had tried to make friends with the Russians, and here was Carter saying there were other things more important than containing Russia.

In reality, neither detente nor the Carter deemphasis on covert operations meant that the two countries stopped harassing and spying on each other. Russia continued to jam Western propaganda beamed into the Eastern bloc through Radio Free Europe. The American embassies in Moscow and the satellite states were subjected to such a barrage of scanning X-rays as to pose health hazards to their employees. Everyone was convinced that the huge Soviet mission to the UN in New York City was heavily staffed by KGB agents who were busy buying information and recruiting new members. The Russians seemed to have little trouble finding Americans willing to sell the relatively small amount of technological information not readily available to the public. An entire family, the Walkers, was charged with selling such secrets in 1986. Leaks made it difficult to maintain secret policies also.

The American intelligence agencies did temporarily put aside their cloaks and daggers and concentrate on data gathering. The volume of new information—scientific, military, political, and technological—and the means of procuring it were both awesome. Satellite surveillance eliminated the need for U-2 overflights, as most spying could be done electronically. With both sides possessing the ability virtually to monitor each other's telephone calls without leaving the comfort of offices in Washington and Moscow, fewer field agents risked their lives à la classic spy thrillers exchanging microdots in back alleys of intrigue-infested cities.

By 1980, with some help from the Russians, the Carter-inspired anomaly had passed. Soviet arms build-ups, their invasion of Afghanistan, clashes over human rights, and disagreement among White House advisers all contributed to the return of acrimonious Soviet–American relations. Carter had chosen men with very different philosophies to serve as foreign policy advisers. A low-key, establishment liberal, Secretary of State Cyrus Vance saw little to be gained from fostering a crisis mentality. National Security Adviser Zbigniew Brzezinski spent two years as the administration's token cold warrior before coming into his own when Russia seemed determined to fulfill his ominous prophesies. In the tense late 1970s, Brzezinski won the day and a strong anti-Soviet stance was again evident in US foreign policy rhetoric. Vance's final break with the administration came over the attempt to rescue American hostages held by Iranian revolutionaries. This military covert operation ended in failure (because of mechanical problems) before it had really begun. Vance had argued against the mission; Brzezinski had supported it.

Brzezinski worried that, because of its acute anti-American orientation stemming from America's support of the Shah, the fundamentalist revolution in Iran would turn to the Soviet Union. Were this to happen, Russia would have an entrée into the oil-rich Middle East and strategically important Persian Gulf. In a direct challenge to the Soviet Union, Carter announced that any outside (read Russian) attempt to gain control of the Persian Gulf would be considered a threat to America's vital interests and be dealt with accordingly.

By the time Carter left office, events had conspired to rekindle a cold war mentality and a concomitant need for secrecy. The renewed Soviet–American contretemps were reflected almost comically in the competition to see who could do the most thorough job of bugging, infiltrating, and X-raying each other's embassies. Nineteen eighty-seven was a highwater mark in this rivalry, with both sides offering the public show-and-tell presentations of the electronic gadgetry uncovered. The stage was also set for a rebirth of covert activity.

With a revived CIA under the directorships of William Casey (1981-87) and William Webster, the Reagan administration spent eight years openly lobbying for congressional and private-sector support for covert aid to the Contra (anti-Sandinista) movement in Nicaragua. Covert support for the Afghan rebels was also public knowledge. Both of these policies supported freedom fighters struggling against Soviet and communist aggression, and were classic extensions of the Truman Doctrine and containment.

The news of secret arms sales to Iran in exchange for help in releasing hostages held by various Arab factions leaked within a year of the event. That story uncovered legally questionable transfers of arms and money to the Nicaraguan Contras through a bizarre sub rosa combination of government and private efforts (reminiscent of the China lobby) to influence events inside, and the American public's attitude toward, Nicaragua. In a throwback to the Dulles view of the world torn between good and evil, Admiral John Poindexter and Colonel North, both of the NSC, confidently told each other that what they were doing was in the best interests of the United States.

Any government would be foolish to ignore the covert side of foreign policy. As North testified at the 1987 hearings into the Iran arms deal and Contra diversion, his job was one of deception, distortion, and lies. The United States has always had a little trouble squaring its democratic, elective political tradition with covert, politically unaccountable policy implementation. Painting The Enemy as black as possible and identifying all "enemies" as extensions of this primary foe may make that task easier; it does not make the contradiction go away, nor does it do much to lift the siege mentality of the cold war.

The Soviet Union has less difficulty with the contradiction of democratic policies and covert unaccountability in part because its government is not democratic in America's sense of the word and in part because the Russian public is less aware of its government's covert operations. Secret diplomacy stays more secret when the government controls most sources of information. In addition, Russians (and most other people, for that matter) expect governments to conduct covert activities. American sensibilities in this area may be peculiarly American.

NOTES

1. Cited in Etzold and Gaddis, *Containment*, 164–68.

2. In 1987 Barbie was brought to trial in France and convicted as a war criminal. The United States had played a major role in his having been able to live the intervening years undetected and unprosecuted in South America. In the 1980s, war criminals were still being extradited from the United States, where they had lived openly or undercover, to such places as Yugoslavia and Israel.

3. Ross Thomas, *The Cold War Swap* (New York: Harper & Row, 1966, 1986), 80.

4. Ibid., 73.

EUROPE IN 1960

NATO

Warsaw Pact

Neutral/
Nonaligned

ICELAND

SWEDEN

FINLAND

NORWAY

SOVIET UNION

IRELAND

DENMARK

GREAT BRITAIN

BENELUX

E. GERMANY

POLAND

W. GERMANY

CZECH.

FRANCE

SWITZ.

AUSTRIA

HUNGARY

RUMANIA

SPAIN

YUGOSLAVIA

BULGARIA

PORTUGAL

ITALY

ALBANIA

GREECE

TURKEY

Europe in 1960.

chapter 6

THE ARMS RACE:
BETWEEN THE DEVIL AND THE DEEP BLUE SEA

The most bilateral and most life-threatening aspect of postwar Soviet–American relations manifested itself in the nuclear arms race. Almost all serious attempts at limiting or regulating nuclear weapons also have been bilateral, although they obviously are of overwhelming international significance. Europeans are caught between two nuclear superpowers whose battles might well be waged on their own soil and at their own catastrophic expense. The Soviet–American nuclear arms race is of stunningly immediate European concern.

Although at least two nations have the power to destroy the planet, nuclear weapons are not the only threat to life. Given that a wide range of wars has been conducted since 1945 without recourse to nuclear power, conventional weaponry still has wide relevancy. Here too, a Soviet–American race dominates the technology.

Our introduction to the nuclear age began with the atomic bomb. Perhaps the best thing that could be said for this technological breakthrough was that it was an American, rather than a German, achievement. The bomb was developed during World War II in shrouded secrecy under the code name Manhattan Project. The first successful test was conducted in the New Mexico desert in July 1945. On 6 and 9 August 1945, over Hiroshima and Nagasaki, Japan, respectively, America dropped the first and only atomic bombs so far to be used in anger.

Compared to today's nuclear weapons, these first bombs were almost toys. They were estimated to have the explosive equivalent of 13,000 and 20,000 tons of dynamite, respectively, whereas a thermonuclear test conducted by the Soviets in 1961 released energy equivalent to 3,000 of the bombs dropped on Hiroshima. Some 200,000 people died in the combined blasts of the 1945 explosions, but even more Japanese had died during the much more conventional fire bombings of Tokyo. Nevertheless, the physical and psychological damage was cataclysmic enough to turn Japan into an arch opponent of nuclear weapons. To this day, it refuses to undertake nuclear weapons research and will not allow nuclear weaponry to be stationed on its soil. Ironically, the devastating success of these prototype bombs led very quickly to an intense, mankind-threatening arms race between the war's two main victors. The results of that race have been bigger, "better," even more devastating weapons.

The United States maintained a monopoly on atomic weapons technology from 1945 to 1949. This seemingly lopsided advantage colored both Soviet and American perceptions of the early cold war years, although just exactly what effect it had on policy, especially Soviet policy, is still a matter of speculation. Russia exploded its first atomic bomb in 1949, and certainly thereafter each new development on either side was entered into the policy formulation equation. Prior to 1957 (and intercontinental ballistic missiles), Russia's shortcomings in delivery technology meant that the United States had little to fear from a direct nuclear attack, much less a conventional invasion.

Europe had no such assurance. Nevertheless, having had no first-hand experience with the atomic bomb, Western Europe's fear of nuclear warfare did not mature as quickly as Japan's. Between 1945 and 1949, while the United States alone had harnessed the power of the atom, the possibility of a nuclear holocaust seemed less worrisome to everyday life than did Europe's very real economic crisis and the shadow of millions of Russian troops still stationed on the Continent. Thus Europe's first postwar military anxieties centered on Russia's superiority in conventional, not nuclear, strength.

Although talk of weapons, whether conventional tanks or nuclear warheads, almost always boils down to comparisons of opposing forces, numerical precision is impossible. For one thing, even Western sources fail to agree on figures, and the Russians have made almost a fetish of secrecy. For another, both sides chronically overestimate their opponent's strengths, sometimes intentionally and sometimes not, and policy may frequently be premised on figures that have little bearing on reality. Each side invariably tries to make the other appear as formidable as possible to justify its own defense spending. That is one of the ironies of arms races.

The numbers game plagues anyone trying to estimate arms capabilities. Should the United States include Western European NATO forces in calculating its military strength? Should estimates of Soviet troop strength include Warsaw Pact members? Whose figures does one use? How many tanks is a bomber worth, and how does one supermissile compare with how many Cruise missiles? While some numbers are necessary for any discussion, they are best thought of as approximations and definitely not as absolutes.

At the end of the war the United States' combined armed forces numbered near twelve million men, the atomic bomb, and the world's largest fleet of strategic bombers. By 1948 troop strength had dropped precipitously, to between one-and-a-half and two-and-a-half million. The United States demobilized quickly, partly because the public insisted, partly because the government did not see a real Soviet threat so quickly after one war had ended, and partly because policymakers expected, in the unlikely event of a need, to use atomic weapons.

If Russia moved, everyone seemed to agree, it would most probably do so in Europe and would use its army still on station in Eastern Europe. Operating on the worst possible eventuality, rather than assuming Russia would behave much like the other victors (which in fact it did), the West projected that the Soviet Union's wartime strength of just over eleven million would stabilize with peace at between four and five million. Governments did little to calm public anxieties based on rather irrational fears that the Soviet Union might take advantage of its superiority in conventional forces to march into the relatively defenseless, war-weary West. In point of fact, Soviet strength had dropped to about three million men by early 1948, and Russia was war-weary too. Nevertheless, most of that number was concentrated in Europe, while any potentially counterbalancing American strength was scattered throughout the Far East and in the United States.

In the immediate postwar years, conventional European forces were no match for the Red Army. Should the Soviet Union launch an attack, Europe's security rested precariously on America's willingness to use its bombs, and on Russia's belief that America was willing and able to do so. We now know that in those early postwar but pre-NATO years, America's atomic arsenal numbered less than 100 bombs, and that its shortage of arming technicians drastically reduced the ability to deploy even that number. We have always known that, even assuming an adequate supply of bombs and personnel, the time needed to deliver bombs across the Atlantic was such that if an advancing Red Army were the target, Europe might have to be destroyed to be saved. Therefore many in the West believed that Europe's security really rested on America's ability to prevent, or deter, a Soviet attack from even happening in the first place. This may have meant that European security rested on quasi-bluff. It may also have meant that Europe's security anxieties were unfounded.

Asked about the West's postwar defense concerns, a Russian might well say that Europe relied on American help against a threat that was not there. Russia was in no position, and had no desire, to attack. A policy of deterrence under those circumstances was a guaranteed winner. The records make clear that Western policymakers thought the actual chances of Soviet aggression were remote, but they nevertheless planned as if it were immediate. As with much of the history of arms races and arms limitations efforts, logic frequently overrode reason. Thus, in spite of what was really a rather nonthreatening situation, both sides paired off against each other and soon an arms race was on.

Within a Russia–Europe–America context at least, conventional and atomic war became inextricably mingled. Having only recently grasped the destructive power of the atom, the world could not now imagine a war in which the master of such power would refrain from using it. Recognizing its own self-interests in preserving as much of a free, anticommunist Europe as possible, the United States accepted the responsibility of guaranteeing European security against Soviet aggression. "Containment" and "deterrence" are mirror-image words describing American policies directed toward that end. Containment aimed literally at keeping Soviet power and communist ideology inside their existing boundaries. Deterrence, more military in connotation, tried to convince the Soviets that a first strike of any kind on their part would be met by such a destructive counterattack as to make any gains not possibly worth the cost.

As the acknowledged leader in nuclear technology and capability, the United States was the primary nuclear deterrent to possible Soviet aggression. Guarding Western Europe against communism was, on the other hand, a joint undertaking in which America and Western Europe worked together. With economic reconstruction dependent on achieving some sense of military security, and with economic reconstruction essential in eliminating the risk of electoral communism, Western Europe and the United States negotiated a peacetime defensive alliance in 1949 (NATO) that paralleled a similar economic alliance (the Marshall Plan, or European Recovery Program). NATO committed all member nations including the United States to mutual defense, and it created a multinational military command center. By the early 1950s, through NATO and expanded defense spending Western Europe had begun to achieve a defensive capability comparable to its economic revival. It was hoped that NATO would develop a conventional force capable of balancing and thus deterring the conventional Red Army. In the meantime, the United States pushed ahead on its own nuclear weapons research.

As further proof of its commitment to Europe's security, the United States stationed troops in Germany. Should the Russians attack, these troops would come instantly under fire, thus giving the United States the strongest of reasons to fulfill its NATO obligations. The American Congress has historically been notoriously reluctant to commit American troops abroad and has been equally reluctant to abandon those already overseas. Having witnessed two world wars during which the United States waited two years or more before sending its own manpower, Europeans were understandably skeptical of promises. The American troops, in the sense that their presence guaranteed prompt American reaction, were reassuring. They were doubly reassuring to Europeans nervous about postwar Germany, since they would, as it were, "keep Germany honest" and prevent a secret German military buildup.

Soviet militance, rhetorical and material, prompted the creation of NATO and a general rearmament in the West. Although Russia repeatedly avowed that it was primarily concerned with its own security, Europe could not be sure how much land, power, and control the Soviets wanted before they would feel "secure." If they believed, as their ideology told them, that the West would try to destroy them, Russians might well decide to beat capitalism to the draw. The large number of Soviet forces stationed in Eastern Europe did nothing to calm Western Europe's fears.

The 1945–49 trauma in Europe came from Russia's conventional, not nuclear, might. That power was dangerous enough, as the Soviets proved with the harshness of their methods used to control East Germany, to keep Europe divided, and to hold Eastern Europe in their grip.

The same year NATO was founded, the Soviets detonated their first atomic bomb and sent a shock wave through Europe. The meagerness of Russia's air force and navy still made its use of the weapon against the United States unlikely, but Europe was a much closer target. The United States accelerated work on the more powerful hydrogen bomb and conducted successful thermonuclear testings in 1951. The Soviet Union was able to do the same shortly thereafter, although it continued to remain technologically behind in weapons development.

In spite of Europe's worst fears, the first military confrontation between East and West occurred not on the Continent but in Korea, and nuclear weapons were not used. In fact one reason for President Truman's dismissal of MacArthur was that general's rather nonchalant suggestion that China be blocked from participation by mining a strip of land several miles wide along the Chinese–Korean border with radioactive nuclear waste. The negotiations at Panmunjom dragged on and on, and the fighting continued. Then, in 1953 Stalin died. This, and the huge number of Chinese casualties in the war, made the North Koreans' supporters less willing to continue. In the United States, a new president took office. Having promised during his campaign to end the war and the war's expense, Dwight Eisenhower made it known that if progress was not made soon, he, unlike Truman, was willing to use atomic weapons. An armistice was finally signed.

In spite of this tag-end excursion into nuclear blackmail, the Korean war showed the atomic age that "small" wars could be fought without recourse to nuclear weapons and that conventional strength was still a very substantial, killing danger. The United States had committed troops to the defense of an ally but had not committed nuclear weapons. How would it respond to the outbreak of a small war in Europe?

By indicating greater willingness to use its nuclear arsenal, the Eisenhower administration may have sought to allay European doubts, or it may simply have been willing to take bigger risks to contain communist (if not directly Russian) aggression. During the 1950s the United States threatened to use the bomb at least three times: if Communist China intervened in Indochina and, on two separate occasions, if that country continued its attacks on the Nationalist Chinese outpost islands of Quemoy and Matsu. It did not use the threat or the weapon when France was losing to the Viet Minh at Dien Bien Phu, and not until 1962 did it directly threaten the Soviet Union. (President Kennedy told Russia that a missile attack launched from Cuba would be taken as a full-scale attack by Russia against the United States and would be responded to accordingly.)

During the Korean war American manpower was held at a much lower level than was Soviet, even though Russia was not a participant. By 1953 Soviet troop strength had grown to about six million men while the American army, on a war footing, had only 3.6 million men under arms. After Korea both forces dropped in size. The Soviet army has fluctuated between three and four million, and American forces have ranged from two to three-and-a-half million (even at the height of the Vietnam war). Numerical manpower per se has become increasingly less important to both sides, however, while the level of training and technological know-how required of military personnel has become increasingly more important. American air and naval technologies required less manpower than did the Soviet land forces.

Korea had shown that nonnuclear war was possible; but it was a very unpopular conflict, and in spite of a number of small, regional hot spots in the 1950s, policy planners did not expect to fight a similar war again; massive retaliation would provide more bang for each increasingly tight congressional buck. In the 1950s and 1960s the United States put its primary anti-Soviet reliance on nuclear weapons and on the Strategic Air Command (SAC) bomber squadrons necessary for their delivery. In the 1950s the underlying policy premises assumed that future wars would be against the Soviet Union directly and would be nuclear. In the 1960s the assumption that any war with the Soviets would be nuclear held firm, but military planners gave more play to non-Russian, nonnuclear military flexibility.

Cynical Europeans wondered whether America's technological nuclear superiority would actually ever be translated into real weapons fired at real targets. Russia's suppression of the 1956 Hungarian uprising proved that, in spite of John Foster Dulles's talk of liberation, the post-Stalin leadership did not have to fear an American nuclear response to conventional Soviet military force used behind the Iron Curtain. What would happen if a small war broke out in Europe outside the Iron Curtain? Would the United States really risk the deadly consequences of nuclear war to protect a small part of Europe?

Dulles's unilateral tendencies encouraged such questions, but the Secretary of State was multifaceted. He worked hard to assuage these and similar fears, and to build a defensive cordon around Russia by building up US commitments to NATO and orchestrating collective security pacts such as CENTO in the Middle East and SEATO in Southeast Asia.

During the 1950s the United States provided conventional weaponry to the collective security pacts it sponsored. In addition, it pursued its own unilateral defense strategy of massive retaliation. The Soviets also busied themselves improving nuclear and conventional strength, and they expanded the scope of their weapons research. Under Stalin, ideological uncertainty (how did it contribute to the building of a socialist state?) had impeded pure research into such things as jet propulsion and rocketry. Stalin concentrated on redeveloping heavy industry, and with it, heavy defense buildup of existing technology. His successors paid more attention to pure research and, having developed an arsenal of thermonuclear weapons, concentrated on rocket-delivery systems. Huge percentages of the Russian budget were devoted to these two areas at the expense of domestic consumer comforts. Contrary to some Western thinking, however, the Soviets never risked undercutting their economic base just to satisfy military ambitions. They were able to continue military *and* make remarkable nonmilitary advances. There was little chance, therefore, of economic pressures forcing major changes in Soviet policy, domestically or internationally. Certainly the West could not realistically expect that the burden of defense spending alone would so disrupt the Soviet economy as to produce the major internal changes such as envisioned in Kennan's analysis of the long-term consequences of a successful containment policy.

The democratic governments of Western Europe and the United States could not make comparable demands on their citizenry and would not match the gross national product percentage rate of Soviet commitment to arms. As long as America had a delivery advantage (the B-52s), it was relatively secure; Europe felt much more vulnerable.

Russia's military programs continued to grow virtually without pause. The 1955 mutual withdrawal of troops from Austria after ten years of joint occupation marked an easing of tensions in and neutralization of that country, but it had little impact on the overall picture. Any reductions in tension were offset by brutal Soviet responses to unrest in East Germany (1953) and Hungary (1956), and by the building of the Berlin Wall (1961). West Germany's 1955 entry into NATO made the French jittery, not to mention a Soviet Union, which was still very edgy about Germany per se and about West Germany as a possible military wedge should Dulles's talk of liberation actually have substance. That same year, the Eastern bloc organized its own defensive alliance, the Warsaw Pact. The Warsaw Pact's nuclear capability was (and still is) really a Soviet capability. Most, if not all, Eastern bloc nuclear weapons are located inside Soviet territory. As a conventional force, however, the pact would be powerful in its own right.

Most of Western Europe, with or without sizeable unilateral national forces, relied heavily on NATO for conventional defense and on the United States for a nuclear umbrella. NATO had no nuclear weapons of its own. The American protection, be it in the form of American- or European-based delivery systems, or tactical nuclear weapons of any kind, was in but not of NATO, with the use of such weapons under the direct control of the president of the United States. The United States had introduced tactical nuclear weapons into Europe in 1952. When West Germany joined NATO, the Soviet Union made it clear that it would consider the deployment of nuclear weapons by the Germans themselves as tantamount to an act of war.

Russia was not alone in its continuing nervousness about Germany. When the British (1952) and the French (1960) became nuclear powers, both refused to integrate their nuclear weapons into NATO command, blocked plans to create a multinational nuclear force, and were adamant about keeping nuclear weapons away from the Germans.

As of 1960 Europe had four nuclear powers (including the United States), and much of the Continent was arranged into two collective defense systems. For whatever reasons, however, none of these nations had ceded control of that power to the collective systems. Nuclear weapons remained in national hands and subject to national security interests.

This exclusivity probably contributed to the interest much of the world expressed in arriving at limits on nuclear weapons. It is perhaps in the nature of humans to wish to eliminate that which they cannot control. It is also in the nature of some humans to want to reduce government expenditures or to lessen the risk of war. Military buildups of all kinds during the 1950s increasingly brought these urges to the fore. People had been calling for arms control and regulation for a long time. In fact, some of the Manhattan Project scientists had asked that the bomb not be used and that research on nuclear weapons be halted. Postwar efforts to stop the spread of atomic technology foundered when the Soviet Union refused to accept means to internationalize atomic research which would have left the US monopoly intact and thwarted Russia's own research and development programs.

Although agreeing that something had to be done to control the 1950s proliferation of thermonuclear stockpiles, the Soviets rejected Eisenhower's 1955 "open skies" proposal to freeze the status quo. The Soviet Union would not, among other things, accept aerial overflights as a means of verifying the companion ban on the development of new weapons of destruction. At that time, such flights were the best available means of monitoring weapons deployment, but, undertaken without official sanction, they were blatant violations of national sovereignty. As a consequence of Khrushchev's rejection of the open skies proposal, the testing of nuclear weapons continued on both sides, with the United States flying covert U-2 missions over Russia.

The Soviets did lag behind American nuclear technology and were unwilling to freeze arms developments while in an inferior position vis-à-vis the Americans. They also continued to refuse to allow on-site or overflight verification. These two refusals, one a mark of inferiority and the other evidence of Russia's demand for secrecy, plagued efforts for arms limitation, much less reduction, throughout the 1950s and 1960s. Since the 1970s, advances in Soviet technology and weapons have narrowed, if not eliminated, the gap between US and Soviet capabilities, thus making them more willing to negotiate. Satellite and other sensor technology has made verification possible without recourse to on-site or overflight inspection. As a consequence of those two factors, plus the cost of the arms race and the obvious overkill dimensions it has reached, the 1970s and 1980s have witnessed a virtual bureaucratization of the arms negotiation process. The cliché about things getting worse before they can get better may have had some applicability here.

Certainly meaningful negotiations were still in the future in 1957, a year that marked a low point in Western security. When the Soviet Union launched Sputnik, the first manmade, earth-orbiting satellite, the implications for space exploration were spectacular; the implications for Western defenses were shattering. The military surveillance and communications values of earth-orbiting satellites would take longer to make themselves felt; the West was most immediately concerned about the technology that allowed such satellites to be launched. If the Soviets had rocket boosters that could put a satellite into earth orbit, they also had boosters that could propel a missile, complete with nuclear warhead, out of and then back into the earth's atmosphere at speeds far greater than any conventional aircraft could attain. The age of intercontinental ballistic missiles (ICBMs) was at hand.

Nuclear weapons are useful only if they can be delivered to a designated target. Prior to 1957, high-flying bomber aircraft were the best available carriers for long-range delivery. Unmanned guided rockets would be much faster, have even longer range without need for refueling, and be difficult to detect and almost impossible to destroy in flight. Ballistic missiles are unmanned guided rockets. "Intercontinental" refers to range. There are also medium-range (Moscow-to-Paris) ballistic missiles (MRBMs) and intermediate-range (Paris-to-Warsaw) ballistic missiles (IRBMs). The 1960s and 1970s introduced SLBMs (submarine-launched ballistic missiles) and MIRVs (multiple independently targetable reentry vehicles) that can carry more than one nuclear warhead, each with its own separate target. Early missile launch sites were stationary and therefore easily found and targeted. The latest generation is, or can be made, much more mobile (such as the submarine-launched missiles) and consequently much more difficult to neutralize.

Sputnik and its launchers burst the West's confidence balloon. Faith in America's technological superiority gave way to fear that the balance of power had tilted toward the Soviets. Although the United States fired its own long-range missile in early 1958, John F. Kennedy lambasted his 1960 Republican presidential opponent, Richard M. Nixon, for the Eisenhower administration's penny-pinching failure to prevent the development of a "missile gap." Once in office, Kennedy initiated a massive space and rocketry program that he could claim had reduced the discrepancy and reasserted American superiority. Although later analysis showed that any gap had been one of confidence rather than of fact and that the accelerated program simply widened an existing American lead in delivery technology, Sputnik and the advance in Soviet rocketry panicked the West and increased the tension surrounding a new Berlin crisis.

In actuality, whether or not there was a gap after 1958 became a matter of definition. As technological shelf-lives would grow progressively shorter, both sides pushed for further advances even though the older systems still "worked." "Worked" is in quotation marks because an ever-present but often-forgotten fact of the ICBM age is that none of these generations of missiles has been tested in a wartime environment. All rely on unbelievably delicate guidance systems, and no one knows for sure how these instruments would function under conditions of nuclear war. Nevertheless, everyone proceeds on the assumption that they will, in fact, work as planned. This is another instance of logic operating at possible variance to reason.

On the assumption that everything would work, in this war-games atmosphere the development of ICBMs, MRBMs, and IRBMs decreased warning time and increased insecurity. For the first time, Americans, long confident that two oceans and an early warning system could protect them (if not Europe) from enemy bombers, felt their own new and physical vulnerability to nuclear weapons. Would that vulnerability cause Americans to reconsider their commitments to NATO? Would the United States be so eager to defend Europe if it ran the risk of its own annihilation by so doing? The Kennedy administration's defense spending tried to allay both American and European fears, but it could not turn back the clock and could not erase Soviet technological advances. Although Soviet submarines carrying nuclear weapons had been patrolling American coastal waters for some time, the 1962 Cuban missile crisis brought American vulnerability into exceptionally stark focus while dramatically reminding other nations that they literally existed at the whims and piques of superpower policymakers. The discovery that Russia had installed missiles in Cuba capable of destroying most East Coast metropolitan centers jolted Americans into an awareness that thirty minutes was not enough time to prepare for a thermonuclear attack.

The crisis electrified the world. American U-2 overflights discovered Russian missile silos in Cuba. Soviet diplomats denied the missiles' presence. During an extended brain-storming session, the Kennedy administration's top advisers considered their options and decided on a policy somewhere between moderate and all-out militant. Kennedy then announced his position to the world in so dramatic a fashion as to give the impression that World

War III was only hours away should Russia not back down. From a noncombatant perspective, the crucial question was whether either the United States or the Soviet Union would be insane enough to wipe out mankind for the sake of something that actually altered the balance of power very little. After all, Russia could launch missiles from Russia just as well as from Cuba. As it turned out, just before a potentially disastrous shoot-out on the high seas, Khrushchev turned his ships around and agreed to remove the missiles from Cuba. Much of the West applauded Kennedy's firm stand, but some people noted that he had risked international nuclear war to prevent Americans from having to face something Russians and Europeans had lived with for years: hostile nuclear weapons very close to them. Some European leaders noted with dismay that the United States had challenged Russia to war without giving its allies advance warning, much less asking for their advice.

Ironically, the Cuban missile crisis led to or coincided with several positive signs that somehow the world might manage to avoid nuclear incineration. One such sign was a change in America's overall defense posture. Kennedy increased America's capacity to retaliate on a massive level, but he also recognized the need for more flexible, limited military responses. Although it still seemed likely that any war involving Europe would be nuclear, the political and military hot spots were the jungles or sand dunes of more remote and much more unstable African, Asian, and Latin American nations. The enemy in such places was likely to be a guerrilla force neither particularly vulnerable to nuclear intimidation nor particularly worthy of the risk of global nuclear confrontation. Kennedy, with his pet Green Beret Special Forces units, adopted counterinsurgency as a more reasonable means of containing communist aggression in such instances.

Another positive sign was the renewed and apparently sincere interest in controlling and limiting through agreement the use of destructive nuclear power. An accident inside Russia the same year it launched Sputnik had prompted the Soviet Union to declare a unilateral suspension of nuclear testing. Although the United States and Great Britain rejected a Russian suggestion that they do likewise, the following year they did agree to halt testing pending the outcome of scheduled arms control talks. These talks stalled. The Eastern bloc proposed, in the so-called Rapacki Plan, the creation of a nuclear free zone in Central Europe. This would have meant the withdrawal of American tactical nuclear weapons from West Germany, with the consequent weakening of Western Europe's defenses, and it was rejected. In 1959, both the West and the People's Republic of China rejected a Soviet call for a nuclear-free Pacific Basin. A monster 50-megaton hydrogen explosion in the Arctic marked the Soviet resumption of testing in 1961, and the United States followed suit shortly thereafter. Coming as it did on the heels of the 1960 U-2 incident, a continuing Berlin crisis, and the Bay of Pigs invasion, and just before the Cuban missile crisis, renewed testing created an atmosphere in which it really did seem possible that such weapons might actually be used.

The Cuban crisis did much to defuse that atmosphere. Coupled with increasing concern about the environmental danger of atmospheric testing, it prompted the 1963 Limited Test Ban Treaty. This first real breakthrough in nuclear controls barred nuclear testing in space, under water, and in the earth's atmosphere. It did not affect the less dangerous underground testing, although even here a limit was later set on the size of each explosion. The ban's original signatories—Great Britain, the United States, and the Soviet Union—were quickly joined by over one hundred nations, none of which was a nuclear power. France and China, the only other nations at the time with nuclear capabilities, refused to sign since such limitations would impede their still-embryonic research programs.

The Test Ban Treaty represented a first step, however halting, in arms regulation. Although it paralleled a general reduction of Soviet–American cold war tensions, it was not followed by any real reduction in arms. The signatories did, however, negotiate a series of treaties that tried to contain nuclear contamination and proliferation. Apparently the United States and the Soviet Union were ready to take to heart a truth so familiar to Europeans. In President Kennedy's words, "We all inhabit this planet. We all breathe the same air. We all cherish our children's future. And we are all mortal."[1]

The Kennedy administration's unilateral actions during the Cuban missile crisis brought a quick reaction from Europe. In 1963 French President Charles de Gaulle decided to reduce his country's NATO participation. He disliked NATO's dependence on the United States and wanted a greater role for Europe in its own defense. During the crisis, and not for the first time, the United States had failed to consult its European allies before making decisions whose consequences were as vital to them as to the United States. France now had its own nuclear capability, and, under its lead, Europe should be able to extricate itself from both American whim and Soviet threat. The passage of time, while increasing the danger from nuclear weapons per se, had lessened European fears of specifically Soviet aggression. In the eighteen years since 1945, the dreaded Russians had engaged in no direct military activities outside their own Eastern European empire. A new generation, not awed by cold war fears of a Red Army on the march, questioned whether that army's restraint was due totally to Western deterrence. Was it possible that Western Europe had avoided Soviet military aggression for the simple reason that the Soviets had never considered aggressing? Was Western Europe the unwitting dupe of cold war hysteria? As much a French and European nationalist as an anticommunist crusader, de Gaulle hoped to ease Europe out of the increasingly non-European American-Soviet rivalry. The Limited Test Ban Treaty suggested that this rivalry was itself changing, that the European psychology of siege could be lifted, and that Europe should reassert its own priorities.

West Germany rejected de Gaulle's initiative, however, and decided to stay in NATO. This meant that NATO could not expect to disassociate itself from Soviet–American relations, so much of which was symbolized by things German. Without Germany, any substitute European alliance would lose a major linchpin in inter-European defense. Germany's decision, therefore, aborted France's plans to wean Europe from America. There remained nonetheless a growing reawakening of European independence. If nothing else, de Gaulle put the United States on notice that it could not expect unquestioning European subservience.

The missile crisis also prompted major changes in the Soviet Union. The bombastic Khrushchev, already under attack for domestic policies and humiliated by having to back down over the missiles, was "retired" from office in 1964. His successors were determined that Russia should never be similarly humiliated again and embarked on a massive, long-term defense buildup. By the 1970s Russia would be able to hold its own militarily against any adversary.

In the interim, Soviet–American relations were generally cool but cordial. Both nations concentrated on new priorities. The imbroglio in Vietnam remained, as had the one in Korea, a limited war. When the United States invaded the Dominican Republic in 1965 and when Russia invaded Czechoslovakia in 1968, no one moved to build these clear acts of aggression into global causes célèbres. Even multinational wars in the Middle East, although fought with Eastern and Western bloc weapons, were limited to conventional carnage and failed to trigger open Soviet–American warfare.

Chances for significant arms regulation seemed to improve even as the destructive capabilities on both sides expanded. In 1960 the United States and the Soviet Union combined possessed a nuclear arsenal of about 30,000 megatons. That represented roughly seven tons of dynamite equivalent for every human being on the planet. Thereafter, missiles, rocket launchers, warheads, and bomber squadrons proliferated at a fearsome rate. Many of them were still aimed at Europe, but the Soviet Union's massive military buildup took its strike capability far beyond Europe now. Although they could not compete with America's global scattering of military bases, Russia's naval and air forces grew dramatically in size, sophistication, and scope of operations. The concept of overkill took on staggering dimensions. The superpowers were spending huge sums of money, which both would much prefer to have spent on more constructive programs. (According to one source, the USSR spent some $40 billion on defense in 1968; the comparable USA figure of $79 billion included its war in Vietnam.[2]) The early 1970s brought into vogue MAD (mutual assured destruction), according to which the buildup of nuclear armaments on both sides should keep pace to assure that if either side launched a first strike, the other, even in its death throes, would be able to retaliate in kind.

Given the number of warheads in each arsenal, MAD assumed not just mutual but most likely global destruction. Deadly serious on one level, MAD and the atmosphere surrounding it suggested to some analysts that the arms race had gone over the top into a kind of warp speed reversal: competition became lunacy that degenerated from idiocy to the ridiculous. The concurrent space race assumed a new black humor significance: mankind might need all those planets when it blew this one up. Also, at that level it did not much seem to matter who—America, Russia, China, or perhaps even some new-comer to nuclear capability—was to blame.

On the other hand, the Soviet Union was now able to approach arms negotiations as a more nearly coequal power. While the reality of Soviet power chilled the West and highlighted NATO's inadequacies, it also made the Soviets more willing to talk seriously about arms limitations. Coequal powers, some analysts reasoned, are more secure in mutual limitations than is a clearly inferior power secure in limiting its defenses against a clearly superior one. The proliferation of nuclear technology among less predictable nations also impelled the elder statesmen of nuclear weaponry to come to grips with their own responsibilities.

Strategic arms limitation talks (SALT) began in 1967 but were halted by world reaction against the 1968 Soviet invasion of Czechoslovakia. They resumed after Richard Nixon won the American presidency and were con-ducted in an atmosphere of ever-increasing global complexity. SALT went hand in hand with detente efforts to improve relations and end long-standing frictions. Detente also went hand in hand with China's increasing stature as a world power.

China's emergence as a political, industrial, and nuclear power could no longer be ignored by the United States and was feared by the Soviet Union. The Chinese had long since broken with the Soviets and were determined to challenge Russian leadership in the communist world. The Russians needed to ease tensions with the West so as not to be fighting political, much less military, battles on two fronts. Thus they welcomed Nixon and Kissinger's offers of detente. For its part, the United States hoped that establishing normal relations with China would not only ease its problems in Vietnam but also pressure Russia into serious arms discussions.

As usual, Nixon and Kissinger excluded Europe from much of their in-ternational intrigue. SALT involved a Soviet–American exchange rather than a more sweeping East–West discussion. In addition, Kissinger's initial contacts with the Chinese were made in complete secrecy. Most of America's allies were as pleased with this long-overdue Sino–American breakthrough as they were displeased by America's proclivity toward unilateralism.

The late 1960s buildup of Soviet arms both rekindled European anxieties and encouraged European nations to reach their own detente with the Soviet bloc. As always, Germany was the potential tinderbox (West Germany being particularly fearful of possible Soviet aggression), but the election of Willy Brandt, a Social Democrat committed to reducing cold war tensions, made possible the tricornered normalization of relations between both Germanies and the Soviet Union. For once the United States found itself following the European lead. By 1974 the two German governments would exchange diplomatic representatives and the United States would formally recognize the German Democratic Republic (East Germany). By agreement, Berlin became less of an open political sore.

These European political initiatives were in the wings during the first round of SALT, but they did not completely eliminate Western Europe's defensive insecurities. Nor did they weaken the American commitment to NATO. Thus, the superpowers discussed only those strategic weapon systems that could span the distance between both nations (i.e., weapons that could hit the United States from Russia, and vice versa) and that were under their respective unilateral control. The talks did not cover most of the weapons located in or aimed at Europe. Nor did they address the inequities between NATO and Warsaw Pact conventional forces. On the other hand, a lessening of Soviet–American belligerency decreased the risk of Europe being caught in the superpowers' crossfire.

Two new weapons systems that destabilized defense balances helped motivate limitation talks. The defensive antiballistic missile (ABM) seeks out offensive missiles in flight and destroys (explodes) them before they can enter the atmosphere. Theoretically, a fail-safe ABM system could protect the defender against any ballistic missile attack, whether launched as a first strike or in retaliation. Again theoretically, ABMs can be deployed around particularly important targets or, at a prohibitive cost, around entire nations. Such a defensive advantage might also encourage offensive action, since the ABM-defended nation would feel less threatened by its opponent's retaliatory capabilities. (As we will see, this same offense-defense ambivalence resurfaced in the 1980s when President Reagan proposed his Strategic Defense Initiative, or "star wars" program.) By increasing the number and variety of incoming missiles with which an ABM system would have to deal, MIRV and Cruise missile technology greatly reduces the feasibility of ABM security. Although the United States had deployed some ABMs around some of its missile bases, the Soviets were pursuing ABM technology with much greater vigor. Reluctant to spend the money for a system that could never adequately defend its many population and defense centers, the United States was nevertheless nervous about the expanding Soviet program.

While Russia built ABMs, the United States worked on its MIRV, which allowed one missile to launch multiple warheads. It is impossible to tell from aerial photography (or even from looking right at the missile) whether a particular missile is MIRVed or, if so, how many warheads it contains and where they are headed. A MIRVed attack would put any ABM system to the severest of tests, and it was assumed that no system could guarantee to track down and destroy all such incoming warheads.

Until agreement could be reached on the number and deployment of ABMs and MIRVs, neither side would feel secure in having attained a stable (and thus less dangerous) balance of terror. But SALT also had the already awe-inspiring task of trying to equalize, limit, and, it was hoped, reduce the size of more traditional strategic arsenals. Here the numbers game was fierce. The United States had 1,054 ICBMs. The Soviet missile count varied depending on source, but everyone agreed it was higher than the American figure. The United States had a strong edge in number of nuclear warheads, while the Soviets had much bigger "throw weights" (i.e., megatonnage of explosive power) per warhead. The United States led in submarine-launched missiles by a margin of three to one and in bombers by a margin of at least two-and-a-half to one. The numbers gave America a clear advantage, but represented delivery capability for both nations more than adequate to obliterate the opponent whether as first (offensive) or second (retaliatory) strike forces. By 1972, just one American MIRVed submarine could quadruple the damage done by all the bombs dropped on Germany and Japan during World War II.

Unfortunately for those who hoped to see major force reductions, when SALT began in earnest the numbers proved less important than the technology. The Soviet Union had not yet perfected a MIRV system, the Americans were behind in ABM deployment, and neither side would scrap either technology. As a consequence, no major offensive weapons reduction came out of the first round of talks. Both sides proceeded apace with efforts to obtain systems superiority (in the American instance) or parity (in the Soviet case), even though the idea of superiority or even parity had in many ways become meaningless. In Europe, which saw itself as the likely target for much of this technology, protests by the so-called Green Parties against the increasing nuclear capability of NATO and Eastern bloc defenses began to play a measurable role in domestic politics.

SALT I (ratified by the US Senate in 1972) did, however, produce agreements, some major and some minor. An upgrading of direct communications promised to minimize chances of accidental war. By agreeing not to interfere with "national verification" technology, the SALT signatories eliminated a long-standing source of contention. Intelligence-gathering facilities located inside the verifier's border, in space, or on ships in and planes over international waters had by now made it possible to spy without recourse to such things as overflights or on-site inspections.

An accord on defensive, ABM technology came rather easily. The Treaty of Antiballistic Missiles Systems limited each nation to two ABM deployment sites of no more than a hundred missiles, and even this was later scaled down to one site each. The United States made no immediate move to expand its ABMs, and the Soviets deployed theirs to defend Moscow. In addition, both sides agreed on the kind of ABM system allowable (among other things, one that was land based and immobile) and made provisions for mutually agreeable technological modification of the systems.

The Interim Agreement on Limitation of Strategic Offensive Arms put a five-year freeze on the construction of offensive missiles and set upper limits on strategic (i.e., intercontinental) missiles and their land and submarine launchers. This did not cover bomber strength, where the United States had a decided advantage. The Soviets maintained numerical superiority in launchers but agreed to limit the number of their supersized missiles. Since limiting launchers did not affect warhead size or preclude the MIRVing of missiles in those launchers, the United States could use multiple warheads to compensate for fewer launchers. By 1977 the United States had roughly 10,000 nuclear warheads to the Soviets' 4,000. Both had been able to double the throw weight of those warheads without violating the terms of the Interim Agreement.

In spite of SALT I's failure to reduce the superpowers' nuclear arsenals, it was nevertheless perceived as a positive advance in Soviet–American relations. Of no small importance, a bureaucracy of arms limitations came into being in the form of a joint Standing Consultative Commission, which would monitor compliance, work on issues of mutual interest, and lay the groundwork for future negotiations. Participants and spectators alike expected SALT I to be followed by successive and more inclusive agreements.

There followed years of rather desultory SALT II negotiating that reaffirmed, rhetorically at least, a mutual desire to respect the legitimacy of each other's interests, and to work toward limiting the risk and expense of armaments. Actually, it did little to reduce the arms race. Both sides acknowledged that efforts to outdo each other did not further the chances for peaceful relations, but each continued to research its own pet projects, such as Cruise missiles and advanced bombers. New agreements proved elusive, with each side haggling over what weapons to include in the talks, how to count weapons, and whether it was possible or desirable to link arms talks with other facets of Soviet–American relations.

As SALT II stumbled forward, Watergate shook America, a new war erupted in the Middle East, and an energy crisis riveted attention on oil prices. The end of America's involvement in Vietnam, followed as it was by a period of international disengagement, seemed from one perspective to decrease the risk of war even as the costs of defense against such a war skyrocketed. From another perspective, American disengagement threatened to leave Europe reliant on its own, primarily conventional defenses. Americans had complained for a long time that their European allies were not shouldering a fair share of the NATO burden; they thought Europe should play a larger role in its own collective defense.

Europe responded to this and to detente by trying to ease long-standing frictions and thus reduce the need for massive defenses. At Helsinki in 1972 and again in 1975, the Conference on Security and Cooperation in Europe (an organization that for years had been struggling to resolve political issues as a first step toward inter-European arms reduction) achieved some remarkable successes. With detente in the air, the United States, the Soviet Union, and most European nations finally agreed to recognize the existing European borders as permanent. By so doing, they did away with many of the sore points that for thirty years had made Europeans live in fear that someone might try forcibly to adjust those borders and thus ignite a new war. When the United States extended recognition to East Germany in 1974, for all practical purposes the issue of reunification was dead. The accords led to expanded trade between East and West Europe in general and, specifically and significantly, between West Germany and the Soviet Union. A slow but perceptible move was under way toward the reintegration of European economies. While few Europeans wanted to disturb this new harmony and a vocal minority joined a growing antinuclear movement, others worried that, as the price for arms agreements with the Soviets, the United States would withdraw its missiles from Europe and leave it open to a Soviet strike.

Even if such a strike were conventional, Europe knew Russia was more than prepared. Fighting the cold war globally, but following policies of limited war, flexible response, and surrogate protagonists, both the United States and the Soviet Union had become major world suppliers of conventional weapons. They used their technology and largesse to gain political influence and advantage far beyond Europe. The French, British, Israelis, and Eastern Europeans joined in the commercial proliferation of conventional arms. Wars in Korea, Vietnam, the Middle East, as well as any number of other conflicts had proved the staying power of war as an integral part of life. The victims of modern conventional weapons were hard pressed to make material, particular distinctions between the damage they could do and the potentially much more destructive power of nuclear weapons.

Even so, everyone might not be willing to abide by the now unwritten cold war rule that small wars be waged conventionally. A slow but steady spread of nuclear technology clouded the international significance of whatever agreements might be reached between Washington and Moscow. The possibility existed that nuclear disaster might be sparked by forces outside the superpowers' control. Events in the Middle East were particularly worrisome in that regard, and while the superpowers had trouble agreeing on their own bilateral arms reduction, they did agree that a nuclear war, regardless of who started it, would not be a good idea.

In 1974 Nixon and Brezhnev signed the Agreement on the Prevention of Nuclear War. They promised to avoid confrontations, bilaterally or with third parties, that might escalate into nuclear war, and they agreed to consult each other should a risk of such confrontation develop. Although reassuring for some and dismissed as meaningless babble by cynics, the agreement caused conservatives in both camps to worry that Soviet–American relations were becoming too cordial and too bilateral. As usual, the Russians had not consulted their Warsaw Pact allies, and the United States had informed its European allies only at the very end of the negotiations. Neither China nor Japan was consulted. Hard-liners and pacifists alike questioned whether

Brezhnev and Nixon were blinding themselves to their ideological principles and to their allies' priorities without, as a justification, making any material reduction in the means of nuclear destruction.

In many ways, this 1974 agreement resembled the 1970 multinational nuclear Nonproliferation Treaty. It satisfied those who already had the technology, was gratifying to those who had no desire for it, and angered those who wished to procure it. The nonproliferation agreement could not guarantee an end to proliferation any more than the prevention agreement could guarantee to prevent nuclear war. Both allowed the United States and the Soviet Union to present a favorable face to world opinion without having to make any hard decisions about numbers and launchers and technologies. Both also did absolutely nothing to end war per se, reduce the profits from conventional arms sales, or significantly influence the course of world events. Nor, in all likelihood, would either agreement prevent a nuclear conflict from erupting should any of the other nuclear powers face defeat in a conventional war.

That is not to say that Nixon and Brezhnev were insincere in wanting to lessen the risk of nuclear war. Neither had as much control over other nations as would be required to guarantee the prevention of third parties from using nuclear weapons, and neither had total freedom of action at home. Brezhnev was not the autocrat Stalin had been, and he had to accommodate both the military and the party hard-liners. Nixon's domestic difficulties (Watergate) undercut his personal negotiating powers, and he could not ignore American military and congressional "hawks" either.

Gerald Ford continued his predecessor's commitment to arms limitation. In November 1974 the Vladivostok accords did in fact achieve a precedent-setting, if tentative, numerical ceiling on even MIRVed missiles. Those ceilings were so high that both nations would have to build to reach them, and more talks were needed to decide which specific weapons were included in the count. In the interim, new technologies increased in importance, making some of the earlier points of contention technologically if not diplomatically obsolete.

Russia raised the throw weight of its allotted missiles. It also made significant advances in bomber technology. Specifically, the Backfire bomber's much longer delivery range now encompassed parts of the United States. The United States developed small, relatively short-range, air-breathing, Cruise missiles. Launchable from land, sea, or air, the Cruise carries a small warhead that can be targeted with great precision. It is almost impervious to detection and much less expensive than ballistic missiles. The Cruise missile destabilized traditional nuclear defenses much the same way guerrilla tactics destablized conventional, set-piece troop movements.

In 1979, five years after Vladivostok, and with the Carter administration now in office, the SALT II accords were signed. Although the treaties were never ratified by the US Senate and were looked upon with suspicion by

Soviet hard-liners, both governments agreed to comply with their ten-year guidelines.

The Treaty on the Limitation of Strategic Offensive Arms allowed each side identical numbers of strategic offensive systems (2,400) that over a two-year period would be lowered (to 2,250). A mix of sanctioned systems included land and sea missile launchers as well as heavy bomber aircraft. In an attempt to stabilize MIRV technology, both sides agreed not to increase the throw weight or number of warheads already tested for given missile systems. Updating of existing missiles had to comply with specified guidelines. Temporary restrictions were placed on deploying or testing mobile ICBM launchers, and the Soviets agreed to limit the production and restrict the range of their medium-range bombers.

SALT II did mean a reduction in launchers for the Soviets and bombers for the Americans. Given the MIRVing allocated to both sides, however, it actually allowed an increase in warheads. Once again, the agreement was clearly intended as an interim measure, with the expectation that later SALTs would decrease both launchers and warheads.

In the seven years between the signing of SALT I and SALT II, however, significant changes occurred on the international scene. Detente did not produce all the hoped-for improvements in America's prestige. In fact, the Soviet Union seemed to be making major advances in places like the Middle East, earlier seen as securely in the West's sphere of influence. The 1970s oil crises wrought havoc on national economies, on the international debt picture, and on traditional cold war priorities. The eagerness with which Western Europe signed natural gas agreements with Russia and provided the sophisticated technological know-how with which to build a pipeline from Siberia illustrated that shift. The one-time arch-enemy had now become an alternative energy source and an alternative to escalating oil prices. Energy, for which there was a proved need, loomed larger than defenses, the need for which rested on seemingly dated fears of Soviet aggression.

As Soviet relations with Western Europe lost much resemblance to their earlier cold war posture, Soviet relations with the United States worsened. Having achieved military parity, and approaching an international prestige parity with the United States, the Soviet Union resented American attempts to affect its internal (human rights) affairs. It was also less reticent in making its presence felt internationally, as was clear from its involvements in Yemen, Ethiopia, and Vietnam. In 1979, the Soviet Union invaded Afghanistan, the first major movement of its troops outside its boundaries and Eastern Europe since 1945. From a leery, neo–cold war perspective (that of National Security Adviser Brzezinski), detente was working to Russia's, not America's, advantage.

This deterioration in Soviet–American relations prompted in the United States an increased defense awareness and decreased willingness to disengage from global anticommunist commitments. The fact that SALT II acknowledged Soviet–American strategic parity did not sit well with a West once again concerned about increasing Soviet adventurism.

The shift could be seen in political as well as military changes. Both the Carter and the avowedly anticommunist Reagan administrations responded to Soviet military build-ups by working to strengthen ties with America's European allies and to upscale European defenses. In England and West Germany, conservative governments sanctioned the stationing of a new generation of nuclear ballistic missiles on their soil. The United States poured billions of dollars into a new MX missile system. Designed to be a kind of shell game mobile launch network that could more easily escape destruction by incoming enemy missiles, the mobile part of the MX system has not at this writing been implemented, and prototype missiles are being housed in old Minuteman silos. Whether MX is or is not in violation of (unratified) SALT II agreements seems to depend on who is doing the interpreting. The MX program has proved extremely costly, and continued appropriations to it underline a resurgent cold war stance and America's commitment to deal from strength in any additional reduction or limitation agreements with the Russians.

The "cold war revisited" atmosphere of the early 1980s allowed little immediate advance past SALT II, although talks (renamed START) continued. A number of factors hindered the SALT/START process. The Soviet invasion of Afghanistan suggested a distressing change in behavior and portended a direct threat to Western control of the Middle East. The US Senate's attempt to link human rights with arms talks not only backfired and helped kill ratification of SALT II, but also soured future Soviet interest in negotiating. Ironically, one consequence of the American attempt to change Soviet emigration policy in exchange for SALT II ratification was a cut-back on Jewish emigration, the intended beneficiary of such linkage, as well as a Soviet pull-back from negotiations. Brezhnev's final years of illness and then the rapid changes in Soviet leadership (Yuri Andropov, November 1982–February 1984; Konstantin Chernenko, February 1984–March 1985; Mikhail Gorbachev, March 1985–) meant that negotiations went on hold until Gorbachev was able to solidify his position.

In response to Russia's continuing weapons expenditures, NATO did increase its preparedness. The very controversial introduction of American Pershing II and Cruise missiles into that system was made with the full approval of the governments involved and reflected a Western Europe reawakened to defense priorities. Ironically, a "double zero" proposal to eliminate all intermediate-range missiles from Europe (originally proposed by the Reagan administration but then adopted with even greater enthusiasm by the Russians) raised serious questions not because of the missiles per se, but because Western Europe had relied on a nuclear defense for so long that its conventional forces had fallen below those of the Warsaw Pact. Without nuclear power, an edgy Western Europe would feel compelled to infuse more scarce money and reluctant manpower to counter Russia's continued build-up of conventional forces.

According to opinion polls, however, the people of Western Europe were, by the middle to late 1980s, more convinced of the sincerity of Soviet arms reduction proposals than of those made by the United States. They accepted Gorbachev's commitment to arms reduction in its own right and as a logical consequence of his nation's hard-pressed economy. President Reagan's flirtation with a new, exorbitantly expensive, and technologically unproved strategic defense initiative (SDI) seemed to cast doubt on just how serious was America's desire to end the arms race.

By 1987 the last remaining holdout NATO members had accepted the double zero option, and talks dealing with the medium-range missiles (INF, or intermediate-range nuclear force) of particular relevance within a European context neared completion. The Reagan administration had sent Pershing II and Cruise missiles to Europe in part to achieve just that result: by increasing NATO's nuclear strength to a level comparable to the Warsaw Pact's, both sides could feel more comfortable about negotiating to eliminate or reduce evenly matched forces.

In December 1987, at a summit in Washington, D.C., Reagan and Gorbachev signed an historic INF treaty, which for the first time in the arms negotiations not just reduced but actually eliminated an entire category of weapons. Over a set time frame, the United States (and West Germany) would dismantle and destroy some 400 warheads housed in Pershing and Cruise missiles; the Soviet Union would do the same with 1,500 warheads in its SS-20s, SS-4s, SS12/22s, and SS-23s. The on-site verification terms marked another landmark in disarmament.

The INF breakthrough would not mean a nuclear-free Europe. Both sides still had nonmissile nuclear capabilities and ICBMs that, if retargeted, could hit Europe. (Great Britain and France also retained their own, independent, nuclear capabilities.) Reagan and Gorbachev both expressed a desire to reduce their ICBM arsenals through START negotiations. Conventional force reductions, also apparently desired by both sides, would involve extensive multinational negotiations.

Bilaterally, the United States and Russia still remained at odds over SDI. Even before the Russians had caught up with Cruise technology, the United States added that space defense system to the arms equation. If deployed, it would once again destabilize any arms balance and perpetuate a much more exotic arms race. Most Europeans were undecided about SDI. As explained in America to Americans, satellite laser technology would provide an orbiting protective shield that could detonate incoming offensive missiles before they entered the atmosphere. This, theoretically, would keep the United States safe from ballistic, if not bomber or Cruise missile, attack. Looked at from a more skeptical vantage point, a star wars umbrella would eliminate MAD's balance of terror stability and open the way to an American first-strike advantage. As of 1987, a sizable portion of the American scientific and political communities was opposed to SDI on principle or because of its cost or was convinced that the project was a technological impossibility. Gorbachev seemed originally to be of this latter leaning and then implied that Russia would develop its own counterpart. After much indignation and many demands that the project be scrapped, Russia agreed to ignore it as an issue in the INF negotiations. As of 1988 SDI still struck much of the world as a science fiction fantasy with an indeterminate potential to evolve into deterrent or demon.

Thus the INF treaty left a great deal of room for further arms limitation. The combined warhead megatonnage in the United States and the Soviet Union had dropped from 30,000 in 1960 to approximately 10,000 in 1984. Since the new systems were more precise and less defensible, however, they represented an increase in overall risk to the planet. The two tons of dynamite equivalent per human being was not only still "adequate" but more likely actually to arrive at the desired target. On the other hand, much of this destructive force, in both the United States and the Soviet Union, was housed in weapons systems built in the 1960s and 1970s that had never been tested in the field. Also, they were dependent on unbelievably delicate guidance systems that might no longer work or might malfunction when passing through a nuclear cloud on the way to their targets.

Any good Soviet or American bomber could deliver payloads inside Europe. Conventional Warsaw Pact troop, tank, and artillary exercises are conducted regularly, and NATO feels a kind of compulsion to stress rather than remedy its own inferiority to those forces. An expanding Soviet navy plies the seas, and the Soviet air force has become a factor that can no longer be ignored. Of course, the other side can paint an equally depressing picture of its defense problems.

Much more than in the United States, there have always been groups in Europe that oppose up-scaling defense systems. People fought the introduction of tactical nuclear weapons; they fought the stationing of Cruise and Pershing II missiles in Europe; they marched in favor of a nuclear freeze or the outright banning of nuclear bombs. Star wars, like all major changes in the rules of any game, also evoked a vocal protest. By the 1980s, increasing numbers of Americans, Russians, and Europeans all saw the arms race as a very expensive game. Few in the West really worried about an actual Soviet military attack, but most firmly believed that it was a game in which the West had to keep ahead. Like MAD, the whole thing may be irrational on one level, but on practical, research, deployment, and budget levels it is a substantiated fear.

In 1985 both the French Socialist and the British Conservative governments rejected Soviet appeals for bilateral arms-limitation talks. In so doing, they made it clear that Europe's defenses were inexorably linked not just to America's technology but also to America's relations with the Soviet Union. In spite of all the differences and complaints Europeans may have with and about American policy and practice, it has not, cannot, and will not cut those ties. Western Europe still prefers to be hostage to its nuclear ally than to a nuclear nemesis. Americans and Russians are, of course, hostage to themselves, their own governments, and each other.

NOTES

1. Cited in Stephen Ambrose, *Rise to Globalism: American Foreign Policy, 1938–1980*, 2nd ed. (New York: Pelican Books, 1980), 270.

2. Woodward McClellan, *Russia: A History of the Soviet Period* (Englewood Cliffs, N.J.: Prentice-Hall, 1986), 344–48.

Celebrating the Camp David accords, 1979: Sadat, Carter, and Begin. *Wide World Photos.*

chapter 7

THE MIDDLE EAST IN SOVIET–AMERICAN RELATIONS

The Middle East is a world of contradictions. Generations of nomads, at home in the desert, mix in urban bazaars with the shopkeepers, engineers, and bankers of a modern, commercial civilization. All of the trappings of air-conditioned and computerized luxury coexist more or less uneasily with customs and traditions that predate the modern era. Nowhere is politics more integral to daily life than among Arabs, and nowhere are political emotions more evident. Here, fiercely independent tribesmen are ruled by hereditary feudal overlords who may owe their authority to inertia, to military strength, to government efficiency, or to foreign backing, but rarely to a vote of the people. There, constitutions, elections, coups, and countercoups come and go with lightning speed in a web of political factions complex enough to overwhelm the participants themselves. Nations faced with debilitating and humiliating external aggression drain their energies in endless internal political turmoil.[1]

The superpowers have tended to see the Middle East's internal politics as extensions of East–West relations rather than as a network of extremely complex dynamics indigenous to the region and only passingly influenced by external events. The area fails to fit nicely into either Soviet or American images of how things are or should be. Most Arabs are not particularly attracted to either of the competing value systems. As a consequence, Soviet–American relations relative to the Middle East have been frustrating for all concerned. Unless these remarkably intricate internal dynamics are understood and accommodated, neither superpower can realistically expect to avoid continual policy disappointments, even failures, in the region.

The Middle East has an old and very rich history. A thriving center of civilization long before Europeans traded in their wooden clubs for more technological means of manipulation, it served as an entrepôt of commerce, culture, religion, and learning. For more than 2,000 years, empire builders from outside took advantage of internal divisions. The petroleum revolution brought in even more outside interest but, in parallel with the decolonization consequences of World War II, also sparked indigenous political, social, and economic changes. Newfound wealth, and awakened nationalist fervor and visions of regional preeminence spurred grandiose plans for economic development and diversification, modernization, and social advancement.

But the Middle East could not bring about a renaissance by itself. Although parts of the area were awash in oil-created wealth by the 1970s, the discrepancies (and consequent suspicions and interest incompatibilities) between haves and have-nots were immense. Technological know-how, modern defenses, and investment capital were available only from outside. Many of the Western industrial nations were stigmatized in the Arab mind by their imperialist past and by their current ties to Zionism. Eastern bloc nations were free of both these black marks, but were obviously eager to use Arab clients to expand communist influence in and access to the area. The anticommunist, anticolonial United States had the most to offer in promoting Middle East development, but it was associated with Israel. This was no small obstacle.

The Middle East is essentially an Islamic world in which everything else, however consuming, is secondary to Allah and necessarily molded to the wishes of Allah. The sporadic successes of various homegrown Communist parties reflect less a popular attraction to atheistic communism than temporary frustrations with rampant corruption, government ineffectiveness, acute economic distress, and nationalistic urges. Religious politics operate regionally as well as nationally, and are subject to sectarian factionalism. Nevertheless, respect for Islam is so strong in most of the Middle East that repressive regimes have been able to suppress popular aspirations by successfully projecting themselves as the true guardians and protectors of Islamic purity. Autocratic monarchies, revolutionary military regimes, and parliamentary social-Islamic governments alike must, with few exceptions, reaffirm their religious commitment to retain any vestige of popular legitimacy. The conditions that sparked Iran's 1979 fundamentalist revolution were very complex, but preeminent among them was the popular perception that, in his headlong dash to modernize, the Shah had forsaken basic Islamic tenets.

Moslems may forsake their own sectarian differences when confronting an enemy. While governments disagree over which tactics should be used to resolve it, almost all Moslems agree that Zionist Israel is indeed their common problem. In its expansionist, militant persona, and seemingly able to call upon endless military and economic resources from Europe and the United States, Israel is an embarrassment, humiliation, and affront to Arab and Islamic sensibilities. The reality all Arabs can agree upon is that Israel has driven hundreds of thousands of Christian and Moslem Palestinians into permanent refugee status.

If our purpose were to describe the Arab–Israeli conflict, a brief for the Israeli point of view would be in order here. Within a Soviet–American–Middle East context, however, the only really relevant issue is that most Arabs *do not like* Israel. That Israel is an anticommunist, very Western nation is relevant to Americans (and probably to Russians) who compile communism-containment equations and policies. It is simply not relevant to the Arabs.

Arab nationalism is relevant. Many Arabs identify themselves first as Moslem, second as Arab, and only third as, for example, Syrian. Pan-Arab nationalism argues for Arab unity, homogeneity, and cooperative support. It abhors outside interference in its affairs. By definition, therefore, Pan-Arab nationalists reject alignment within the Soviet–American East–West bipolarity. Egypt's Nasser, the hero of Pan-Arab nationalism, was a cofounder of the nonaligned movement, and his aim was to legitimize nonparticipation in East–West confrontations and to reject the necessity of adopting foreign values and foreign ideological values.

Talk of Arab nationalism should not obscure the reality of political and geographic borders. Nationalism in the classic Western sense pulls citizens of specific political entities together or apart. The modern boundaries of, for example, Syria were determined less by ethnicity or history than by the administrative needs of mandate bureaucrats. History recalls a time when Syrians controlled a much larger area. One variety of nationalism dreams of resurrecting that historic "Greater Syria." Equally nationalistic Lebanese and Jordanians may well view this as blatant expansionism. Such historical legacies can easily lead to doubts about the sincerity of expressions of Arab nationalism. When Russophobe Americans see a leftist Syrian government actively involving itself in Lebanese affairs, they are more inclined to credit that interest to the machinations of Soviet expansionism working through a Syrian surrogate than to see the continuity of regional historical forces, the support by one group of Arabs to another, or even the aggression of one Arab nation against another.

As if regional, national, and religious nationalism were not enough, prenational tribal identities still dominate parts of the Middle East. These identities can cut across national boundaries and lead to international disputes. They can also, as in the case of the United Arab Emirates, result in internationally recognized nations that in reality are little more than large tribes. Since Westerners like to think that they have long since stopped killing each other for reasons so primitive as tribal feuds, they find it easy to ignore the intensity of tribal loyalty and to assign more meaningful and conspiritorial motives to tribal intrigues. They would probably be on much firmer ground using their sophisticated interdisciplinary social and political analyses to understand, for example, Kurdish unrest inside Iran and Iraq. The Kurds are one of several distinct ethnic minorities that find themselves trapped inside someone else's nation. They feel abused, discriminated against, and deprived of their right to self-determination. Willing to use violence, intrigue, and foreign assistance to secure their ends, these minorities further upset the Middle East's always precarious equilibrium.

The Middle East enjoys an infinitely richer political life than do either the United States or the Soviet Union. Stereotypically Marxist class divisions vie with each other for political control and economic advantage. In less Marxist terms, the array of organized parties, political orientations, and individual opinions is virtually endless. The Middle East also suffers from its share of territorial and resource controversies, Israel's occupation of Egyptian, Jordanian, and Syrian lands being the most familiar. All of these provide issues around which shifting political alliances coalesce, argue, and act. The actions sometimes ignite into street riots, electoral rebellions, and ultimately, even revolution. It is perhaps not surprising that outsiders schooled in the relatively bland Soviet and American political environments are often misled and always befuddled by the maze of Middle East politics.

The public policies of nations ruled by families that inherit their power tend to be nepotistic, paternal, undemocratic, anticommunist, and conservative. That does not preclude their supporting economic development, high standards of living, and constructive contributions to international diplomacy. The West tends to smile on such regimes. They are, after all, anticommunist; heavy purchasers of military, industrial, and consumer goods; stable, and predictable, with a vested interest in maintaining the status quo. Governments like that of Saudi Arabia have found the Israeli problem particularly distressing since their mandated support of the Arab position puts them at odds with the international powers with whom they feel most comfortable, that is, the West. How reflective these governments are of their citizenry is one of the unknowns of Middle East life that, should they ever have a chance to become known, could dramatically alter conditions. With the examples of Iran's revolution and Lebanon's continuing civil war so close at hand, insiders and outsiders alike wonder how strong repressed political emotions are and what form they would take if released.

In a very different tradition from the hereditary rulers, one wing or another of the Baath party has dominated Syrian and Iraqi politics for the last quarter-century. The Baathist wishes to free his own nation and the Middle East as a whole from foreign intervention. The party advocates economic socialism, adapted to Middle East conditions, that has more in common with Eurosocialism than with Marxist communism, but that is still repugnant to classic capitalism and to the property-owning upper classes. During the time of the noisiest cold war sabre rattling (and parallel to Arab–Israeli conflicts), Americans rather uncritically assumed that Baath dealings with the Soviets meant Baath domination by the Soviets. In fact, the Baath are no more interested in subordinating themselves to Soviet than to Western intervention. Baath regimes have normally been intolerant of internal communist organizations even as they maintained friendly Eastern bloc relations. Since its war with Iran began, the Iraqi Baath party has tried to improve its relations with the West. For reasons that relate at least in part to its proximity to Israel and the situation in Lebanon, Syria has maintained closer ties with the Eastern bloc.

How does all of this tie into Soviet–American relations? In their competition for allies and vassals, both nations have, often to their own great discomfort, regularly tried to pull Middle East nations into their own camps. The superpowers, in other words, have tried to mold Middle East dynamics into an extension of their own rivalries. Both have found their efforts frustrating.

The Middle East's role in Soviet–American relations really began in Iran, with which many Arabs do not identify because it is not an Arab nation. During World War II allied and Soviet troops occupied Iran jointly to protect supply routes. By 1945, and with Soviet encouragement, separatist movements in the northern provinces and the leftist Tudeh party were both challenging the Teheran government. The Soviet Union itself demanded oil concessions from the shaky Iranian government and refused to withdraw its troops as scheduled. The Iranian parliament's selection of a prime minister reportedly friendly to the Tudeh party led British and Americans alike to fear that Iran was about to fall under Russian sway. The battle for Iran stands as one of the first cold war confrontations.

Iran's Prime Minister Qavam proved much craftier and more single-mindedly nationalistic than anyone expected. He immobilized a violently anti-Soviet parliament, maneuvered the Soviets into accepting Iran's suppression of the separatist movements, and signed a concession favorable to the Soviets but requiring parliamentary ratification. Soviet troops withdrew, and when parliament predictably rejected the concession terms, Moscow had little recourse. Western accounts credit the Soviet retreat to world opinion and sharp words from Washington, but Iranian savoir faire certainly played as important a role in securing the withdrawal and protecting Iran from Russian interference.

Qavam's victory went unrewarded. He quickly lost power, and years of political turmoil followed during which the West worried about Soviet intentions and Iran worried about the West. Nationalist sentiment and legitimate grievances over the country's financial returns from an Anglo-Iranian oil agreement dating back to the 1930s led to protracted Iranian efforts to renegotiate the agreement and, ultimately, to threats of nationalization. The

British-dominated oil cartel was adamant in its opposition and seemed unmoved by America's postwar priority of winning friends in order to contain communism. In theory, the United States government supported Iran's right to a more equitable return from its oil resources. In practice, it withheld economic aid from Iran pending settlement of the oil dispute.

That boycott continued when Mosaddeg, a nationalist with no announced East or West affiliation, assumed power in 1951 and obtained parliamentary authority to proceed with nationalization. Most Iranians cheered this assertion of national sovereignty and also expected dramatic improvements in the economy to follow immediately. The oil cartel had a very different interpretation. Successful nationalization by Iran might well lead to similar attempts elsewhere and was to be discouraged at all cost. Since any drop in Iranian production could now be offset by output from huge new oil finds nearby, two years of lethargic negotiations ensued during which Iran's oil production virtually ceased, as did the oil royalty payments that had assured the government's popular support and financed its budget. National frustrations sparked domestic violence, and Mosaddeg was forced to rely more and more heavily on the Soviet-friendly Tudeh party, thus further alienating the United States to which Iran continued to look for desperately needed financial help. Mosaddeg's last-ditch power play in 1953 led to his arrest, the assumption of authority by the young, pro-West Shah, resolution of the oil contretemps, granting of American aid, and repression of communist and other internal opposition. For the next twenty-five years Iran and the Shah remained firmly aligned with the anticommunist West in return for enormous amounts of economic and military support.

As the first Middle East nation to become rich from oil, and as a strong, heavily militarized ally of the West, Iran put itself forward as a model for and leader of the Middle East. But not everyone agreed. Iran was not Arab and was too closely aligned with the West; it was also unwilling to take a firm stand against Israel.

Iran did, however, serve as model for the Arab oil-producing states. The terms of the oil agreement finally reached in Iran allowed both sides to profit. Iran nationalized its oil and established the National Iranian Oil Company (NIOC), which would pay $700 million over ten years as compensation to the oil cartel, but which would receive fifty percent of the industry's profits. Actual operations were run by a consortium of international oil firms empowered to extract, refine, and market petroleum products for NIOC in return for half of the proceeds. As new fields opened, NIOC negotiated even more advantageous terms with other private companies, greatly expanded the scope and sophistication of its operations, and assumed more and more control over oil strategy. Many other Middle East oil-producer governments patterned their relations with private oil companies after Iran's. They learned to use petroleum as leverage to reduce outside interference and to gain interregional and international support in their competition for regional leadership roles.

Rather than having to depend on royalty payments from foreign oil concessionaires, oil-producing nations found that they themselves could assume control of production and revenue. Collectively, they had become a major economic-political force in the world by the 1970s.

All of this was watched closely by cold warriors. Neither side wanted to pass up the chance to expand its influence and contain the other, and both, especially the West, had vested interests in the control of and profits from oil.

It took several decades after the war for the term *oil-producing nation* to translate into significant international status and for sufficient money to become available to propel those nations toward a level of development that added new dimensions to their value as cold war prizes. In the interim, another issue came to dominate Middle East politics.

For Arabs, the creation of Israel in 1948, followed as it was by the exodus of Christian and Moslem Palestinians and the start of a now forty-year-old Palestianian problem, was much more traumatic than any highly publicized early cold war European hot spots. Syria, Jordan, Iraq, Egypt, and the Sudan united against what they saw as an unwelcome, non-Arab extension of Western imperialism. By the time West Germany joined NATO and the Soviets responded with the Warsaw Pact, Israeli incursions into the Egyptian Sinai had prompted Egypt, Saudi Arabia, Syria, and Yemen to sign an anti-Israeli military alliance. Among other things, this alliance highlighted the intensity and commonality of concern felt by disparate Arab nations against a common enemy. The alliance needed armaments, however, and the West refused to provide them to be used against so committedly anticommunist a nation as Israel. Therefore Nasser traded cotton for Eastern bloc weapons. The United States, and especially the CIA (which spent most of the 1950s trying rather ineptly, insensitively and unsuccessfully to Americanize a Middle East body politic fully occupied in searching for its own, not America's, soul) had already labeled Egypt as unreliable and interpreted this apparent shift to the left as verification.

Israel's aggression during the Suez crisis reaffirmed the need for strong Arab unity against both the enemy within (Israel) and the old enemy without (European imperialism). It also reaffirmed the southern tier's earlier decision not to align itself in the Baghdad and CENTO anti-Soviet alliances, the terms of which allowed foreign troops on Arab soil. Arab nations increasingly looked to their own Arab League for mutual defense and for guidance in regional and international diplomacy.

The Suez crisis was a Soviet victory by default. The United States was horrified by its allies' actions, but because of its firm ties with all three nations, could not avoid some guilt by association. Russia's role in bringing the crisis to an end raised its prestige in the area and opened the door to expanded relations. (Ironically, England's and France's decision to violate Egypt's sovereignty made it possible for the Soviet Union to invade Hungary, an equally heinous act, with virtual impunity.) Israel's role in the crisis was no more and no less than what anti-Zionist pessimists had expected all along. Arab states, in desperate need of capital and technology, were at best suspicious of, and at worst dismayed by, the West's behavior. Those without financial self-sufficiency or without conservative, obsessively anticommunist leadership sought Soviet assistance.

Aware of but apparently unpersuaded by the dilemma Israel created for Arab policy makers, the United States announced in the Eisenhower Doctrine a Middle East version of the earlier Truman Doctrine. Mute on the subject of Israeli aggression, the doctrine pledged to assist any Middle East nation threatened by communist aggression. The first such "threat" showed itself in Lebanon.

The heavily Westernized Lebanese people, with their extraordinary religious diversity, were for years held together by a tacit division of political power along religious and ethnic lines. By 1958, however, Arab nationalism, Christian conservatism, Druze provinciality, charges of favoritism and misapportionment, and Western efforts to align Lebanon, together with an influx of stateless Palestinian refugees, had produced a civil war. Lebanon's president issued a half-hearted request for American assistance in defending the tottering government against domestic Arab opposition and its Syrian supporters.

The short-lived presence of US Marines had little lasting impact on the outcome of Lebanon's 1958 crisis, which owed its resolution more to the efforts of Lebanese themselves and other concerned Arabs. Similarly, American troops sent to Lebanon as one of several participating UN forces in 1982, after a new civil war had weakened the government and while the country was also under siege by Israeli and Syrian forces, made no constructive contribution.

The rest of the Middle East learned several lessons from these two visits. In neither instance were the American forces willing or able significantly to influence events. Military might notwithstanding, the United States proved impotent in dealing with the tumult of Lebanon's political conditions. Second, American policy makers never really came to terms with the complexities involved, which argues for the inevitable failure of their efforts, however well intended. Middle Easterners, especially in 1958, found America unable to disassociate Arab socialism or nationalism from Soviet bloc rhetoric. Third, most Arabs saw the presence of foreign troops—whatever their nationality, ideology, or purpose—as a humiliating affront to Middle East sovereignty. (The same feelings would hold toward UN peacekeeping forces in the Sinai; their presence, however necessary, implied Egypt's inability to handle its own affairs.)

Soviet diplomacy in the Middle East had its own shortcomings, as would be evident in Egypt and later in Afghanistan. The sad difference, however, is that the Middle East continues, perhaps irrationally, to expect more support and sympathy from America, and consequently feels more disillusioned with each American failure to understand the region.

After the 1962 Cuban missile crisis, both the United States and the Soviet Union recoiled from the risk of direct confrontation. Increasingly, Soviet–American relations assumed the sometimes even amicable veneer of diplomatic cordiality. Although the United States flexed its muscles in Vietnam and fifteen years later the Soviets did the same in Afghanistan, most often they were content to subsidize rival factions in developing nations that waged mini–cold wars at minimal risk to their principals' own finances and manpower.

Soviet intervention in Czechoslovakia in the Prague Spring of 1968 did prompt the Brezhnev Doctrine's blanket justification for military intervention to safeguard socialism (a kind of Russian Truman Doctrine), but the Kremlin has acted under the auspices of that doctrine infrequently. Its behavior in the 1970s put it more in line with the Nixon than the Brezhnev Doctrine. The 1969 Nixon Doctrine announced that future aid to America's allies would stop short of involving American troops and seemed dramatically to decrease the chance of direct American military involvement in the Middle East or elsewhere.

The confrontational side of Soviet-American relations was played out by understudies in the 1960s and the 1970s. Since these understudies had to rely on their principals for fire power, if not for manpower, the worldwide demand for state-of-the-art weaponry escalated. The much more public bilateral nuclear arms race was paralleled, therefore, by conventional arms proliferation that, in day-to-day life, had a remarkably high casualty rate.

Not illogically, antagonists in both superpowers interpreted the Arab-Israeli arms race as an extension of their own race for allies; logical perhaps, but inaccurate. The Middle East arms obsession was not new and could be justified by a variety of reasons not related to Israel; for example, to defend oil fields, to assure internal order, to protect contested boundaries, and even to defend against possible communist aggression. The most visible reason, however, was, in fact, Israel.

Although by the late 1960s much of the Middle East could finance its own arms purchases, those groups with the most at stake in the Arab-Israeli conflict (Egypt, Syria, Jordan, and Israel) could not. Their consequent reliance on outside military assistance allowed hostilities that had nothing intrinsic to do with Soviet–American relations, and that would have been fought had there never been an America or a Russia, to assume cold war dimensions.

The United States became Israel's chief arms supplier, either indirectly through economic aid, which allowed Israel to funnel its own funds into arms, or directly through arms shipments. Thus Israel became perhaps the most heavily militarized nation per capita in the world.

Throughout the 1960s, in spite of Egypt's deteriorating economic conditions, Nasser remained the chief spokesman for and architect of Arab unity.

Sharing disputed borders with Israel, the Arab nations of Egypt, Jordan, and Syria resented Israel's existence, felt threatened by its expansionism, and struggled to resolve their own problems brought about by large Palestinian refugee populations. Denied access to American weapons capable of countering the Israeli build-up, Arabs relied on Eastern bloc weapons and Soviet military advisers.

In 1967 full-scale war erupted when Israel launched "preventive" attacks on the Sinai, the west bank of the Jordan River, and Syria's Golan Heights. It refused to evacuate occupied territories even after a cease-fire was reached. America's role as provisioner in this Six-Day War prompted half the Arab states, including Egypt, to break diplomatic relations with it. When the next year America sold Israel fifty new jet fighters, the Arabs were determined to defend themselves through whatever means available.

The Six-Day War left an array of consequences over and above the humiliating Arab defeat. It created an enlarged, increasingly militant Palestinian problem. Financed by the oil revenues of sympathetic Arab nations, the Palestinian Liberation Organization (PLO) began aggressively to bring the refugees' plight to world attention. In addition, Israel's occupation of Arab lands fostered a perpetual series of border skirmishes and aerial dog-fights. Middle East news made international headlines on a regular basis. Given the ever-growing importance of oil, the willingness of Arab nations to act together against Israeli expansionism, an enlarged Soviet presence and its identification with the Arab cause, and America's continued identification with Israel, the Middle East began to assume even greater significance in superpower calculations.

The Soviet Union was now taking an active and ameliorative role in the area. The 1960s witnessed a change in Soviet leadership, global expansion in Soviet commitments and capabilities, and increased sophistication in Soviet–Middle East policy. Official visits to Ankara and Teheran reflected Russia's success in alleviating tensions with its southern neighbors. Intervention in the Yemeni civil war in 1967 suggested an expanded familiarity with and assertiveness in Middle East affairs, as did Russia's role in the 1967 Six-Day War and its aftermath. Many of the countries, including Egypt, that broke ties with the United States now opened their ports to the Soviets, which added a naval dimension to Russia's presence and also strengthened Russia's global capabilities.

The Soviet Union was instrumental not only in achieving a 1967 cease-fire but also in securing passage of UN Resolution 242. A cornerstone of the Arab position on any termination of the Arab–Israeli conflict, the resolution supported the Arab demand for Israeli withdrawal from occupied territory before meaningful peace negotiations were possible, and demanded a just settlement of the refugee problem. The United States reaffirmed its own support of the resolution in principle, in 1969 and 1973, but Israel made little move toward any compliance that would be acceptable to the Arabs.

Arabs read this as meaning the United States was giving lip service only, whereas the Soviet Union, with no Israeli connections, seemed sincere if self-serving in its support of the Arab cause. The Arabs also took note of changing Soviet–American relations.

Russia had, after all, pulled itself nearly equal militarily to the United States. By 1972 America accepted Soviet nuclear parity and, although the gap here was still sizeable, a Soviet military presence was making itself more and more apparent throughout the world. The Middle East's emergence as a center of globally strategic resources, communication links, and military bases made it a logical focus of Russian interest. The Soviet Union had access to Egyptian and Yemeni port facilities, provided thousands of military advisers and other personnel to already volatile Arab polities, and could, really for the first time, live up to America's long-held fear of the spread of Soviet influence.

Russian penetration of the Middle East was limited by the Arabs themselves, however. By the late 1960s and early 1970s the area was strong enough to take a more aggressive role in protecting its own interests. Discovery of new oil fields coincided with a climbing world demand for oil on one hand and with greater national control over that oil by the Arab nations themselves on the other. Formed in the early 1960s, the Organization of Petroleum-Exporting Countries (OPEC) and its subgroup of purely Arab members (AOPEC) were on the threshold of becoming global powerbrokers. Oil revenues assured many Arab states greater economic independence, more freedom to shop around for arms and technology, and less willingness to succumb to external pressures.

On to this scene came a new American president and his energetic foreign policy adviser, Henry Kissinger. Kissinger was the first secretary of state to slough off the good guy–bad guy dichotomy of the cold war and begin to see Middle East dynamics as internal to the region. Concerned about Soviet global aggrandizement, the Nixon-Kissinger team nevertheless recognized that, in the Middle East at least, the traditional bombast of bipolarity actually benefited Soviet ambitions. Less belligerent relations between the two superpowers would reduce friction and thereby eliminate entry points (such as Egypt had been) by which the Soviets could expand their international influence. Kissinger decided, if possible, to withdraw the Middle East from Soviet–American competition.

Thus, one purpose behind the Nixon–Kissinger drive for Soviet–American detente was to undo some of the harm done by America's support of Israel and to find an acceptable way to move the Soviet Union out of the Middle East. This could best be done, of course, by ending the Arab–Israeli conflict. If that proved illusive, the next best thing would be to eliminate either side's need for recourse to the Soviet Union. The United States began a campaign to restrain its Zionist ally. Temporarily, at least, the superpowers worked in tandem for peace in the Middle East.

Progress did not come easily. For one thing, the Soviet Union did not obligingly fade into the night. For another, the Israelis proved no more tractable than the Arabs. Israel rejected calls to have the conflict resolved through international tribunals and insisted that any negotiations take place bilaterally between itself and individual Arab nations. Seeing Israel as a regional problem, the Arabs, in the main, demanded regional negotiations and were leery of divide-and-conquer tactics. The Soviet Union supported their position but also wanted to promote Middle East peace, apparently without realizing that cessation of hostilities would probably be more to America's advantage than its own. Russia pressured Egypt to moderate its militant anti-Israel stance. At the same time, the efficiency of Egypt's Soviet-trained air force undermined Israel's longtime air superiority and renewed the Arab world's military self-confidence.

Anwar Sadat, Nasser's successor, was torn between anticommunist and anti-Israeli forces, as well as other kinds of domestic opposition. He appeased the first by launching a major crack-down on the Egyptian Communist party and, in 1972, by expelling all Soviet military personnel. The humiliated Russians had to accept Sadat's demands in order to maintain their antiimperial credibility and preserve their footholds in other Arab nations. Shortly there-after, Sadat tackled the second, even stronger source of domestic frustration by spearheading a Pan-Arab retaliatory attack on Israel. The fourth Arab–Israeli war broke out in 1973.

The United States and the Soviet Union were both caught off guard and immediately pushed for a cease-fire. The full-scale war ended in an Israeli victory, with new territorial conquests. Sporadic fighting continued, how-ever, and these repeated cease-fire violations led at one point to the super-powers putting their own forces temporarily on alert against each other. That threat may have had the single advantage of warning all sides that the current alignment of forces could not afford to continue.

At this point the Arabs took matters into their own hands. Unable to dislodge Israel militarily, they struck at Israel's support. An oil boycott was implemented against selected nations (e.g., the United States), and a trade boycott blocked companies with extensive Israeli dealings from Middle East markets.

The oil embargo brought much of the world up short, especially when it was followed by dramatic increases in oil prices. The United States was forced to reexamine its national security interests; that is, to weigh Israel's contri-butions to America's security against those of the Arab oil-exporting nations, and to recognize the dependency of developed and developing nations alike on Middle East oil. A postembargo shift in American policy emphasis led to an intense interest in resolving the whole Arab–Israeli conflict, which in-terest was heightened by continuously rising oil prices and a consequent worldwide recession. Americans came face to face with the realization that they could no longer afford to ignore or misread the Middle East's priorities. Nor could they blame Middle East turmoil on Soviet agitation alone.

On the other hand, there was little the United States (or any outsider) could do about the Palestinian problem, which had grown in size and become more radical each time Israel expanded its borders. All Arabs and Moslems espouse the Palestinian grievance against Israel, a common enemy that is one of the mainstays of Arab unity. At the same time, each individual Arab state is reluctant to absorb too many Palestinians into its own midst (even if the Palestinians were willing to be resettled), and most are hesitant to become further embroiled in a conflict that has no easy solution and risks upsetting relations with Europe and the United States.

In this sense, Israel is a conduit that has allowed Soviet–American tensions to afflict the Middle East. Arabs rightly or wrongly hold the United States responsible not only for the existence of Israel and Israel's ability militarily to humiliate them, but also for the plight of the Palestinians. From this perspective, America's response often left Arabs with little choice but to appeal to the Soviet Union for military defenses against Israel. It was thus in America's interests with respect to containment as well as to its oil-related security to try to resolve the issue.

The Middle East peace talks that America sponsored between 1973 and 1980 were, unfortunately, to the Arab–Israeli conflict what SALT was to arms limitations. Well publicized "successes" dominated Western headlines, but the underlying issues were not solved. Neither Kissinger's nor Carter's diplomacy produced any real meeting of minds. The United States' success in freezing the Soviet Union out of the negotiations did, however, revalidate the intrinsically Middle East nature of the conflict, since Russia could no longer be blamed for obstructing peace.

Watergate brought an end to Nixon's presidency and gave Jimmy Carter a chance to mediate Egyptian–Israel negotiations. The imperatives of Egypt's threatened economic collapse did indeed produce a peace agreement with Israel in 1979. By its terms, both countries agreed to establish diplomatic and economic relations, and Israel agreed to a scaled withdrawal from the Sinai. But the Carter administration's hope that Egyptian–Israeli peace would lead to a more general Arab–Israeli settlement came to nought. In fact, by signing with the Israelis, Sadat spelled Egypt's demise as spokesman for Arab nationalism. As of 1988, Egypt has been the only Arab nation to crack under pressure, and much of the Arab world continued to hold it at arm's length.

In the years after the signing of the Camp David Accords in 1979, Lebanon disappeared, for all intents and purposes, under a combination of internal and external pressures many of which fed directly or indirectly back to Israel. Palestinian despair and the terrorism it engendered increased rather than decreased. The Middle East armed itself as never before. If these weapons were not for use within an Arab–Israeli context (and both sides swore they were not), the only other explanations were their use to suppress internal opposition (which, at least in the Arab states, was to a large extent a consequence of the reluctance of conservative pro-Western governments to tackle the Israeli problem head on) or to fight each other in conflicts such as the Iran–Iraq war, which threatened to engulf the entire region. In other words, America's profitable, new-found skill at playing both ends against the middle did not end the Arab–Israeli conflict or halt war in the Middle East. A cynic might even suggest that in order to dislodge Russian influence, the United States shifted from a staunchly pro-Israel stance to that of mediator and arms broker *for both sides* without really coming to grips with the fundamental issues. Some may well debate the probable chances of any outside agent being able to resolve these issues and consequently, find America's inability to do so no surprise. On the other hand, by approaching the problems with the attitude that they were solvable and then not being able to solve them, the United States helped fuel frustration and, ironically, a kind of anti-American backlash for interfering, raising expectations, and failing to deliver the desired results.

The overall situation in the Middle East in the 1970s did represent a kind of American victory. The Soviet Union found itself squeezed out of much of the region or associated with people such as Libya's Muhamar Qaddafi, whose extremism even the Arabs viewed with mixed emotions. By the end of that decade, however, the United States saw reason to revive its fears of the Middle East as a central arena in a renewed cold war.

Some Americans worried that Soviet–American relations in the Middle East had come full circle, with the Soviet Union finding a new entry through revolutionary Iran. To blame the United States, as many Iranians did, for the Shah's twenty-five-year reign was to give outsider forces too much credit. To see Iran's anti-Americanism as an automatic Soviet gain was to give the Soviet Union too much credit. The United States did fail to see, much less understand, the groundswell of frustration and dislocation that ultimately led to the Shah's downfall. The revolution blamed the United States because that country had the audacity to think it understood Iran and because it was such an easy scapegoat. In late 1979 the revolutionaries took out some of their anti-American frustration by capturing fifty-two US embassy personnel and holding them hostage for over a year. With Iran suddenly a real threat to American lives, no one could realistically have expected friendly US–Iranian relations. It may nevertheless have taken peculiarly East–West mentalities (the Russians had hopes of converting the revolution) to build from that contretemps an image of this radically fundamentalist, religiously dominated, social and political revolution jumping out of the Western fire into an atheistic, Eastern frying pan. Revolutionary Iran's cold war ramifications were much more perceived than real, although under pressure of war and ostracism it has opened economic ties with its neighbor to the north. The inept timing of Russia's invasion of Afghanistan was guaranteed to reduce any real probability that Iran would welcome an increased Soviet presence in their Islamic utopia.

The Soviet invasion of Afghanistan also gave new life to the cold war. President Carter was dismayed at the move in and of itself. He also feared the Soviet action as a possible preamble to expansion that, if not contained, might take Russia (through revolutionary Iran?) south to control the Arabian Gulf and its oil-shipping lanes. The resulting Carter Doctrine, which seemed to reverse the Nixon Doctrine's retrenchment of US forces, designated the Arabian Gulf as vital to American and free world interests, and pledged that the United States would take whatever actions necessary to guarantee free access.

When in the mid-1980s the Iran–Iraq war spilled over into the Arabian Gulf and threatened oil shipments, the Reagan administration brought a kind of Carter Doctrine into play, not against the Soviet Union but against Iran. As the largest and most publicized component of a truly international flotilla of military and commercial vessels in the Arabian Gulf, the United States stood on the brink of a quasi-war with Iran by 1987. The rather comfortable image of Soviet–American hostility playing itself out in the Middle East had once again turned in on itself. The reality proved to be much much more complicated. As proof that internal Middle East politics seem destined to torment American policy planners, by 1987 hand-held heat-seeking missiles that the United States had provided the Afghani freedom fighters had found their way into Iranian hands and were being used against American allies in the Arabian Gulf. The Soviet forces, against which the Afghani freedom fighters had been using these missiles quite successfully, were now so bogged down in Afghanistan that most Americans saw it, with a certain amount of glee, as the Russian version of Vietnam. Rather than using Afghanistan as a stepping stone to the Arabian Gulf, Russia seemed desperately to be trying to find a way out of its own quagmire.

Other aspects of the Middle East also dominated news headlines in the 1970s and 1980s. The Iranian revolution (in Iran and as an apparently exportable product), the Iran–Iraq war, and the precipitous drop in oil prices forced outsiders to recognize that the roots of these problems were Middle Eastern and only indirectly related to the larger Soviet–American picture.

The PLO and international terrorism offered perhaps the most complex challenge to contingency analysis. Much of the PLO holds the United States responsible for Israel's ability to annex Palestinian lands, and feels that only the United States can force Israel into withdrawing. As an alternative to renewed direct Arab–Israeli conflict, Arab nations have been willing covertly to sponsor PLO, and even terrorist activities, and have in many ways anointed the PLO with the mantle and mandate of Arab nationalism. This allows governments that wish to maintain friendly relations with the United States to support, at one and the same time, diplomatic and even terrorist efforts seen by that same United States as most unfriendly. While Arabs and Arab governments may not concur with the general concept of terrorism as optimal means to any end, support of the PLO has become a sine qua non for membership in the Arab brotherhood; attacks against the PLO have become, by definition, attacks against the Arab cause.

In 1986 the Reagan administration decided to get tough on PLO-associated terrorists whose activities had killed several Americans. Reasoning that Qaddafi was providing the support and sanctuary necessary for terrorist actions, the United States launched a lightning one-time strike on Libyan military targets. Rather unexpectedly, this strong response was followed by at least a temporary drop in terrorist activity by both Libya and the PLO. It is not impossible that the Soviet Union, which had been supplying economic and technical assistance to Libya, exerted some pressure to cool Qaddafi, who was having troubles of his own with his Saharan neighbors.

Terrorism was not, however, limited to the PLO, and if one star was waning another was on the rise. Moslem Shiite fundamentalist incursions into terrorist activities and hostage taking seem to have paralleled the rise of revolutionary Iran and have been particularly active in Lebanon. For whatever reason, Russians have rarely been the focus of bombings, hostage takings, or other terrorist actions. Americans, on the other hand, have been particularly attractive targets, and several American hostages have been held by a variety of factions in Lebanon for literally years; more continue to be taken periodically. The air strike against Libya and the PLO seemingly had no deterrent impact on terrorism from this source.

In taking a principled, "we will not negotiate" stand against PLO terrorism, the United States seemingly sided against Arab nationalism and denied the validity of Palestinian grievances against Israel. America's clandestine attempt, in violation of its own principle, to trade arms for hostages and to negotiate with fundamentalist terrorists made its 1986 "principled" attack on Libya and the PLO seem particularly Janus-like and pro-Israel to many Arabs.

In dealing with terrorism, the Soviet government took a page from Arab government tactics. While denouncing terrorism in general and on principle, it has demonstrated continued support for those PLO-related organizations and nations that were often the targets of America's antiterrorist crusades. In so doing it has been able to maintain a positive, if not particularly activist, image in the Arab world.

NOTES

1. For a solid survey of Middle East history see Sydney N. Fisher, *The Middle East: A History*, 3rd ed. (New York: Alfred Knopf, 1979).

Testing the SALT waters.

Don Wright, *Miami News*, 1971.

Partners in Detente—Nixon and Brezhnev—Washington, 1973.
Dirck Halstead, GAMMA-LIAISON.

chapter 8

THE 1970S AND 1980S:
NIXON, FORD, CARTER, AND REAGAN

HEADLINE HISTORY, 1969–87

Many people never know much more about world events than what they learn from headlines, political cartoons and well-publicized quotations in or out of context. The news media can make, reflect, and distort history as it happens. To review history through headlines is to recapture the contemporaneous perspective often overwhelmed by hindsight when day-by-day events are later weighed and summarized. The following items are from *Time Magazine*, which, as a weekly, is itself flavored by a little instant hindsight.

The Nixon Administration

Almost immediately after his inauguration, Richard Nixon and his National Security Advisor Henry Kissinger began their quest for detente. The path was not always smooth, with many of the same old issues attracting attention together with some very new initiatives. Much of the first Nixon administration was occupied with Vietnam, references to which have not been included.

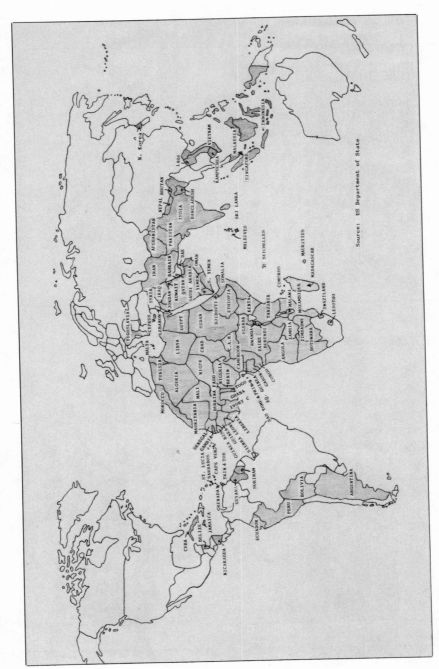

The Nonaligned Movement.

Source: US Department of State

Detente Bread.

Don Wright, *Miami News,* 1973

Cooperation.

Michael Witte, 1973.

"The Soviet Flight from Egypt"
(31 July, p. 18)

"East–West: Historic Tea Party in Helsinki"
(4 December, p. 19)

"Soviet Union: Crackdown on Dissent"
"[East Bloc:] Detente Stops at Home"
(18 December, p. 31; 25 December, p. 16)

1973

"Brezhnev Comes Courting"
"And Now, Moscow's Dollar Diplomat"
"Russia: The View Beyond the Cold War"
(25 June, cover story, p. 26; 2 July pp. 9, 10)

"East Germany: The Last Cold Warrior"
(13 August, p. 39)

"The Bloody End of a Marxist Dream [Allende]"
(24 September, p. 35)

"Black October: Old Enemies at War Again
[Middle East]"
(15 October, p. 30)

"Was the Alert Scare Necessary?"
"Are the Russians the Real Winners?"
(5 November, pp. 15, 38)

The Ford Administration

America's open and active involvement in Vietnam ended in January 1973. Plagued by the Watergate scandals, President Nixon resigned in the middle of his second administration. Gerald Ford kept Kissinger on, now as secretary of state, but some of the spark had gone out of detente. Much of Kissinger's attention was focused, unsuccessfully as it turned out, on trying to bring Egypt and Israel together.

1974

"Arming to Disarm in the Age of Detente"
(11 February, p. 15)

"The Third Summit: A Time of Testing"
(1 July, p. 19)

The Carter Administration

The Carter administration initiated a campaign to improve human rights worldwide but found itself sidetracked by problems in Iran and Afghanistan and by the energy crisis. Its major achievement was mediation of an Egyptian–Israeli peace and conclusion of a SALT II agreement. Both turned out to be less successful than originally hoped and both were overshadowed by rising Soviet–American tensions.

Crew patch of the joint Apollo-Soyuz Test Project, 1975.   *NASA.*

"Then it's all settled—he gets Eastern Europe and we get détente, Park Place and Marvin Gardens . . ."

Mike Peters, *Dayton Daily News*, 1975.

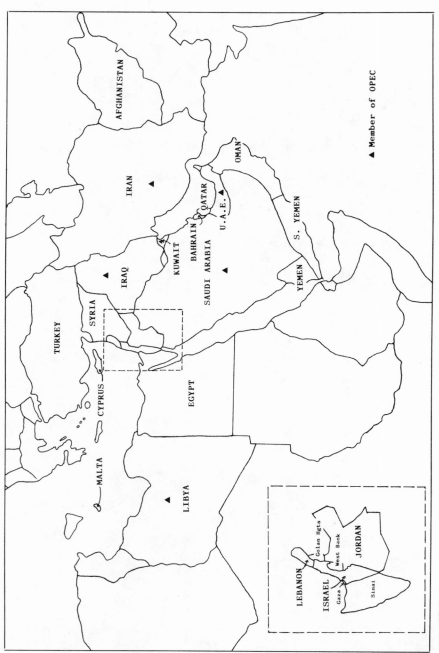

The Middle East.

1977

"Carter's Morality Play"
(7 March, p. 10)

"After Moscow's Frost, a Thaw in Geneva [SALT II]"
(30 May, p. 6)

"Danger: Eurocommunism"
(20 June, p. 49)

"Cold War? Nyet. But It's Getting Chilly"
(18 July, p. 10)

"SALT: Toward a Breakthrough—The Kremlin changes nyet to da"
(10 October, p. 41)

"Spooked Spooks at the CIA"
(28 November, p. 22)

1978

"Diplomatic Blues in Peking:
Guess who's mired in Indochina now?"
(6 February, p. 43)

"Peeking at the Chinese Card [Brzezinski's Visit]"
(22 May, p. 52)

"U.S.–Soviet relations worsen as Carter and Brezhnev trade accusations"
(12 June, p. 16)

"The Shcharansky Trial: A convicted dissident becomes the symbol of
U.S.–Soviet tension"
(24 July, p. 24)

"A Sudden Vision of Peace: Jimmy Carter stages an extraordinary summit
that has old [Middle East] foes embracing"
(25 September, p. 9)

" 'I Can Move Damned Fast' [Alexander Haig]
Maybe even fast enough for NATO to stop a Soviet blitz"
(11 December, p. 40)

1979

"Tying the Sino–American Knot:
Fireworks, protests and a solemn call for peace"
(15 January, p. 34)

"SALT: Now the Great Debate
Moscow was tough, but the Senate won't be easy"
(21 May, p. 22)

"The Storm over Cuba:
Soviet troops, Senate fury, and suddenly
SALT is endangered"
(17 September, p. 12)

"Getting Tougher: End of a Viet Nam hangover"
(24 December, p. 19)

1980

"The View From Red Square:
Our Containment is Their Encirclement"
(4 February, p. 18)

"Afghanistan: Moscow's Murky Morass"
(25 February, p. 32)

"What Ever Happened to Detente?"
(23 June, p. 32)

" 'The U.S. Is No Longer No. 1'
Europeans take a bleak new view of their chief ally"
(30 June, p. 12)

"Rethinking the Unthinkable:
Carter revises the new game plan for fighting
a nuclear war"
(25 August, p. 30)

"Killing the Spirit of Helsinki: A tough new crackdown
on dissidents [in the Soviet Union]"
(1 December, p. 45)

The First Reagan Administration

Ronald Reagan's first administration saw a dramatic outburst of overt cold war rhetoric and a consequent increase in Soviet–American tension. While events in the Middle East continued at crisis levels with a war between Iran and Iraq and chaos in Lebanon, Reagan became particularly concerned about Central America.

1981

"Closing a Window, Slowly:
Reagan decides to build the MX and B-1,
but leaves a few doors open"
(12 October, p. 18)

"Arming the World: out of control and no limits in sight"
(26 October, p. 28)

"Moscow's Aim: Split NATO.
The 'peace' offensive against Europe tries to
block U.S. missiles"
(2 November, p. 38)

"Schmidt fails to convince Brezhnev that the U.S.
wants serious arms talks"
(7 December, p. 36)

1982

"Reluctant to Follow Reagan:
With a different point of view, the allies reject sanctions"
(11 January, p. 26)

"Nicaragua: A left-wing military buildup worries Washington"
(18 January, p. 36)

"Linking the Unlinkable:
Tying arms control to Soviet acts:
a noble aim that often fails"
(8 February, p. 44)

"To Save El Salvador:
Fearful of a leftist victory, the U.S. steps up
its aid to a beleaguered regime"
(15 February, p. 22)

"U.S. officials oppose dealing with the Salvadoran rebels"
(15 March, p. 23)

"Thinking the Unthinkable:
Rising Fears about Nuclear War"
(29 March, cover story)

"Stay Just on the Horizon, Please:
Worried Arab rulers want U.S. help, but not if it
is too obvious [re Yemen]"
(25 October, p. 47)

"A TOP COP TAKES THE HELM
Yuri Andropov becomes the first KGB boss to
run the country"
(22 November, p. 18)

1983   "Sizing Up the Enemy:
The U.S. details the 'lengthening shadow' of Soviet power
'They seem to aim at world domination' [-Casper Weinberger]"
(21 March, p. 16)

"Reagan appeals for aid against the menace in
Central America"
(9 May, p. 20)

"Showing the Flag
Not since Viet Nam has the U.S. flexed so much
muscle abroad"
(22 August, p. 10)

"D-Day in Grenada"
(7 November, p. 22)

"Andropov's Ultimatum: If the missiles go in [to Europe],
the Soviets pledge to walk out at Geneva"
(7 November, p. 70)

"A Soviet Walkout
Bonn's vote for missiles triggers the inevitable"
(5 December, p. 12)

"Trouble on Two Fronts:
El Salvador's guerrillas make progress as
right-wing violence increases
(12 December, p. 32)

1984   Hopes fade for a spring thaw between Moscow and Washington
(16 April, p. 21)

"Growls from a 'Wounded Bear'
Moscow angrily rejects Western inquiries about Sakharov"
(11 June, p. 40)

"With relations on hold
the superpowers hurl weighty words at each other"
(3 September, p. 48)

Angola.

Doug Marlette, *The Charlotte Observer*, 1976. *Reprinted by permission of Doug Marlette*, The Atlanta Constitution.

Jeff MacNelly, *Chicago Tribune*, 1984.
Reprinted by permission of Tribune Media Services.

The Americas.

"Gromyko Comes Calling"
(1 October, p. 12)

"Back on Speaking Terms"
(3 December, p. 16)

1985   "Star Wars is the big obstacle as the U.S. and Soviets
return to Geneva"
(11 March, p. 12)

"[Gorbachev] Ending an Era of Drift"
(25 March, p. 16)

"[Nicaragua] Raising the Stakes:
The U.S. imposes an embargo, and Ortega
goes calling in Moscow"
(13 May, p. 32)

"The Soviets soft-shoe toward the summit with slick P.R."
(26 August, p. 12)

"GENEVA SUMMIT
High Hopes, Low Expectations"
(25 November, p. 32)

"Spies, Spies Everywhere: Four more espionage arrests
add to a year of selling dangerously"
(9 December, p. 28)

The Second Reagan Administration

The second Reagan administration was caught up in South Africa's furor, its own Irangate-Contra diversion scandals, and tensions in the Persian Gulf. Negotiations toward the double zero option of eliminating all intermediate-range nuclear forces moved forward in fits and starts but with ever-increasing likelihood of success.

1986   "This Year in Jerusalem.
At last, Scharansky is released to Israel and freedom"
(24 February, p. 36)

"The Man Who Makes Reagan See Red [Ortega]"
(31 March, cover story)

"Triumph in Moscow
Pianist Vladimir Horowitz"
(5 May, cover story)

"MELTDOWN AT CHERNOBYL"
(12 May, cover story)

"Moscow Takes a Hostage:
In a risky game of tit for tat, the KGB
imprisons an American newsman"
(15 November, p. 22)

"Iceland Cometh"
(13 October, p. 26)

"NO DEAL
Star Wars Sinks the Summit"
(20 October, cover story)

"The Dangers of a Nuclear-Free World"
(27 October, p. 4)

"Holding Hands in Europe:
Shultz reassures the allies that U.S. foreign
policy is alive and well"
(22 December, p. 40)

1987   "The Call to Reform:
Gorbachev condemns past Communist Party mistakes
and offers bold plans for change"
(9 February, p. 28)

"Wooing the West:
Gorbachev uses glitz to push Glasnost"
(2 March, p. 22)

"Let's Make a Deal:
Gorbachev seizes the initiative with an offer
to remove missiles"
(16 March, p. 38)

"Soviets in San Diego?
Washington proposes a sweeping on-site
inspection plan"
(23 March, p. 14)

"Welcoming Back the Bear:
Exploiting U.S. Woes, Soviet Diplomacy Is Again
on the March [Middle East]"
(13 July, p. 38)

"WILL THE COLD WAR FADE AWAY?"
(27 July, p. 40)

"Coping with the Unfathomable [Iran]"
(17 August, p. 39)

"Captain Ahab vs. Moby Dick: Reagan throws yet another
harpoon at Managua"
(19 October, p. 28)

"We Meet Again.
Why all the world loves a summit"
(14 December, p. 16)

". . . detente makes a comeback
(21 December, p. 16)

THE NEW COLD WARRIORS

Ronald Reagan's election put US foreign policy back on an old, familiar track. Once again, the United States was telling the world that the Soviet Union and its communist surrogates were doing and saying anything to further their aim of world domination. Reagan reestablished the overt cold war and gave new life to its covert counterpart. For a while at least, hardliners in both countries had the security of knowing where their nations stood in relation to one another.

Richard Nixon had turned away from the cold warriorism he had voiced as representative and vice president. As president, he immersed himself in the triangular riddle of relations with the People's Republic of China, detente with the Soviet Union, and America's war in Vietnam. He paid much less attention to the places of less historic note where, in the 1980s, a Reagan White House would rediscover international communism at work.

While President Carter directed much more attention to the little nations of the world than had Nixon, he was as prone to castigate conservative regimes that violated human rights as he was to upbraid communist governments. Carter never really saw the distinction between authoritarianism and totalitarianism, which would be so central to the Reagan administration's choice of friend or foe. He saw Nicaragua's Somoza be defeated by the revolutionary Sandinistas without giving much heed to the conservative conviction that so motley a hodgepodge of idealists would inevitably itself fall victim to a well-disciplined, Moscow- and Havana-trained cadre of communists. One of Reagan's first moves was to cut off aid to the Sandinistas and work overtly and covertly to ensure that the communist virus, carried by Sandinista reformers, was not spread into the rest of Central America.

Early Reagan oratory evoked images of evil empires against which the free world needed always to be vigilant. The US defense budget soared and American–Soviet arms talks stalled. Any new negotiations would be made from strength, which meant a push for new technologies at home and a buildup of military defenses in Europe. Until a sufficient level of strength was achieved, Reagan saw little advantage to serious negotiations.

In any case, there really was no one with whom to negotiate. The early Reagan years coincided with an unparalleled series of literally dead and dying Russian leaders. The resultant power transitions stagnated Soviet foreign policy behind a self-protective hard-line veneer.

In the early 1980s, most Americans defined the Soviet Union's occupation of Afghanistan as unmitigated aggression. Russia took much of the blame for Poland's suppression of the Solidarity movement. The Soviet air force shot down a South Korean airliner. After a brief post-Helsinki spurt, the emigration of Russian Jews was curtailed. Well-known dissidents such as Andre Sakharov were imprisoned, sent into internal exile, or deemed psychologically disturbed and put in mental institutions. All in all, Reagan had little trouble finding reasons to roll back the clock and drum detente out of Washington's diplomatic lexicon. Conservatives had a field day venting their ten years of detente-induced frustration. Commentators glibly discussed the "winnability" of a nuclear war and projected American deaths in an "acceptable" range of thirty to forty million. Liberals watched in horror as the country's population as a whole turned more conservative and accepted Reagan's view of the world at face value.

The Reagan administration believed that arms control often worked to Russia's advantage. Compromise meant a slow but certain loss of ground to the enemy. Reagan also believed that nuclear arms control was, in an immediate sense, irrelevant. Whether nuclear weapons were controlled or whether they proliferated might someday determine the fate of mankind; however, the immediately relevant issue was to roll back communist advances made in remote places while America's attention had been focused elsewhere. For people living under the constant threat of death by machine gun or sniper bullet, the risk of a nuclear holocaust was existentially meaningless. Bullets had meaning; anarchy had meaning; guerrilla insurgency had meaning. From a conservative perspective, old-fashioned communism, the revolutionary and bloody overthrow of those principles by which "reasonable" people wish to live, represented a greater threat than did any science fiction rendition of the morning after. Russia, it seemed, and with the aid of its Cuban allies, had been conscientiously picking away at the stability and cohesiveness of small, often economically weak nations convinced, because of the post-Vietnam syndrome, that an irresolute America would do little to stop them. Americans might march to ban the bomb, but how far would they go to stop communism in countries with little name recognition and even less political appeal?

Reagan foreign policy, especially during his first four years, reaffirmed that Soviet–American relations did not simply involve each other. The two superpowers had assumed such gigantic proportions that they and the life-styles they each represented dominated both international relations and many countries' domestic politics. Through Reaganite eyes, America and the Soviet Union were the actual and the symbolic protagonists in a great and ponderous ideological morality play that spoke to all mankind. As a very human symbol of life and light, the United States was admittedly flawed, but it must nevertheless accept its responsibilities, or the world would be enveloped in a godless blanket of darkness. According to this philosophy, the Soviet Union not only possessed evil weapons of nuclear war, but it also, more insidiously, fueled discontent, fomented disorder, and financed class war.

This imagery fit especially well in an early 1980s Central American context. Historically, the US government had played a double-edged game there. Willing to take extreme action to ward off even the rumor of leftist regimes, it had, on the other hand, given "reliable" governments free rein to run their own domestic affairs. Generally speaking, the United States expected Central America to control its own population, provide American investors with substantial profits, and stay out of trouble. It trained Central American national guard armies and supported regimes, however corrupt or nepotistic, that guaranteed profits, lambasted communism, and kept anti-American sentiment under control.

Then in 1979 and during the Carter administration, the Sandinista revolutionaries toppled one of those strong-man regimes. Worried that communists would use the reformers to eliminate Somoza and then eliminate the reformers, conservatives saw the Sandinistas as easy targets for Cuban and Soviet co-option. One Cuba was more than enough. If the communists gained control, they would use Nicaragua as a staging ground from which to spread revolution. Americans suddenly took note that some of Nicaragua's neighbors were, indeed, already having domestic problems; Nicaragua might not be the only Central American nation at risk. Also, Central America, unlike Afghanistan, Vietnam, or even Berlin, was right in America's back yard.

Reagan assumed office just in time to witness the unfolding of this self-fulfilling conservative prophesy. Fears of Soviet–Cuban infiltration through Nicaragua surfaced both at home and in Central American nations where embattled ruling classes faced opposition from both Left and Right. Americans took out their atlases and began paying more attention to Central America, and they discovered something about themselves. Most of them had envisioned that area as if it were one country. They had mixed together the political histories of Nicaragua, Guatemala, Honduras, El Salvador, and Costa Rica and emerged with an image of constant turmoil, and, more often than not, they washed their hands of the "corrupt" Latinos. After Vietnam, and with detente not far behind them, some even suggested that a little leftist reform might not be all that bad for "those people," and certainly the area was not worth risking American lives to keep men like Somoza in power. But when Cuba and the Soviet Union sent troops and material into Nicaragua, fence sitters who had not yet made up their mind about Nicaragua decided a reassessment was in order.

El Salvador, with a strong insurgent movement, was most immediately at risk. Well-publicized reports of right-wing death squads regularly assassinating anyone they disliked, centrist or leftist, disturbed some Americans as much as did the leftist guerrillas. With rebels boycotting elections and the death squads killing opposition leaders, stability, much less democracy, was hard to come by. The Reagan administration worked long and hard with the centrists, who in turn made deals with the rightists. In 1983 a relatively stable government under General Duarte was elected, and with American military and economic assistance, held its own against the leftist insurgents whom Reagan had now designated as agents of international terrorism.

Costa Rica, a showcase of democracy and high living standards, had little to fear from insurgent movements. A much poorer Honduras, enjoying the stability of military rule and close ties to the United States, was also able to maintain domestic order even when fighting between the Sandinistas and their military opposition, the Contras, spilled over the border.

Unlike Honduras, El Salvador, and Costa Rica, Guatemala does not share a border with Nicaragua and therefore did not have to worry about direct cross-border infiltration. It was, however, very worried about social upheaval, domestic turmoil, and communism. Guatemala was the first Central American country to witness the cold war firsthand. In the early 1950s, Jacob Arbenz Guzman instituted reforms that disturbed the property-owning middle and upper classes. Prompt action by the Eisenhower administration stopped him. Thereafter, the Guatemalan government remained staunchly anticommunist, taking whatever measures necessary to suppress domestic unrest.

Guatemala faced a peculiar problem because its large Indian population had never been fully integrated. Almost feudalistic in their own traditional, apolitical life-style, these people did not experience the prosperity many middle- and upper-class Latinos had come to enjoy partly through entrepreneurial efforts and partly through legislative exploitation. The restive Indian population, augmented by poor Latinos and sometimes manipulated by power-hungry opportunists, might, under the right circumstances, be putty in the hands of political malcontents, anarchists, revolutionaries, and outside agitators.

Arguing that there is nothing inherently free, democratic, or admirable about people who are poor, ignorant, and gullible, the Guatemalan government imposed tight controls to ensure responsible citizens the benefits of economic freedom. The various centrist political parties disagreed as to means and even as to specific ends. They argued over what role the army should play in protecting stability. But they agreed that communism, whether from inside or from outside, was anathema, and that only through discipline and responsible behavior could liberty be maintained. They had not been pleased by President Carter's obsession with human rights. In fact, many Central Americans argued that the human rights issue obscured a slow but steady communist advance. President Reagan saw Guatemala's authoritarian tradition as one that could, unlike intractable communist totalitarianism, be guided toward democratic libertarian reform. Sympathizing with the government's need to preserve order, he offered little criticism of strong-arm tactics to control against instability. With minimal US intervention, Guatemala has in recent years maintained a precarious status quo against leftist opposition.

Unfortunately, like El Salvador, Guatemala has a very activist right-wing fringe. Reflecting a segment of the middle class gone berserk, this minority driven by racism, religion, personal ambition, or simply fear, uses death squad tactics of indiscriminate violence and terror against not only the peasant population but also the centrist majority.

Death squads have given Latin America a bad name, a statement that is not as simple-minded as it seems. Insular Americans see political violence and cannot distinguish its minority, almost terroristic source from the majority that abhors both wanton violence and communism. Americans then ask themselves whether they should help a country in which responsible, educated people, theoretically the leaders of society, seem not only to sanction but actually to support assassination and terror. Such extreme right-wing vigilantism has made it difficult for the Reagan administration and its Latin American allies to garner as much international support as they would like, and has, of course, provided the left with a bounty of propaganda.

Central America problems dominated the first Reagan administration, but by the mid-1980s, cold war tensions there had eased even though the region remained in political and especially economic crisis. The American press and public focused their attention on Nicaragua, the anti-Sandinista Contra movement, and on the administration's battle to gain congressional support for covert aid to the Contras. As had Vietnam but without the added complication of US troop involvement, the war in Nicaragua divided Americans as well as Nicaraguans. Congressional hearings into the public and private means by which Americans were supporting the Contras made it clear that, whatever its impact on Soviet–American relations, the new cold war, as had the old one, was putting a strain on the accountability of America's representative government.

The Reagan administration remained firmly committed to Contra efforts to overthrow the Sandinista government in Nicaragua or, at the very least, to force elections and win a coalition voice in a democratic government. In 1987, a joint initiative by all five Central American governments, acting together and aimed at ending regional tensions, was threatened with derailment by an American insistence that the Contras be included in any such agreements. Nicaragua refused to accept that condition. In compliance with the agreement signed between the Central American governments, it did, however, take tentative steps toward a dialogue with the Contras, and direct negotiations began in March 1988. Critics of the Reagan policy suggested that, having come to political grief over the Iran-Contra diversion scandal, the administration was still willing to back the Contras even at the risk of obstructing interregional harmony, which could do much to ease Central America's overall economic and political problems.

At bottom, the Reagan administration wanted to keep communism and the Soviet Union out of Central America. As Americans had done so often in the past, they not only lumped those two together, but saw hard-line communism where others might have seen Marxism, agrarian reform, or economic discontent. Thus Colonel North's almost fanatic dedication to funding the Contras, and thus Reagan's unwillingness to let Central Americans work out some of their interregional difficulties on their own.

Strangely, Latin America is a cold war tug of war, over the outcome of which the Soviet Union may have little control. Hypothetically, Russia could refuse ever again even to talk to a Nicaraguan Sandinista and that would not dissipate American fears.

For one thing, whatever position Russia takes, Fidel Castro is unlikely to give up his campaign to expand socialism into Latin America. With or without Soviet support, the Cubans use each country's internal problems to court the discontented (of which there is no shortage) and inspire rebellion. Although the Soviet Union is contributing some $10 million a day to keep the Cuban economy afloat, if push comes to shove it may have little control over Castro's missionary diplomacy. (A similar relationship between the United States and Israel makes it clear that aid does not necessarily mean control.) Thus even if the Soviet Union stays away, communism, in the form of Cuba, will be close at hand.

The Soviet Union can also do little about the fact that Central American economies are in tatters and, with the possible exception of Costa Rica (and now Nicaragua), plagued by grossly uneven distribution of wealth. Any group that goes outside the procedurally democratic but substantively oligarchical political structures to obtain remedies will probably face strong military opposition internally, be embraced by Castro as a revolutionary comrade whether it wants to be or not, and be branded as revolutionary communist by conservative American administrations. The success or failure of any such effort will be chalked up as an anticommunist victory or defeat. All of this could well happen without the Soviet Union having lifted a finger.

Although the Soviet Union did, in fact, lift a finger to help Nicaragua, the Reagan cold war was in this sense self-perpetuating. Fuel for a cold war fire was harder to come by during the second Reagan administration. As noted, tensions in Central America eased off, making the spectre of communism oozing out of Nicaragua into neighboring countries more difficult to sustain. A defensive policy of containment evolved into an offensive one of liberation: save Nicaragua from Sandinista-Cuban-Russian rule by financing a Contra victory.

Problems in the Middle East—terrorism, the PLO, the Iran-Iraq war, and even Qaddafi's Russian connections and America's raid on Libya in 1986—simply refused to adopt cold war colorations. Certainly the world was not running out of crises, but many of those crises seemed to have outgrown cold war simplicity.

It also looked as though Russia had finally hired a public relations firm to upgrade its almost byzantine image. Firmly in power by 1986, Mikhail Gorbachev was the first Soviet leader since Lenin who could hold his own in civilized, mixed company. Mr. and Mrs. Gorbachev took the West by storm, dissipating in a remarkably short time its image of Russian leaders as old, stodgy, dour, and bombastic. Gorbachev was young, charming, and urbane. He was also the Soviet Union's first leader to have been born after the Bolshevik Revolution and the first to use Western media tactics to Russia's advantage. After a shaky first week or so, Gorbachev even managed to turn the 1986 nuclear disaster at Chernobyl into a tragic accident of human error about which the entire world could mourn. Those responsible were found, tried, and convicted. Assessing responsibility for this and other Soviet shortcomings, military as well as economic, gave Gorbachev the wherewithal to replace old-guard personnel with men more committed to his own view of Russia's future. A policy of *glasnost*, or openness, combined with personal charisma to convince many in the West that Gorbachev was sincere in his desire to limit or even eliminate nuclear weapons, certainly more sincere than was arms control skeptic and mastermind of star wars initiatives, Ronald Reagan. Gorbachev's appointment of the totally unknown Eduard Shevardnadze as foreign minister raised eyebrows everywhere, but also suggested a desire to wipe the tradition-stagnated, hard-line cold war slate clean, to launch a new, less acrimonious chapter in Russia's history. Thanks in large part to Gorbachev's skill as an image maker, the Soviet Union and the Soviet people seemed to become more real and more approachable. To call this man the ruler of an evil empire was to label Hopalong Cassidy the bad guy. It was bad casting, it did not wash, and it forced a change in Reagan's policy.

No slouch in public relations and image making himself, Reagan found himself waging a popularity contest unimaginable when Stalin, Khrushchev, or Brezhnev had been in office. He retreated from his cold war stance. Direct attacks on the Soviet Union decreased, although neither Russia nor communism was remotely rehabilitated. A chilly 1986 summit in Iceland produced no arms negotiation breakthroughs, but it did reopen high-level personal diplomacy. The Washington summit one year later not only produced signature of the INF treaty but also witnessed Gorbachev holding news conferences, hosting meetings with top American businessmen, and, to everyone's amazement, plunging into astonished American lunchhour crowds.

The INF treaty represented a major coup for Gorbachev personally and for the Soviet Union nationally. As the area most affected, Western Europe's willingness to lift at least part of its nuclear defense umbrella (it could still rely on long-range missiles based in the United States) suggested readiness to take Gorbachev at his word, and to accept Russia perhaps more fully than ever before in history as an honorable, if not necessarily lovable, neighbor. Steps, in 1988, toward a Russian withdrawal from Afghanistan also enhanced Russia's public relations (if not its military) image.

Whatever its level of success, Gorbachev's crusade to reform, streamline, and liberalize Russia will not end the suspicion that underlies Soviet–American relations. Misunderstandings, tensions, rivalry, and probably even crises will inevitably continue. But a new, less beetle-browed Russia may, of itself and prompted by a new American perception, lift the cold war veil that has distorted those relations for most of the past forty odd years.

The Summit at Reykjavik, 1986: Reagan and Gorbachev.
Eric Bouvet, Daniel Simon, Alexis Duclos, GAMMA-LIAISON.

EPILOGUE

WHY THE COLD WAR IS STILL WITH US—OR IS IT?

In his collection of cold war documents published in 1967, historian Walter LaFeber included the lyrics to a then current Beatles song, "Sergeant Pepper's Lonely Hearts Club Band." Those lyrics talk about a show that the band had been performing for twenty years "going in and out of style" but "guaranteed to raise a smile." LaFeber was suggesting that the cold war had been playing for twenty years (1947–67) and that, like the band's performance, it was time for it to go. In 1987 both the Beatles and the cold war still had devotees. For a variety of valid and invalid reasons, the Soviet Union and the United States continue to view each other with hostility and suspicion. Neither is particularly good at accepting, much less dealing with, change. Both find it hard to imagine that the cold war, that nice stable framework through which they saw each other and the world, may simply have melted away and left something with which they are both uncomfortable—a diplomatic unknown—in its place. What would that unknown be? Might it not be even worse? Would it mean America's (or Russia's) demise as a world power? Better, many cold war devotees reason, the known than the unknown.

Trying to preserve the known is, by one definition, conservative. By another definition, it is inherently defensive. Within a context of the arms race and negotiations, neither side would ever dream of coming out and saying it was building an offensive weapons system. By the same token, few leaders on either side have had the courage to announce a new diplomatic offensive that would significantly change the familiar rules of the game. Nixon and Carter both tried, with only limited success. Faced with an entrenched and inert bureaucracy schooled in the cold war, Gorbachev will need a long time to see how fundamental a change he can bring about, even if he wants to. His particular disadvantage is that the Soviet Union has almost always had to play catch-up.

Even today, economically, technologically, and militarily, the Soviet Union is first, second, third, even fourth runner-up internationally. Its much-publicized boast that socialism is ultimately superior to capitalism would give Russia a vested interest in seeing the game continue even if there were no militarized national security issues at stake. An ambivalent fear/disdain has characterized America's attitude toward the Soviet Union pretty much ever since the Bolshevik Revolution. Through luck and, after World War II, national policy, the United States has maintained the advantage in the bilateral rivalry and is determined to continue to do so. Ironically, the obsession of the two nations with each other may have blinded both to the reality that third parties have, in terms of quality of life, been able to outdistance both, usually through ignoring excessive military spending.

On the other hand, it is unrealistic to expect that such ideological, military, and economic power centers would not be rivals. History offers few instances of contemporaneous major world powers that have lived together in peace and harmony. Perhaps the most that can be anticipated is that they do not blow up each other (and everyone else). In this regard, to date and in terms of concrete as opposed to rhetorical measurements, Soviet–American relations have been much better than might be expected. Both sides have refrained from direct military confrontation. Europe, the territory over which both have competed most strenuously, has enjoyed forty years of peace and unprecedent prosperity. So too have both the United States and the Soviet Union.

KILLING WITH KINDNESS

As someone who is no more impressed than most other Americans with communist rule as practiced in Russia, Eastern Europe, Cuba, or China, I sometimes find myself daydreaming about how things might have been had the West (and I really mean the United States) taken a different approach. My vision is applicable to almost all of the now communist nations and could be applicable in the future to nations, such as Nicaragua, that find themselves caught between a rock and a hard place.

The vision is based on a few unsubstantiated assumptions: faced with intense opposition and ostracized from normal diplomatic relations, revolutions are more likely to go to extremes than they would if they were welcomed or even treated as if nothing much had happened; people are corruptible;

and it is easier to influence from inside with carrots, than from outside with sticks.

The West's response to revolutions has historically been negative. War is declared on them; their leaders are written off as expendable; economic relations are often curtailed and boycotts of the renegade region are imposed. The American revolutionaries turned to the French for help and received it only because the French wanted to hassle England. No one helped the French, most of the nineteenth-century revolutions in Europe were squashed, and no one helped the Russians. The Chinese won their revolution pretty much on their own; Cuba and Nicaragua turned to the Soviet Union only after they had been ostracized by the United States and their neighbors.

What would Lenin have done if in 1917–18 the United States had responded positively to the Bolshevik Revolution; flooded Russia with food, progressive reformers, reporters, urban planners, and teachers; and proceeded to help the revolutionaries define their ideological goals pragmatically? The Bolsheviks had, in fact, expected a much more positive response from America than they received, and some had even looked to America for guidance and support. Could the United States have corrupted, redirected, or manipulated the Bolshevik Revolution while still projecting friendship and aid?

Or what if, after World War II, the United States had loaned Russia the money it needed and decided that Soviet–friendly East European regimes warranted sympathy and support at least as much as did Italy and Germany? What if the United States had simply refused to let Russian paranoia fluster it and had responded to Russian war damages with a veritable deluge of war surpluses?

The situation is a bit more complicated in China and Cuba. Both countries could, and sometimes did, argue that the United States had been at least partly responsible for the presence of social, political, and economic conditions that demanded revolutionary rectification. To have killed these revolutions with kindness, the United States would probably also have had to admit some degree of culpability and promise to change its ways. That might have demanded too much in bruised ego, but from budgetary, military, and ideological points of view, may well have been worth the effort.

A blanket policy of killing with kindness would not necessarily always be successful. If, after two, three, four years, the revolution were still out of control, however, the United States could do what it now does as an immediate matter of course—cut ties, impose sanctions, organize military resistance, or send in the CIA. The wait would have caused no irreparable damage and would have prevented a monopoly of Soviet influence on the revolution. As I see it, there is very little to lose and a fair amount to gain. Approaching revolutions from this perspective of cooperation, the United States might even learn some things from them that would be to its own domestic benefit.

As I say, this is a recurring daydream of mine but, based on past American behavior, I seem to be in the minority.

CHRONOLOGY

Wilson	Lenin	Oct. 1917	Bolshevik Revolution
		Aug. 1918– April 1920	US troops in Russia
	Stalin		
Roosevelt		Nov. 1933	US recognizes USSR
		June 1941	Germany attacks USSR
		Nov. 1941	US begins lend-lease programs to USSR
		Dec. 1941	US enters World War II
		Nov. 1943	Teheran Conference
		Feb. 1945	Yalta Conference
Truman		July– Aug. 1945	Atomic age begins; Potsdam Conference
		1945–1948	Soviets solidify hold on Eastern Europe
		March 1947	Truman Doctrine
		June 1947 –1952	Marshall Plan
		June 1948	Berlin blockade begins
		June 1948	Yugoslavia expelled from Cominform (end of monolithic communism)
		July 1949	NATO ratified by Congress

		1949	Communist victory in China; de facto division of Germany
		Sept. 1949	USSR explodes atomic bomb
Eisenhower		June 1950 –July 1953	Korean War
		1952	US explodes hydrogen bomb
		March 1953	Stalin dies
		Oct. 1953	USSR explodes hydrogen bomb
		1954	Overthrow of Arbenz government in Guatemala
	Khrushchev	July 1955	Eisenhower-Khrushchev Geneva summit (first meeting of heads of state since 1945)
		Oct.– Nov. 1956	Suez crisis; Hungarian uprising
		Oct. 1957	Sputnik launched
		1958–1961 1959	Periodic Berlin crises climax with building of Berlin wall; Khrushchev visits US
		1960	Eisenhower-Khrushchev summit; U-2 incident
Kennedy		June 1961	Kennedy-Khrushchev summit
		Oct. 1962	Cuban missile crisis
		1963	Nuclear Test Ban Treaty
	Brezhnev	1963–1972	US engaged in Vietnam
		1965	US invasion of Dominican Republic
Johnson		June 1967	Six-Day War
		1968	Brezhnev Doctrine (Czechoslovakia)
		1968–1972	SALT 1 negotiations
Nixon		1969	Nixon Doctrine (Vietnam)
		1972	US reestablished contact with China
		1972	Nixon visits Moscow and Beijing
		1972	SALT 1 ratified
		1972–1979	SALT 2 negotiations
		June 1973	Nixon-Brezhnev Washington summit
		Oct. 1973	Yom Kippur War
		1974	Nixon visits Moscow
Ford		Nov. 1974	Ford travels to Vladivostok
		July 1975	Helsinki agreement
Carter		June 1979	SALT 2 signed (never ratified)

		Dec. 1979	Soviet invasion of Afghanistan; US imposes grain embargo
		1980	US boycott of Moscow summer Olympics
		1980	Carter Doctrine
Reagan	Andropov Chernenko	1980–1983	Unrest in Poland
	Gorbachev	1982	START talks begin
		May 1986	Nuclear accident at Chernobyl
		1986	Reagan-Gorbachev Reykjavik summit
			Reagan-Gorbachev summit
		Dec. 1987	Reagan-Gorbachev Washington summit; INF treaty signed
		May 1988	Reagan-Gorbachev Moscow summit

GLOSSARY

Appeasement The granting of concessions in order to maintain peace. Most often applied pejoratively to the Munich 1938 meeting at which France and England conceded Germany's absorption of Czechoslovakia's Sudetenland in return for Hitler's promise that he had no further territorial ambitions. In a postwar context, is often used in reference to charges that American policy makers have failed to be tough enough with the Soviets.

Brezhnev Doctrine (1968 in a Czechoslovak context) Announced that the Soviet Union had the right to aid its allies in defending "proletarian internationalism" and Socialist solidarity. Applied to intervention in Afghanistan in 1979.

Camp David A presidential retreat in Maryland that has been used periodically for high-level meetings between heads of state. "The spirit of Camp David," in the context of the Carter administration's mediation of the Egyptian–Israeli peace settlement, refers to a positive, optimistic atmosphere consequent to such meetings.

Carter Doctrine (1980 in a Middle East context) "An attempt by any outside force to gain control of the Persian Gulf region will be regarded as an assault on the vital interests of the United States of America, and such an assault will be repelled by use of any means necessary, including military force." Reversion to unilateral action option. (*See* Nixon Doctrine.)

Cold Warrior Someone who sees hostile, bipolar US–USSR relations as the dominant feature of international relations. Soviet cold warriors (or hard-liners) see the United States as their arch-enemy; American cold warriors see themselves in a death struggle against communism and the Soviet Union.

Containment Originally associated with George Kennan and the theory that preventing, through nonmilitary means, the expansion of Soviet territorial and political control would both protect the world from communism and eventually lead to dramatic, liberal changes within the Soviet Union. More generally, refers to continuing American efforts, using whatever means, to prevent the spread of Soviet and communist influence.

Detente (associated with the Nixon–Ford administrations) An attempt to reduce tensions worldwide, but especially between the United States and the Soviet Union, thereby decreasing the chances of conflict and increasing the time, attention, and resources that could be concentrated on other domestic and international problems. While detente usually carries with it the concept of increased cooperation, *disengagement* and *neoisolation* have been used in the 1970s and 1980s to suggest a pullback in American involvement internationally without any necessary improvement in superpower relations.

Disengagement (*See* Detente).

Domino Theory (usually associated with the Eisenhower–Kennedy years) The idea that if one country falls to communism, its immediate neighbors may do so also. In the 1950s American policymakers projected a line of nations from the Middle East at one end to Vietnam at the other falling to communism unless adequate defensive measures were followed.

Eisenhower Doctrine (1957 in a specifically Middle East–Lebanon context) US forces could be called into play should a Middle East government request assistance or protection against "overt armed aggression from any nation controlled by International Communism."

Geneva Site of many summits, high-level negotiations, and international conferences. "Spirit of Geneva" implies a positive, optimistic atmosphere after successful meetings or negotiations. Often refers to the 1955 Eisenhower–Khrushchev summit and the ensuing thaw in Soviet–American relations.

Geneva Accords Since Geneva has been the location for any number of meetings, negotiations, and agreements, this term has any number of specific references. Usually refers to the 1954 agreements relating to French Indochina (Vietnam, Cambodia, Laos).

Helsinki Site of, among other things, SALT negotiations and meetings of the Conference on Security and Cooperation in Europe.

Helsinki Agreements (1975) A series of multinational agreements by the Conference on Security and Cooperation in Europe that, among other things, recognized existing national boundaries in Europe and exchanged pledges to increase East–West cultural exchanges and to respect human rights.

Johnson Doctrine (1965 in a Latin American context) Committed the United States, unilaterally if necessary, to preventing any communist government from taking office in the western hemisphere and to defending any noncommunist government so threatened. By insisting that change occur peacefully, the policy rejected the legitimacy of revolution.

Linkage (associated with the Nixon and Carter administrations) The tying together of seemingly unrelated issues in order to achieve desired ends, e.g., increased American economic aid to Russia would encourage it to pressure North Vietnam into peace negotiations; or no trade agreement unless Russia modified its emigration policies.

Marshall Plan (European Recovery Program, or ERP) Massive US economic assistance program focused on Europe (1948–1952) to encourage economic recovery, promote inter-European cooperation, and decrease the ideological appeal of communism.

Munich (*See* Appeasement).

Neoisolationism (*See* Detente).

Nixon Doctrine (1969 in a Vietnam context) Announced that US support to nations engaged in defending themselves would be limited to military and economic support and would not include manpower. Seemed to reject future unilateral military actions in defense of another nation.

Nonalignment Movement Begun in the 1950s, a movement in many nations of people who wanted to disassociate themselves from the East–West tug-of-war. Membership is heavily developing nations. Founded by Egypt (Nasser), Yugoslavia (Tito), and India (Nehru).

SALT (Strategic Arms Limitations Talks, 1968–1979) The term is increasingly generic and used in reference to any arms negotiations. The Reagan administration's efforts to divorce itself from association with these earlier rounds of negotiations by renaming the process START was not particularly successful.

Spirit of Camp David (*See* Camp David).

Spirit of Geneva (*See* Geneva).

START Strategic Arms Reduction Talks (*See* SALT).

Titoism The Yugoslav heresy that demonstrated that a country could be communist without being under Soviet control.

Truman Doctrine (1947 in Greek civil war–Turkey context but later having a much broader application)   The United States pledged itself to "support free peoples who are resisting attempted subjugation by armed minorities or by outside pressures." Carried an understanding that the armed minorities or outside pressures were communist. First open-ended cold war policy that acknowledged America's acceptance of peacetime, international responsibilities. A mainstay of postwar American foreign policy.

Yalta (February 1945)   Crimean site of a wartime Big Three (Roosevelt, Churchill, Stalin) meeting at which major postwar policy agreements were reached. After the fact and in light of cold war tensions, many of these agreements and the ways in which they were interpreted and implemented became the subjects of controversy.

BIBLIOGRAPHIC ESSAY

Literature on Soviet-American relations is already virtually endless and continues to grow at an awesome rate. This bibliographical essay will help students begin exploring the subject in greater depth, but should not be seen as inclusive of all the available research. It is limited to books (although there is a rich fund of research in article form as well), especially those most likely to be available in even rather small libraries. The material covered here is much more narrowly focused on bilateral Soviet-American relations than is the preceding text.

The best available bibliography of US diplomacy is Richard Burns, ed., *Guide to American Foreign Relations since 1700* (Santa Barbara: ABC-Clio, 1983) published in conjunction with the Society for Historians of American Foreign Relations. If one accepts the idea that the consequences of post-World War II Soviet-American relations have extended far beyond any narrow bilateral context, serious scholars must explore the broadest range of diplomatic interactions, and the Burns bibliography provides an excellent research aid. Leo Okinshevich, comp., *United States History and Historiography in Postwar Soviet Writings, 1945–1970: A Bibliography* (Santa Barbara, Calif.: ABC-Clio, 1976) is a valuable key to the Soviet perspective.

The best readily available primary source material can be found in the Department of State, *Papers Relating to the Foreign Relations of the United States* (Washington, D.C.: U.S. Government Printing Office) series. These now go through at least 1954, and some more recent volumes are forthcoming. The documents selected by Thomas H. Etzold and John Lewis Gaddis, eds., *Containment: Documents on American Policy and Strategy, 1945–50* (New York: Columbia University Press, 1978), are very useful.

Any number of perfectly acceptable textbook treatments of American diplomatic history in general provide more than adequate factual and chronological information.

Comparison of one book with others can, in and of itself, offer intriguing insights into the problems to be encountered in trying to arrive at historical "truths."

A small number of surveys tackle the full sweep of Russian-American (as opposed to Soviet-American or postwar Soviet-American) relations. Written during the early cold war years, Thomas A. Bailey's rather anecdotal approach in *America Faces Russia: Russian-American Relations from Early Times to Our Day* (Ithaca, N.Y.: Cornell University Press, 1950) emphasizes two centuries of friendly, if infrequent, relations. William Appleman Williams's *American-Russian Relations, 1781–1947* (New York: Rinehart, 1952) sees antagonism where Bailey saw friendship, and places much of the blame on America's post-Bolshevik Revolution containment policies. John Lewis Gaddis's *Russia, the Soviet Union and the United States: An Interpretive History* (New York: Wiley, 1978) covers much the same material, plus thirty years and minus Bailey's frills and Williams's biting critique.

Adam B. Ulam, *Expansion and Coexistence: Soviet Foreign Policy, 1917–1973*, 2nd ed. (New York: Holt, Rinehart & Winston, 1974) offers a reliable Western interpretation of Soviet policy, while Nikolai V. Sivachev and Nikolai N. Yakovlev, *Russia and the United States: U.S.-Soviet Relations from the Soviet Point of View*, (trans. Olga Adler Titelbaum) (Chicago: University of Chicago Press, 1979) give their American audience a truly enlightening glimpse into how they view us.

The formative period in Soviet-American relations was not the cold war but rather World War I and the concurrent Bolshevik Revolution. The two volumes that put Wilson and the Bolshevik Revolution into the most complete historical context are still Arno Mayer's *Political Origins of the New Diplomacy, 1917–1918* (New Haven, Conn.: Yale University Press, 1959) and *Politics and Diplomacy of Peacemaking: Containment and Counterrevolution at Versailles 1918–1919* (New York: Knopf, 1967). John M. Thompson, *Russia, Bolshevism, and the Versailles Peace* (Princeton, N.J.: Princeton University Press, 1967), George F. Kennan, *Soviet-American Relations, 1917–1920*, 2 vols., (Princeton, N.J.: Princeton University Press, 1956–58), and Linda Killen, *The Russian Bureau: A Study in Wilsonian Diplomacy* (Lexington, Ky.: University Press of Kentucky, 1983) all deal, in progressively narrower focus, with aspects of America's response to Revolutionary Russia.

Soviet-American relations during the 1920s and 1930s have as yet not been thoroughly documented. Nevertheless, there is a variety of remarkably diverse studies. Joan Hoff Wilson, *Ideology and Economics: U.S. Relations with the Soviet Union, 1920–1933* (Columbia, Mo.: University of Missouri Press, 1974) highlights the division that developed between Americans with economic interests in Russia and Americans with political fears of Russia. Peter G. Filene, *Americans and the Soviet Experiment, 1917–1933* (Cambridge: Harvard University Press, 1967) studies the American public's response to Russia during the years of nonrecognition. Beatrice Farnsworth, *William C. Bullitt and the Soviet Union* (Bloomington, Ind.: Indiana University Press, 1967), paints an excellent portrait of one of the central figures in pre-World War II American-Russian relations. The issue of recognition and the high expectations consequent thereto is explored in depth in Edward M. Bennett's *Recognition of Russia: An American Foreign Policy Dilemma* (Waltham, Mass.: Blaisdell, 1970). A sequel volume by Bennett, *Franklin D. Roosevelt and the Search for Security: American-Soviet Relations, 1933–1939* (Wilmington, Del.: Scholarly Resources, 1985) carries the story through to the beginning of World War II. A more global examination of diplomacy during the Roosevelt years can be found in Robert Dallek, *Franklin D. Roosevelt and American Foreign Policy, 1932–1945* (New York: Oxford University Press, 1979).

Robert Beitzell, *An Uneasy Alliance: America, Britain, and Russia, 1941–1943* (New York: Knopf, 1972), discusses the first two years of wartime diplomacy. Gabriel Kolko, *The Politics of War: The World and United States Foreign Policy, 1943–1945* (New York: Random House, 1968), takes a much different point of view, but serves as a chronological sequel to Beitzell. John Lewis Gaddis, *The United States and the Origins of the Cold War, 1941–1947* (New York: Columbia University Press, 1972), focuses on Soviet-American relations during and right after the war. Martin J. Sherwin, *A World Destroyed: The Atomic Bomb and the Grand Alliance* (New York: Knopf, 1975) discusses atomic diplomacy during the war.

Specialized studies linking World War II and the cold war include George C. Herring, Jr., *Aid to Russia, 1941–1946: Strategy, Diplomacy, the Origins of the Cold War* (New York: Columbia University Press, 1973); and Leon Martel, *Lend-Lease, Loans, and the Coming of the Cold War: A Study of the Implementation of Foreign Policy* (Boulder, Colo.: Westview, 1979).

Athan G. Theoharis, *The Yalta Myths: An Issue in U.S. Politics, 1945–1955* (Columbia, Mo.: University of Missouri Press, 1970) explores American domestic cold war politics as well as the realities of wartime diplomacy. Charles L. Mee, Jr., *Meeting at Potsdam* (New York: Evans, 1975), studies the last of the major wartime conferences, and is critical of the behavior and motives of all of its participants.

Early cold war literature continues to proliferate and has developed a very complex historiography. Thomas G. Paterson, ed., *The Origins of the Cold War*, 2nd ed. (Lexington, Mass.: Heath, 1974), offers a good starting point for the first twenty-five years of debate. Daniel Yergin, *The Shattered Peace: The Origins of the Cold War and the National Security State* (Boston: Houghton Mifflin, 1977), concentrates on the immediate postwar years and offers a synthesis of orthodox and revisionist interpretations. Yergin's rather dispassionate appraisal can be contrasted to a much more passionate critique written at the height of the Vietnam war: J. and G. Kolko, *The Limits of Power: The World and United States Foreign Policy, 1945–1954* (New York: Harper & Row, 1972). Zbigniew K. Brzezinski's *The Soviet Bloc: Unity and Conflict*, rev. ed. (Cambridge: Harvard University Press, 1971) offers a study of Soviet policy and insight into one person—Brzezinski—who would play his own role in formulating American policy toward the Soviet Union during the Carter administration. John Lewis Gaddis, *Strategies of Containment: A Critical Appraisal of Postwar United States National Security Policy* (New York: Oxford University Press, 1982), approaches postwar diplomacy thematically. While Stephen E. Ambrose, *Rise to Globalism: American Foreign Policy Since 1938* (Baltimore: Penguin, 1971), has written an intriguing but general survey of postwar American diplomacy, Walter LeFeber, *America, Russia, and the Cold War, 1945–1984*, 5th ed. (New York: Wiley, 1984, 1967), takes a critical, revisionist approach focused specifically on Soviet-American relations.

Dean Acheson, Harry Truman, James Byrnes, and Averell Harriman, among others, have all left first-hand accounts of American cold war policy formulation in the 1940s and later. In addition, there are many very good biographies of prominent American policy makers, including Townsend Hoopes, *The Devil and John Foster Dulles* (Boston: Little, Brown, 1973). George Kennan, as both a participant in and a historian of the cold war, is essential reading: *Russia and the West Under Lenin and Stalin* (Boston: Little, Brown, 1960); *Memoirs, 1925–63*, 2 vols. (Boston: Little,

Brown, 1967, 1972); and "The Sources of Soviet Conduct," *Foreign Affairs* [25:4(1947):566–82]. Lloyd C. Gardner's *Architects of Illusion: Men and Ideas in American Foreign Policy, 1941–1949* (Chicago: Quadrangle, 1970) studies a number of the major figures in American early cold war policy making.

America's domestic response to the early cold war can be glimpsed through Richard M. Freeland's *The Truman Doctrine and the Origins of McCarthyism: Foreign Policy, Domestic Politics, and Internal Security, 1946–1948* (New York: Knopf, 1962) and Richard Rovere's classic *Senator Joe McCarthy* (Cleveland: World, 1959).

A sampling of specialized early cold war studies should include Geir Lundestad, *The American Non-Policy Towards Eastern Europe, 1943–1947: Universalism in an Area Not of Essential Interest to the United States* (New York: Humanities Press, 1975); B.R. Kuniholm, *The Origins of the Cold War in the Near East: Great Power Conflict and Diplomacy in Iran, Turkey, and Greece* (Princeton, N.J.: University of Princeton Press, 1980); John Gimbel, *The Origins of the Marshall Plan* (Stanford, Calif.: Stanford University Press, 1976); and Lawrence S. Kaplan, *A Community of Interests: NATO and the Military Assistance Program, 1948–1951* (Washington, D.C.: Office of the Secretary of Defense, Historical Office, 1980). Burton I. Kaufman, *The Korean War: Challenges in Crisis, Credibility, and Command* (Philadelphia: Temple University Press, 1986) looks at the war as a study in foreign policy rather than military history. John C. Campbell, *Tito's Separate Road: America and Yugoslavia in World Politics* (New York: Harper & Row, 1967), is one of the very few studies of US-Yugoslav relations.

Soviet-American relations after 1954 have been given less attention than the early cold war years, in large part because State Department records for these years are not yet open to researchers. Nevertheless, there is enough material to keep one reading for a lifetime. A number of American participants, including Dwight D. Eisenhower, Robert Kennedy, Henry Kissinger, and Richard Nixon, have published memoirs or narratives. Robert Divine, *Eisenhower and the Cold War* (New York: Oxford University Press, 1981), offers a sympathetic interpretation about a president about whom scholars are still very undecided. Richard J. Walton's *Cold War and Counterrevolution: The Foreign Policy of John F. Kennedy* (New York: Viking, 1972) is a revisionist critique of a brief but important and transitional period of Soviet-American relations.

A sampling of studies looking at Soviet policy can be found in Stephen Cohen, Alexander Rabinowitch, and Robert Sharlet, eds., *The Soviet Union Since Stalin* (Bloomington, Ind.: Indiana University Press, 1980). The two volumes of Nikita Khrushchev's memoirs, *Khrushchev Remembers* (1970) and *Khrushchev Remembers: The Last Testament* (1974), both translated and edited by Strobe Talbott and published in Boston by Little, Brown, offer very rare personal glimpses into Soviet history. A sampling of Leonid Brezhnev's speeches and writings can be found in *Peace, Detente, and Soviet-American Relations: Public Statements by Leonid Brezhnev* (New York: Harcourt Brace Jovanovich, 1979).

Specialized studies of the post-1954 years include Dennis L. Bark, *Agreement on Berlin: A Study of the 1970–72 Quadripartite Negotiations* (Stanford, Calif.: Hoover Institution Press, 1974), which provides background material on the history of this volatile city; Herbert S. Dinerstein, *The Making of a Missile Crisis, October 1962* (Baltimore: Johns Hopkins University Press, 1976), which gives attention to the Soviet perspective; Paula Stern, *Water's Edge: Domestic Politics and the Making of American Foreign Policy* (Westport, Conn.: Greenwood, 1979), which discusses the Jackson Amendment to the Trade Reform Act of 1974 and the whole idea of linkage;

and Connie M. Friesen, *The Political Economy of East-West Trade* (New York: Praeger, 1976). Richard Mahoney, *JFK: Ordeal in Africa* (New York: Oxford University Press, 1983), sees indecision and cold warriorism as the dominant themes in Kennedy's approach to African nationalism.

G. R. Urban, ed., *Detente* (New York: Universe Books, 1976), offers a wide range of views on detente compiled from interviews with American and European policy makers and scholars. Fred Warner Neal, ed., *Detente or Debacle: Common Sense in U.S.-Soviet Relations* (New York: Norton, 1979), presents a series of essays generally favorable to detente. Richard Pipes, *U.S.-Soviet Relations in the Era of Detente: A Tragedy of Errors* (Boulder, Colo.: Westview, 1981), offers a very critical appraisal of the policy. Charles E. Timberlake, ed., *Detente: A Documentary Record* (New York: Praeger, 1978), has compiled the multitude of Soviet-American agreements, treaties, pacts, and protocols associated with detente.

For an introduction to American-Middle East relations see either William R. Polk, *The United States and the Arab World*, 3rd ed. (Cambridge: Harvard University Press, 1975), or Robert W. Stookey, *America and the Arab States: An Uneasy Encounter* (New York: Wiley, 1975). Kermit Roosevelt, Jr., *Countercoup: Struggle for the Control of Iran* (New York: McGraw-Hill, 1979) recounts America's role in the overthrow of Mosaddeg. Donald Neff, *Warriors at Suez: Eisenhower Takes America into the Middle East* (New York: Linden/Simon & Schuster, 1981), looks at the Suez crisis. As a policy insider, William B. Quandt, *Decade of Decisions: American Policy Toward the Arab-Israeli Conflict, 1967–1976* (Berkeley: University of California Press, 1977), gives an intriguing look into the global aspects of American policy in the Middle East. Oles M. Smolansky, *The Soviet Union and the Arab East Under Khrushchev* (Lewisburg, Pa.: Bucknell University Press, 1974), emphasizes the problems Russia had in dealing with the region.

Richard D. Burns, *Arms Control and Disarmament: A Bibliography*, vol. 6 of *War/ Peace Bibliography Series* (Santa Barbara, Calif.: ABC-Clio, 1977) provides an invaluable research aid. Samuel B. Payne, Jr., *The Soviet Union and SALT* (Cambridge, Mass.: MIT Press, 1980), provides a rather rare look at arms control from a Soviet perspective. Alexander L. George and Richard Smoke, in *Deterrence in American Foreign Policy: Theory and Practice* (New York: Columbia University Press, 1974), offer a case study approach to the American side of the arms race and its practical implementations. Chalmers M. Roberts's *The Nuclear Years: The Arms Race and Arms Control, 1945–1970* (New York: Praeger, 1970) is a journalistic survey that concentrates on the pre-SALT years. In *The SALT Experience* (Cambridge, Mass.: Ballinger, 1979), Thomas W. Wolfe carries the story through SALT II and feels the United States has gone too far in trying to satisfy the Soviets.

There has as yet been little proven scholarship on the 1980s. Glimpses can be found in Lawrence T. Caldwell and William Diebold, Jr., *Soviet-American Relations in the 1980s: Superpower Politics and East-West Trade* (New York: McGraw-Hill, 1981), and Nish Jamgotch, Jr., ed., *Sectors of Mutual Benefit in U.S.-Soviet Relations* (Durham, N.C.: Duke University Press, 1985).

INDEX

ABM. *See* Antiballistic missiles
Acheson, Dean, 46–47, 61
Afghanistan, 92, 93; Soviet invasion of, 116, 137; Soviet withdrawal from, 164
Africa: during World War II, 23, 25; nonrecognition of South Africa, 3; Soviet involvement in, 91; U.S. involvement in, 83–84, 90; *see also* Angola; Mozambique; South Africa; Zaire
Agreement on the Prevention of Nuclear War, 114
Alaska, purchase of, 1
Albania, 40, 71
Allende, Salvador, 89
American Communist Party. *See* Communist Party of America
American Relief Administration, 8
Amtorg, 9
Angola, 90
Antiballistic missiles, 111, 112
AOPEC (Arab Organization of Petroleum Exporting Countries), 133

Appeasement, 45; definition of, 175; during World War II, 22, 39; Poland's role, 41
Arab-Israeli conflict, 65, 125, 134
Arabs: nationalism, 65, 66; nonalignment policy, 125; support from the Eastern bloc, 132
Arbenz Guzman, Jacob, 51–52, 82, 160; *see also* Guatemala
Armistice: Korean, 62, 101; Soviet-Japanese, 21
Arms control, 104; Ford Administration and, 115; Reagan Administration views, 158; Soviet attitudes to verification, 105; Soviet power and, 110; *see also* Strategic Arms Limitations Talks
Arms race, 87, 97–120, 131; difficulties of numerical estimates, 98–99; European attitudes after World War II, 98; U.S. monopoly of nuclear technology (1945–1949), 97–98

Arms sales, 22, 93
Aswan Dam, 66
Atomic bomb, 20, 44; development
of, 97–98; impact on policy
formulation, 26, 98; Russian, 47,
98, 101; testing of, 97–98
Atomic research, 44
Atomic weapons technology, 98
Axis alliance, 23

Baath party, 126–27
Baghdad Pact, 82; see also Iran;
Mossadeg, Mohammed
Ballistic missiles, 85, 105, 106;
intermediate-range (IRBM), 105,
106; long-range, 105–6; medium-
range (MRBM), 105, 106;
"missile gap", 105–6; submarine-
launched (SLBM), 105; see also
type of ballistic missile
Baltic provinces, Soviet relationship
with, 22
Barbie, Klaus, 80
Baruch Plan, 44
Bay of Pigs, 84, 85–86; see also Cuba
Belgian Congo. See Zaire
Berlin, 42; airlift, 43; blockade, 43
Berlin Wall, 85
Big Three, 24, 26; agreements, 27–
28, 30
Bilateral coexistence, 79
Bilateral treaties, xv
Bipolarity, 35, 58; American, 39;
concept of, xii, xiv, 59–60, 136;
and containment, 49; examples
of, 35; fallacy of, 70; versus
nonalignment, 68; and
Yugoslavia, 55
Bolshevik government: payment of
Provisional Government war
debts, 6, 7, 12
Bolshevik Revolution, 1, 4, 21;
impact of, 23; reaction to, 5, 169
Brandt, Willy, 110
Brest-Litovsk, Treaty of, 21
Brezhnev Doctrine, 130; definition of,
175
Brezhnev, Leonid, 114

Brinkmanship, in Cuban missile crisis,
86
Brzezinsky, Zbigniew, 92
Bulgaria, 56
Bullitt, William, 14–15

Cambodia, 63
Camp David: Accords, 135; definition
of, 175
Capitalists, definition of, 36
Carter administration issues, 146
Carter Doctrine, 137, 175
Carter, Jimmy, 91
Casey, William, 93
Castro, Fidel, 85, 162; see also Cuba
CENTO. See Central Treaty
Organization
Central America, 9; joint initiative,
162; and Reagan administration,
150; U.S. expectations in, 159
Central Intelligence Agency. See CIA
Central Treaty Organization, 82, 103,
129
Chauvinism, Soviet, 57, 58
Chernobyl, 163
Chile, U.S. policies toward, 89–90
China: after World War II, 30;
communist takeover of, 47; and
nonaligned movement, 70;
rapprochement with the U.S.,
78; revolution in, 69–70; U.S.
nonrecognition of, 15; U.S.
nuclear bomb threats, 102
Chinese Communist Party, 47
Churchill, Winston, 24, 27–28
CIA, 71, 88; and the Bay of Pigs,
85–86; covert operations, 84;
functions of, 76; in the Middle
East, 82; and the Nixon
administration, 91; support of
Iran, 81; on Vietnam, 83; see
also Dulles, Allen
Coexistence, 87; bilateral, 79;
economic, 8, 11
Colby, Bainbridge, 5–6, 9
Cold peace, 33, 52
Cold war: beginnings of, 34; causes
of, 29, 34; current situation, 167;

definition of, 33, 35; re-establishment of, 157; strategy, 35

Cold warriors, 59, 77, 81; definition of, 175–76; in the Reagan administration, 157

Colonialism, 60

Cominform, 57

Communism, Soviet: definition of, 36

Communist International meeting, 13

Communist Party of America: Soviet involvement in, 11, 13

Conference on Security and Cooperation, 113–14

Containment policy, 61–62, 66, 89; in Africa, 83; in Central America, 162, 163; covert, 83, 86, 93; definition of, 49, 176; and European security, 99, 102; implementation, 76; and Jimmy Carter, 91; in the Middle East, 135; and Vietnam, 64

Contras: U.S. aid to, 81, 93, 161; see also Iran-Contra affair; Nicaragua

Costa Rica, 160

Counterinsurgency, 86, 107

Counterintelligence, 80

Covert diplomacy, 91

Cruise missiles, 111, 115, 118

Cuba: American nonrecognition of, 3; revolution, 85; support of Nicaragua, 160; see also Bay of Pigs

Cuban Missile Crisis, 86, 106–7, 108–9

Czechoslovakia: defense treaty with the Soviets, 21; overthrow of government, 35; Soviet invasion of, 109, 110, 130; U.S. involvement in, 48; in World War II, 22

Davies, Joseph, 14

Death squads in Latin America, 161

Declaration on Liberated Europe, 29, 39

Decolonization, 91, 124

Defense spending: motives for, 98;

Soviet, 103, 109; U.S., 109, 117, 158

Democracy, definition of, 36

Detente: in 1970s, 66; definition of, 176; during the Nixon administration, 88–89, 141; during the Reagan administration, 158; European response to, 113; reasons for, 133; results of, 92; and SALT, 110; see also Disengagement

Diem. See Ngo Dinh Diem

Diplomatic recognition: advantages of, 2, 7, 12; of the Bolshevik Revolution, 1; criteria for, 2; de facto, 3, 7; during the Roosevelt administration, 11; economic benefits of, 6; of Germany, 44; results of, 2–3, 13–14; Russian concept of, 5; versus national recognition, 2

Disengagement, 89, 133; see also Detente

Dominican Republic, 87

Domino theory, 64, 82; definition of, 176

Donovan, William, 75

"Double zero" option, 117, 118, 155

Duarte, Jose Napoleon, 160

Dulles, Allen, 81; see also CIA

Dulles, John Foster: Aswan Dam offer, 66; as a cold warrior, 81; on communism, 51, 62; liberation policy, 103

Eastern Europe after World War II, 40

East Germany, 44; see also Germany

Egypt: modernization effort, 66; nationalism, 65; peace with Israel, 135, 145, 146; support from the Eastern bloc, 66

Eisenhower Doctrine, 130; definition of, 176

Eisenhower, Dwight D.: and anticommunism, 62; change in foreign policy, 67; McCarthy charge, 79; nuclear weapons

policy, 101–2; "open skies" proposal, 104
El Salvador, 160
ERP. *See* Marshall Plan
Ethnocentricity: American, 23, 30, 36; definition of, xiv; Soviet, 30–31, 36; and views of World War II, 19; *see also* Universalism
European Recovery Program. *See* Marshall Plan

FBI. *See* Federal Bureau of Investigation
Federal Bureau of Investigation, 76
Fifth Column, 50
Finland, 14, 22, 40
Five-Year Plans, 9, 23
Ford administration issues, 145
Ford, Gerald, 115
Ford, Henry, 8–9
Foreign policy: effect of atomic technology, 98; *see also* Diplomatic recognition; Soviet foreign policy; U.S. foreign policy
France: defense treaty with the Soviets, 21; in World War II, 22

Gaulle, Charles de, 71; policies toward NATO, 108–9
Geneva Accords, 63, 176
Geneva Summit, 84, 176
German Democratic Republic. *See* East Germany
German Federal Republic. *See* West Germany
Germany: invasion of Poland in World War II, 22; invasion of Russia, 41; non-aggression pact with Russia, 14; occupation zones, 42; reparations to, 29, 42, 43; reunification, 42, 43, 114; as symbol of bipolarity, 44; Treaty of Rapallo, 7; *see also* Hitler, Adolf
Glasnost, 163; *see also* Gorbachev, Mikhail

Goldwater, Barry, 87
Gompers, Samuel, 9
Gorbachev, Mikhail: difficulties confronting, 168; popular success in West, 163–64; reforms, 53, 117
Great Patriotic War: beginning of, 22; Russian defeat of Nazis, 20; significance to Russia, 23; *see also* World War II
Greece, 27; British support, 45; civil war, 35, 45; U.S. role in, 46, 48; Yugoslavian aid to, 56
Green Beret Special Forces, 107
Green Parties, 112
Guatemala: social problems in, 160–61; U.S. support, 51–52, 82; *see also* Arbenz Guzman, Jacob

Hamilton, Alexander, 3
Harding, Warren, 6
Harriman, W. Averell, 9
Helsinki Agreements, 113–14, 176
Hiroshima, 98
Hiss, Alger, 79
Hitler, Adolf, 19, 21, 23; invasion of U.S.S.R., 22–23, 24; neutrality agreement with Russia, 21–22; and Poland, 22; rise to power, 43; *see also* Germany
Ho Chi Minh, 63, 64
Honduras, 160
Hoover, Herbert, 6, 79
House Un-American Activities Committee, 78–79
HUAC. *See* House Un-American Activities Committee
Hughes, Charles Evan, 6
Hull, Cordell, 21
Human rights issue, in the Carter administration, 146, 157, 161
Hungary, Russian invasion of, 65, 67, 102
Hydrogen bomb, 101

ICBM. *See* Intercontinental ballistic missiles
Iceland summit, 163

Security, national, 77–78
Selassie, Haile, 91
Service, John S., 78
Shah of Iran, 77, 91, 92; and Islam, 124; ouster of, 136; takeover of Iran, 128; see also Iran
Shevardnadze, Eduard, 163
Siberian pipeline, 116
Sino-Yugoslav relations, 70
Six-Day War, 132
SLBM. See Ballistic missiles, submarine-launched
Socony-Vacuum Oil, 9
Solidarity movement, 158
Somoza, Anastacio, 91, 157–58, 159; see also Nicaragua; Sandinistas
South Africa: Africa's nonrecognition of, 3; during Reagan administration, 155; Transkei, 3
South East Asia Treaty Organization, 83, 103
Souvana Phouma, 82–83; see also Laos
Soviet-American relations: in the 1920's, 9–10; in the 1930's, 10; after diplomatic recognition, 14; ban on Russian gold imports, 10; before the Bolshevik Revolution, 1; deterioration of, 39; during Wilson administration, 4; during World War II, 21; effect on Middle East, xiv, 123–40; influence on the world, xii; see also Soviet foreign policy; U.S. foreign policy
Soviet-British relations, 7, 8
Soviet-European relations, 10
Soviet foreign policy: collaboration with capitalist governments, 10; glasnost, 163; intervention in Africa, 91; peaceful coexistence, 9, 11, 68; in post-war Finland, 40; post-World War II European strategies, 99–100; toward United Nations Security Council, 61; see also Soviet-American relations
Soviet-German relations, 7, 14, 21

Soviet-Japanese relations, 12, 21
Soviet-Nicaraguan relations, 160
Soviet-Yugoslavian relations, 69
"Sphere of coprosperity", 19
"Spheres of influence", 27, 39, 91
Sputnik, 85, 105, 106
Stalingrad, Battle of, 23, 24
Stalin, Josef: Big Three negotiations, 28; decision on Poland, 22; definition of friendly government, 40; plan to oust Yugoslavia from Cominform, 57; purges, 12, 14
Standing Consultative Commission, 113
START. See Strategic Arms Limitations Talks
Star Wars program. See Strategic Defense Initiative
State Department, U.S., 75, 76
Stimson, Henry, 6, 21
Strategic Air Command, 102
Strategic Arms Limitations Talks, 110, 116, 117; definition of, 177; purpose of, 112; SALT II ratification, 115, 146; SALT II talks, 113; SALT I ratification, 112
Strategic Defense Initiative, 111, 118–19
Suez Canal crisis, xiv, 66, 67; Israeli aggression, 129; see also Egypt; Middle East; Nasser, Gamal Abdel
Syria, 125, 127

Taft, Robert A., 77
Technology, impact on cold war, 34
Teheran summit meeting, 26
Terrorism, 138
Test Ban Treaty of 1963, 86, 108
Thermonuclear tests, 101
Third Reich, 21, 23, 24; see also Germany; Hitler, Adolf
Titoism, 58, 59, 177
Tito, Joseph Broz, 27, 56; acceptance of U.S. aid, 57–58; and nonaligned nations, 67

Soviet neutrality agreement with
Hitler, 21–22; *see also* Great
Patriotic War
World War I recession, 38

Yalta agreements, 26, 27–28, 29;
description of, 178; deterioration
of, 39; violation of, 40–41
Yalta Declaration on Liberated
Europe. *See* Declaration on
Liberated Europe
Yugoslavia, 90; aid to Greece, 56;

attitude toward the Soviet
Union, 56; communism, 40, 55;
denunciation of the Soviet
Union, 7; expulsion from
Cominform; nonalignment
policy, 55, 59; re-establishment
of ties to the Soviet Union, 69;
relationship with China, 70; split
from Soviet socialism, 57, 58;
U.S. aid to, 57–58, 59

Zaire, 84

ABOUT THE AUTHOR

Linda R. Killen is a professor of history at Radford University, where she has taught since 1976. She received her B.A. in literature from the University of Wisconsin in Madison and switched to history in graduate school. She earned both her M.A. and Ph.D. from the University of North Carolina in Chapel Hill. Her field of specialization is American diplomatic history, and her current interests are Soviet–American and Yugoslav–American relations. In addition to several articles, she has published *The Russian Bureau: A Case Study in Wilsonian Diplomacy* (Lexington: University Press of Kentucky, 1983), a monograph exploring Woodrow Wilson's economic policy toward revolutionary Russia, and is coauthor of *Versailles and After* (New York: Garland, 1983), a bibliographical guide to American foreign relations, 1919 to 1933.

Professor Killen spent much of her childhood overseas, and in 1986 spent five months in Yugoslavia on a Fulbright research grant. Her teaching career has highlighted the need to introduce Americans to different perspectives.